Postcolonial Theory and International Relations

What can postcolonialism tell us about international relations? What can international relations tell us about postcolonialism?

In recent years, postcolonial perspectives and insights have challenged conventional understanding of international politics. *Postcolonial Theory and International Relations: A Critical Introduction* is the first book to undertake a comprehensive and accessible examination of how postcolonialism radically alters our understanding of international relations. It offers a postcolonial critique of the discipline of IR, as well as essays that provide alternative, postcolonial readings of key aspects of international politics.

Each chapter is written by a leading international scholar and the topics covered include the nation and nationalism, the historical origins of the modern international system, war, political economy, race in international thought, and Empire. In so doing it provides scholars and students with a valuable insight into the challenges that postcolonialism poses to our understanding of global politics.

Sanjay Seth is Professor of Politics and Director of the Centre for Postcolonial Studies at Goldsmiths, University of London. He has published extensively on postcolonialism, social and political theory, and modern Indian history and is a founding co-editor of the journal *Postcolonial Studies* (1998–present).

Interventions
Edited by: Jenny Edkins,
Aberystwyth University and
Nick Vaughan-Williams,
University of Warwick

'As Michel Foucault has famously stated, "knowledge is not made for understanding; it is made for cutting." In this spirit the Edkins–Vaughan-Williams Interventions series solicits cutting edge, critical works that challenge mainstream understandings in international relations. It is the best place to contribute post disciplinary works that think rather than merely recognize and affirm the world recycled in IR's traditional geopolitical imaginary'.
Michael J. Shapiro, University of Hawai'i at Mãnoa, USA

The series aims to advance understanding of the key areas in which scholars working within broad critical post-structural and post-colonial traditions have chosen to make their interventions, and to present innovative analyses of important topics.

Titles in the series engage with critical thinkers in philosophy, sociology, politics and other disciplines and provide situated historical, empirical and textual studies in international politics.

Critical Theorists and International Relations
Edited by Jenny Edkins and Nick Vaughan-Williams

Ethics as Foreign Policy
Britain, the EU and the other
Dan Bulley

Universality, Ethics and International Relations
A grammatical reading
Véronique Pin-Fat

The Time of the City
Politics, philosophy, and genre
Michael J. Shapiro

Governing Sustainable Development
Partnership, protest and power at the world summit
Carl Death

Insuring Security
Biopolitics, security and risk
Luis Lobo-Guerrero

Foucault and International Relations
New critical engagements
Edited by Nicholas J. Kiersey and Doug Stokes

International Relations and Non-Western Thought
Imperialism, colonialism and investigations of global modernity
Edited by Robbie Shilliam

Autobiographical International Relations
I, IR
Edited by Naeem Inayatullah

War and Rape
Law, memory and justice
Nicola Henry

Madness in International Relations
Psychology, security and the global governance of mental health
Alison Howell

Spatiality, Sovereignty and Carl Schmitt
Geographies of the nomos
Edited by Stephen Legg

Politics of Urbanism
Seeing like a city
Warren Magnusson

Beyond Biopolitics
Theory, violence and horror in world politics
François Debrix and Alexander D. Barder

The Politics of Speed
Capitalism, the state and war in an accelerating world
Simon Glezos

Politics and the Art of Commemoration
Memorials to struggle in Latin America and Spain
Katherine Hite

Indian Foreign Policy
The politics of postcolonial identity
Priya Chacko

Politics of the Event
Time, movement, becoming
Tom Lundborg

Theorising Post-Conflict Reconciliation
Agonism, restitution and repair
Edited by Alexander Keller Hirsch

Europe's Encounter with Islam
The secular and the postsecular
Luca Mavelli

Re-Thinking International Relations Theory via Deconstruction
Badredine Arfi

The New Violent Cartography
Geo-analysis after the aesthetic turn
Edited by Sam Okoth Opondo and Michael J. Shapiro

Insuring War
Sovereignty, security and risk
Luis Lobo-Guerrero

International Relations, Meaning and Mimesis
Necati Polat

The Postcolonial Subject
Claiming politics/governing others in late modernity
Vivienne Jabri

Foucault and the Politics of Hearing
Lauri Siisiäinen

Volunteer Tourism in the Global South
Giving back in neoliberal times
Wanda Vrasti

Cosmopolitan Government in Europe
Citizens and entrepreneurs in postnational politics
Owen Parker

Studies in the Trans-Disciplinary Method
After the aesthetic turn
Michael J. Shapiro

Alternative Accountabilities in Global Politics
The scars of violence
Brent J. Steele

Celebrity Humanitarianism
The ideology of global charity
Ilan Kapoor

Deconstructing International Politics
Michael Dillon

The Politics of Exile
Elizabeth Dauphinee

Democratic Futures
Revisioning democracy promotion
Milja Kurki

Postcolonial Theory
A critical introduction
Edited by Sanjay Seth

More than Just War
Narratives of the just war and military life
Charles A. Jones

Deleuze & Fascism
Security: war: aesthetics
Edited by Brad Evans and Julian Reid

Feminist International Relations
'Exquisite Corpse'
Marysia Zalewski

The Persistence of Nationalism
From imagined communities to urban encounters
Angharad Closs Stephens

Interpretive Approaches to Global Climate Governance
Reconstructing the greenhouse
Edited by Chris Methmann, Delf Rothe and Benjamin Stephan

Postcolonial Encounters with International Relations
The politics of transgression
Alina Sajed

Postcolonial Theory and International Relations

A critical introduction

Edited by Sanjay Seth

LONDON AND NEW YORK

First published 2013
by Routledge

2 Park Square, Milton Park, Abingdon, Oxon OX14 4RN
Simultaneously published in the USA and Canada
by Routledge
711 Third Avenue, New York, NY 10017

Routledge is an imprint of the Taylor & Francis Group, an informa business

© 2013 Sanjay Seth for selection and editorial matter, contributors their contributions.

The right of Sanjay Seth to be identified as editor of this work has been asserted by him in accordance with the Copyright, Designs and Patents Act 1988.

All rights reserved. No part of this book may be reprinted or reproduced or utilised in any form or by any electronic, mechanical, or other means, now known or hereafter invented, including photocopying and recording, or in any information storage or retrieval system, without permission in writing from the publishers.

Trademark notice: Product or corporate names may be trademarks or registered trademarks, and are used only for identification and explanation without intent to infringe.

British Library Cataloguing in Publication Data
A catalogue record for this book is available from the British Library

Library of Congress Cataloging-in-Publication Data
Postcolonial theory and international relations : a critical introduction / edited by Sanjay Seth.
　p. cm. — (Interventions)
Includes bibliographical references and index.
1. International relations—Philosophy. 2. Postcolonialism.
I. Seth, Sanjay, 1961–
JZ1305.P68 2012
327.101—dc23　　　　　　　　　　　　　　　　　　　　2012027482

ISBN: 978-0-415-58287-2 (hbk)
ISBN: 978-0-415-58288-9 (pbk)
ISBN: 978-0-203-07302-5 (ebk)

Typeset in Times New Roman
by Cenveo Publisher Services

Printed and bound in Great Britain by the MPG Books Group

Contents

Notes on contributors ix

Introduction 1
SANJAY SETH

PART I
Critique 13

1 Postcolonial theory and the critique of International Relations 15
SANJAY SETH

2 The other side of the Westphalian frontier 32
JOHN M. HOBSON

3 Slavery, finance and international political economy: postcolonial reflections 49
BRANWEN GRUFFYDD JONES

4 Time and the others 70
CHRISTINE HELLIWELL AND BARRY HINDESS

PART II
Performance 85

5 War, armed forces and society in postcolonial perspective 87
TARAK BARKAWI

6 Deferring difference: a postcolonial critique of the 'race problem' in moral thought 106
SIBA N'ZATIOULA GROVOGUI

7	IR and the postcolonial novel: nation and subjectivity in India	124
	SANKARAN KRISHNA	
8	The 'Bandung impulse' and international relations	144
	MUSTAPHA KAMAL PASHA	
9	The spirit of exchange	166
	ROBBIE SHILLIAM	
	Bibliography	183
	Index	200

Contributors

Tarak Barkawi is associate professor in the Department of Politics, New School for Social Research. He earned his doctorate at the University of Minnesota and specializes in the study of war, armed forces and society, with a focus on conflict between the West and the global South. He has written on colonial armies, 'small wars' and imperial warfare, the Cold War in the Third World, and on counterinsurgency and the War on Terror. More generally, he is interested in the place of armed force in histories and theories of globalization, modernization and imperialism, especially from a postcolonial perspective.

Siba N'Zatioula Grovogui is professor at Johns Hopkins University. He is the author of *Sovereigns, Quasi-Sovereigns, and Africans* (University of Minnesota Press, 1996) and *Beyond Eurocentrism and Anarchy* (Palgrave, April 2006). Grovogui is currently completing two manuscripts: the first on the genealogy of order, entitled *Future Anterior: The International, Past and Present*, and the second on the meaning of the 'human' in human rights traditions under the rubric of *Otherwise Human: The Institutes and Institutions of Human Rights*. Grovogui has also been conducting a ten-year-long study of the rule of law in Chad, in the context of the Chad Oil and Pipeline Project, funded by the National Science Foundation.

Branwen Gruffydd Jones is senior lecturer in International Political Economy at Goldsmiths, University of London. Her teaching and research address Africa in the global political economy, and Africa in the global politics of knowledge. She is currently working on a collaborative project on African political thought, and engaged in longer-term research on the politics of the African city.

Christine Helliwell is Reader in Anthropology at the Australian National University in Canberra. She has published widely in the area of social/cultural theory; much of her work is concerned with the inappropriateness of Western analytic categories for the study of non-Western peoples. She has carried out extensive ethnographic research in Indonesian Borneo; her ethnography of Gerai, *'Never Stand Alone': A Study of Borneo Sociality*, appeared in 2001. Apart from her work (some with Barry Hindess) on the place of time in academic discourses of otherness, she is currently researching Western representations of clitoridectomy.

Barry Hindess is Emeritus Professor in the Australian National University's School of Politics and International Relations. After working as a sociologist in Britain, he joined the ANU in 1987, later moving to ANU's Research School of Social Sciences, where he learned to pass as a political scientist. Like many senior academics he has published more than he cares to remember, but he is happy to recall *Discourses of Power: from Hobbes to Foucault* (Wiley-Blackwell, 1996); *Governing Australia* (with Mitchell Dean) (CUP, 1998); *Corruption and Democracy in Australia* (Democratic Audit of Australia, 2004); *Us and them: elites and anti-elitism in Australia* (with Marian Sawer) (API Network, 2004); and papers on neo-liberalism, liberalism and empire and the temporalizing of difference.

John M. Hobson is Professor of Politics and International Relations at the University of Sheffield. He has published eight books, the most recent of which is *The Eurocentric Conception of World Politics: Western International Theory, 1760–2010* (CUP, 2012). While this book reveals how international theory has been Eurocentric ever since 1760, it also argues that Eurocentrism is a complex, polymorphous discourse that takes different forms and can be anti-imperialist as well as imperialist. This follows on from his earlier book, *The Eastern Origins of Western Civilisation* (CUP, 2004), which produces a non-Eurocentric account of the rise of the West.

Sankaran Krishna teaches politics at the University of Hawaii at Manoa. His most recent book was *Globalization and Postcolonialism: hegemony and resistance in the 21st century* (Rowman & Littlefield, 2009). His research interests are in critical international relations, postcolonial studies and South Asia. He is currently working on some essays on the disappearance of the commons in neo-liberal India; competing ideas of the nation before and after the Partition of the subcontinent in 1947; and related topics.

Mustapha Kamal Pasha is Sixth Century Chair and Head of International Relations at the University of Aberdeen, UK. He specializes in International Relations theory, Political Economy, Human Security, and Contemporary Islam. Currently, he is Vice President of the International Studies Association. Professor Pasha is the author/editor of several books, as well as recent articles in *International Politics*; *Critical Review of International Social and Political Philosophy*; *Global Society*; *Annals of the American Academy of Political and Social Science*; *Journal of Developing Societies; Alternatives; Millennium*; and *Journal of International Studies*. He also serves on the editorial boards of *Globalizations*; *International Political Sociology*; *Critical Asian Studies*; *Asian Ethnicity*; and *Critical Studies on Security*. Currently, he is completing a book on the confluence of Islam and International Relations.

Sanjay Seth is Professor of Politics and Director of the Centre for Postcolonial Studies at Goldsmiths, University of London. He has published extensively on social and political theory, postcolonialism, and modern Indian history. He is the author of *Subject Lessons: The Western Education of Colonial India* (Duke University Press, 2007) and a founding co-editor of the journal *Postcolonial Studies* (1998–).

Robbie Shilliam is Senior Lecturer in International Relations at Queen Mary College, University of London. He has previously worked at Victoria University of Wellington, New Zealand, and the University of Oxford. He has published on slavery, anti-colonial struggles and political theory in, for example, *Thesis Eleven*, *Comparative Studies in Society and History*, and *Millennium*. He is author of *German Thought and International Relations* (Palgrave, 2009) and editor of *International Relations and Non-Western Thought* (Routledge, 2010).

Introduction

Sanjay Seth

The title of this book, *Postcolonial Theory and International Relations*, requires explanation. What is 'postcolonial theory'? Does 'international relations' refer to relations between states and nations, war, diplomacy and so on, or to the discipline which takes these matters as its object? Does the 'and' in the title suggest that 'postcolonial theory' is being 'applied' to better understand the international arena, or does it signal that postcolonial theory is being employed to engage and critique the discipline of International Relations?

The purpose of this introduction is to address these questions, to explain why this volume is divided into two parts, and to introduce the essays which comprise it. I will not begin by providing a definition of postcolonial theory,[1] because such a definition cannot be summarily provided in an introduction; the reader will gain a sense of this from reading the essays. I will, however, commence by seeking to clear possible misconceptions, by specifying what postcolonial theory is not; doing so will also provide the beginnings of an understanding of what postcolonial theory is, and what possibilities an engagement with it might afford the scholar of international relations.

The 'post' in postcolonial theory does not signify the period or era 'after' colonialism came to an end, but rather signifies the entire historical period after the beginnings of colonialism. It is of course impossible to assign a precise date to such epochal changes but, if pressed, one would be forced to nominate 1492; it is first with the 'discovery' and subsequent conquest of the Americas, and later the European conquest of large parts of Asia, Africa and other parts of the world that, in Stuart Hall's words, 'different temporalities and histories have been irrevocably and violently yoked together.'[2] The historical and theoretical claim signalled by the 'post' in postcolonialism, as I explain in greater detail in the first essay of this volume, is thus not that we are in the era after colonialism, with the implication that it now belongs to the past but, on the contrary, that the world has been decisively shaped by colonialism, and that one cannot even begin to understand the contemporary situation if this fact is not acknowledged, taken into account, and explored in all its ramifications.

Second, postcolonial theory is not an attempt to elaborate a theory of the world as it would look from the vantage point of the Third World or developing world or the global South. It is certainly true that the intellectual genealogy of postcolonial theory includes anti-colonial nationalism and anti-imperialism in its various forms (including the thoughts of Frantz Fanon, Mao, Fidel Castro and others), and more generally, that the critical, political and ethical energies that fuel postcolonialism have much to do with anti-imperialism and Third Worldism.[3] But while postcolonial theory draws upon and is politically allied with anti-imperialism, it is not simply the continuation, and contemporary version, of this. This is in part because postcolonialism is critical of all 'essentialisms', that is, of all approaches which take national and ethnic identities for granted, by assuming them to be 'fixed', 'natural' or 'primordial' – and this includes the essentialist claims of anti-colonial nationalisms and Third Worldism.[4] If the world as we know it is the product of the violent and coercive linking together of different histories within the same temporality, then there are no 'pure' identities: 'Europe' or 'the West', and Asia or Africa or the 'non-West', were historically constituted, each defining the other. Thus while postcolonialism is indebted to anti-colonial nationalism, it is also critical of the essentializing claims of nationalisms; while it is keenly aware of the fact that some nations are more sovereign than others, it seeks to deconstruct sovereignty, not simply to advocate equal sovereignties; and while it draws attention to the many ways in which the inequalities which characterize our world have helped produce poverty and suffering, it also casts a critical eye upon the discourses of 'development', 'modernization' and 'catching-up'.

These are epistemological issues, and they bring me to the third and final misconception that needs to be avoided. Postcolonial theory is not an attempt to foster a 'non-Western IR'. The discipline of IR, as has often been observed, is principally an Anglo-American affair, with a strong base in Europe. A non-Western IR would thus be a welcome development: a plurality of voices in the discipline, actually reflecting the plurality of voices in the world that the discipline seeks to describe and comprehend, would be a very good thing indeed. But postcolonialism is not that thing.

A non-Western IR would still be IR; it would mobilize the concepts and categories of IR (state, national interest, sovereignty and the like) but now from the viewpoint of the poor and weak nations of the world, or of the emergent but not yet hegemonic powers. Such a development would, as I say, be welcome: but the ambitions of postcolonial theory are other, and go further. Postcolonial theory has at its heart an epistemological concern, namely to question the universality of the categories of modern social scientific thought, and of the disciplines into which it is divided; it is an epistemological challenge to, and critique of, existing disciplines, including IR. For the insistence upon the centrality of colonialism in the making of the modern world has, as its theoretical correlate, a call for rethinking the categories through which we have hitherto narrated and understood that history. The categories of civil society, state, nation, sovereignty, individual, subjectivity, development and so on, emerged in the course of seeking to think through and understand a particular slice of history, that of the region of the world we now know as 'Europe'. These categories are not necessarily universal ones, to be found anywhere and everywhere: postcolonial theory is in part a project to 'explore the capacities and limitations of certain European social and political categories in conceptualizing political modernity.'[5]

The above remarks, on the meaning of postcolonial theory, also serve to clarify the answer to the second question posed at the beginning of this introduction: this book is about both international relations and the discipline of International Relations. To write about war, international political economy and the other topics covered here cannot be done without also engaging the discipline which takes these topics as its specific subject matter, and without indicating why and how it is necessary to go 'beyond' such treatments. While some of the essays place the emphasis more on international relations as a field for investigation, and others on International Relations as a discipline, they are all concerned with both, and this is not the axis along which the book is divided into two parts. This division instead registers the fact that some essays are principally concerned with critique, with showing why the dominant accounts and understandings of the international are deficient, and why a postcolonial 'take' on it is necessary; while others seek to provide, or perform, a postcolonial interpretation of the international. Hence the two parts of this volume, 'Critique' and 'Performance'. All but one of the essays were specially written for this book, and were commissioned from scholars whose work is well known in the field, as well as younger scholars whose work has made an impact in International Relations, postcolonial theory, or both.

The essays

The first essay seeks to outline the three core elements of any postcolonial critique of the discipline of IR. Seth contests the dominant account of the emergence of international society, which sees it as a European invention which then radiated outwards, until it came to encompass the world. Drawing attention to the fact that the events privileged in this account of the emergence of the present international order, such as the Peace of Augsburg and the settlement of Westphalia, roughly coincide with the subjugation of the Americas, the rise of the slave trade, and the founding of the British and Dutch East India Companies, Seth asks whether it is plausible to think that these latter processes did not significantly shape the development of the international order. His answer, of course, is that any satisfactory account of the emergence of the modern international system cannot be the story 'of how an international society that developed in the West radiated outwards, but rather needs to explore the ways in which international society was shaped by the interaction between Europe and those it colonized'. He further argues that not only is the historical account of the emergence of international society deeply Eurocentric, so also is its understanding and explanation of the functioning of that international society. In one influential account, the modern international order is the first to acknowledge that the world's peoples are irreducibly heterogeneous, and that their differences cannot be 'ranked' such that some are deemed superior to others. This being so, the question confronting this international system was how to respect differences, while formulating rules that

4 *Introduction*

allowed for the interactions, including conflicts, which are also a feature of international society: rules that needed to be immune from the accusation that they favoured one set of peoples, and their values, over others. The principles of equal state sovereignty, self-determination and non-intervention are the solution to this puzzle in this account, because they are merely procedural 'form', and not substantial values or commitments. Against this, Seth argues that international law, diplomacy, and the very idea of state sovereignty are not mere neutral 'form', but in fact work to reinforce the dominance of some nations over others.

The third element in Seth's critique concerns epistemology; specifically, the idea that knowing is a representational act or process: postcolonial theory, he suggests, 'has been especially sensitive to the role of knowledge not simply as a "mirror" which represents the "real", but as a potent force for shaping what is "out there", and has been especially attentive to the many circumstances in which knowledges born in Europe are inadequate to their non-European object.' Applied to the international domain, this sensitivity can lead to the recognition that much of what IR takes as axiomatic – including the idea that there are states and nations, and that these pursue 'their' interests' – are not facts of the world that IR recognizes, but rather contingent, and contested stabilizations of meanings. The contingency and instability of these stabilizations is especially apparent in the international domain – more so, usually, than in the sphere of 'domestic' politics; and Seth concludes that the problem with IR, the discipline that takes the international as its object, is that it naturalizes and obscures this contingency and these contestations, rather than illuminating them.

John Hobson calls the conventional and widely accepted account of the emergence of sovereignty and the modern system of states the 'Eurocentric big bang theory of world politics'. This theory has a number of recensions, but all of these assume that modern sovereignty emerged in Europe and was then exported to the rest of the world, and thus that 'it is an autonomous and self-constituting Europe that we must exclusively focus upon if we are to tease out the origins of modern sovereignty'. It is this theory – through repetition, it has assumed the status of an axiom – that Hobson challenges, through a detailed historical account of the crucial role played by 'the East', and by the 'discovery' of the New World, in the emergence of modern sovereign states. Hobson shows that it is not that the sovereign state came first, and was then globalized, but rather that globalization was a necessary precondition for the rise of sovereignty; that the globalization which made the emergence of sovereignty possible was an 'Oriental globalization', centred around trade routes that had Muslim West Asia and China as their fulcrum, with the small continent of Europe connected to, but a relatively minor player in, this globalized system; and that these connections gave Europe access to material, technological and intellectual resources which proved critical to the emergence of sovereign states in Europe. In this account, sovereignty, instead of being the consequence of Europe's 'unique' or 'exceptional' economic, cultural and intellectual attributes, is rather the historical outcome of a globalizing process that includes what we have learned to call the West, the East, and (the conquest of) the New World, with the East playing the leading role. The importance of this lies not, of course, in according the non-Western world due 'credit' for founding institutions, practices and a system which arguably are of dubious value, but rather in the fact that a Eurocentric (mis)understanding of the past has as its correlate a misunderstanding of the character and functioning of the present: 'only by bringing the wider global context and the relations between civilizations into focus can we properly understand the sovereign state in particular, and world politics in general.' Hobson's important essay is thus at once and simultaneously a necessary preliminary to, as well as an important element in, enabling us to understand and practise the study of globalization differently.

Branwen Gruffydd Jones's essay begins with a striking paradox: 'the eighteenth century, the historical moment of the birth of political economy as a branch of knowledge, was also the historical moment when the economies of Britain and France were fundamentally enmeshed in the transatlantic economic system based on the slave trade and slave-labour', and yet classical political economy had very little to say about the connection between transatlantic slavery and the emergence and subsequent development of capitalist modernity. Drawing upon a body of work mostly produced by Caribbean, African and African American scholars, Gruffydd Jones shows that the transatlantic slave trade was of critical importance to the development of industry and capitalism in Europe, including the emergence of modern forms of credit and financial institutions. Why, then, was this fact not adequately registered, let alone explored, in classical political economy? Gruffydd Jones shows that this was in part because political economy took the national economy as its basic unit of analysis, thus occluding international linkages and systemic connections from its analytic frame. Just as John Hobson insists that we cannot properly account for the emergence of modern structures and practices of sovereignty by taking the nation or even Europe as our basic unit of analysis, so Gruffydd Jones shows that we cannot begin to account for the role slavery played in the emergence of the capitalist modern without regarding the global economy as 'a complex, integrated entity', rather than as a sum of national economies.

The fact that classical political economy failed, for the most part, to adopt such an approach, and instead took the national economy as its point of departure, was itself due to a deeper reason: a philosophy of history which assumed a linear conception of historical time in which societies 'progressed' from savagery to civilization, and which further assumed that the past was 'dead', and had no direct influence on the present. Against this, Gruffydd Jones argues for a different historical imagination, one for which the essential features of the era of translatlantic slavery 'constitute forms which have continued to develop, which remain embedded ever more strongly in our own present', and belong 'firmly within the history of our own present global condition'. To rethink the importance of slavery in the making of the global capitalist economy is not just a matter of correcting the historical record, but requires that we rethink the foundational assumptions of political economy, root and branch. The development of an international political economy (IPE) adequate to its subject matter requires not simply addition and correction, but critique; the problem is not simply one of inadequate knowledge, but of the politics of knowledge. Gruffydd Jones ends with a judgment that is shared by all the essays in this volume: 'To acknowledge and take seriously the centrality of colonialism to world history and the modern condition is to question the underlying assumptions, imaginations and epistemologies of disciplinary forms which have ignored, overlooked or forgotten colonialism; it is to question the politics of social inquiry and disciplinary formation.'

Just as Hobson and Gruffydd Jones unpack the history behind the emergence of the modern world system, Christine Helliwell and Barry Hindess seek to bring to light one of the most important, if usually unacknowledged, intellectual assumptions that governs the practice, and sometimes the study, of international politics and war.

As is well known, while there has been a scrupulous and agonized counting of the war dead of the 'coalition of the willing' – those willing, that is, to invade Iraq in an illegal and immoral war – there is no equivalent counting of the Iraqi dead. In the absence of any serious effort to keep track of Iraqis killed and maimed, there are only estimates – estimates that vary widely. Nor is the case of Iraq in any way an exception; it has been a consistent if usually undeclared feature of international politics that the lives of non-Western peoples have been assumed to be less valuable than those of Westerners. 'The Oriental doesn't put the same high price on life as does a Westerner ... Life is cheap in the Orient.' Beginning with this quote from the commander of American forces in Vietnam, Christine Helliwell and Barry Hindess enquire into the intellectual presuppositions that undergird and enable this presumption, one which can constantly be seen at work in international politics and war, even if it is not often articulated with the forthrightness of General Westmoreland. What makes it possible, even unremarkable, to think this otherwise extraordinary thought? Helliwell and Hindess show that the answer lies in a combination of two ideas, both of which have deep roots in Western intellectual traditions. The first they label, borrowing a phrase from the anthropologist Johannes Fabian, the 'denial of coevalness' – the idea that some peoples who are very much our contemporaries (for how else could we wage war on them?) nonetheless are in some sense relics of a past (they are 'backward', 'underdeveloped', 'medieval' and so on) who have survived into the present. The second idea or presupposition is that 'the individual' is a figure who first becomes fully visible in the present, in the Western modern. When the latter idea is made to map onto the former, it results in the conclusion that societies and peoples who belong to the past, even if they inhabit the present, are not composed of individual subjects, and are not 'like us'; they are swarms, mobs and crowds, not individuals. Lacking full individuation, they do not value life as we do, and our estimation of the value of their lives, consequently, also cannot be equated to the value 'we' attach to our own. Non-Western lives, in short, are worth less than ours: indeed, are cheap. No one can seriously doubt that this unstated presumption governs global politics and conflict; the evidence lies not only in Iraq and Vietnam, but also in Afghanistan, Pakistan – indeed, anywhere outside of the charmed circle of wealthy, mostly Western countries.

The study of war and peace is often thought to constitute the core of international relations; war, then, is an apposite topic for the first of the essays that comprise Part II of this volume, essays which seek to show how a postcolonial rereading of international relations can lead to new insights. Tarak Barkawi argues that 'postcolonial critique helps us see war and armed forces anew, phenomena whose meaning and significance both traditional and critical scholars have all too often taken for granted.' How so? The study of war in IR, Barkawi argues, is invariably subordinated to the study of security and strategy, and it is, for the most part, states that seek security and pursue strategies. Thus, treating war as a moment or aspect of security studies reinforces IR's 'nation-state ontology of the world', a world always already divided into discrete, bounded units. By contrast, the 'relational ontology' which is at the heart of postcolonial theory – exemplified by 'its insistence that the modern world was formed in and through imperial encounters', and thus that the colonizer and colonized each shaped the other – is more appropriate for the study of war. For, in an argumentative reversal which is characteristic of many of the essays in this volume, Barkawi contends that it is not simply that war is one of the consequences of a world divided into discrete units, but that war has helped produce a world divided into discrete states; that it is never simply a confrontation between nations or ethnic groups, but rather one of the chief historical means by which identities and states have been made and remade. That is why, even where they result in victory for one side, wars leave none of the participants unchanged: World War II, for instance, 'consumed one world order and spat out another'.

Like capitalism, bureaucracy and other major processes that have shaped the modern, war and the military are inherently transnational, and thus attending to colonial armies, to the wars in French Indochina or British India (note the complication of state units here) and to 'small wars' between imperial powers and irregular forces is not principally a matter of rectifying the neglect of the non-Western world, but rather a way of better understanding war and the military as such, and of accounting for the role of war and armies in the making of the modern. Barkawi's original and stimulating essay not only demonstrates the fecundity of postcolonial theory to one of the prime subjects of IR; in doing so it also makes a point that is a fundamental and recurring one in this volume, namely, that bringing the West and the non-West into the same analytical frame is important not principally as a way of attending to the non-West, but because it is a prerequisite to an adequate understanding of the global and the international. As Barkawi elegantly puts it, 'As always with the postcolonial, the journey out to the periphery helps understand better the metropole.'

Various essays in this book challenge the historical centrality accorded to Europe in most accounts of modernity, and this usually leads them to, or is accompanied by, re-examination and critique of the disciplinary configurations through which knowledge of the modern world is produced. Siba Grovogui's essay addresses the assumed moral centrality of the west. Grovogui shows that this centrality takes the specific form of ascribing universality to moral categories which in fact bear the mark of their parochial histories. In contesting this ascription,

8   *Introduction*

Grovogui ranges widely – from Hegel to Hannah Arendt and others, and from the civil and political rights of Jews to the civil rights movement of black Americans in the 1950s and 1960s – to show that the texts and categories which liberal understandings of justice and morality draw upon do not escape the historical and cultural circumstances of their production, including, and perhaps especially, the importance of racial assumptions and racial thinking to these historical and cultural circumstances. 'Philosophers cannot jump over their own historical and empirical shadow', as Grovogui puts it, and neither can philosophy do so. The empirical tinge or thread of particularity is always woven into the texture of abstract moral judgment, and thus liberal notions of justice and morality invariably have a racial tincture, for the simple reason that their 'historical and empirical shadow' was one in which race played a large part. Grovogui examines, as one of his examples or 'cases', Arendt's disapproving judgment on the use of Federal troops to compel the integration of a high school in Little Rock, Arkansas. Arendt acknowledged the oppression suffered by black Americans, but felt that in this case 'the most important constitutional question was whether citizens or persons could freely decide to enter into associations of their own liking without government interference mandating the inclusion of everyone, regardless of the ends of such associations.' This abstract argument is perfectly reasonable, *provided* one ignores the ways in which the freedom of association of citizens Arendt defends and elaborates is one that was racialized from the beginnings of the American republic, when slaves were counted as three-fifths of a man, and no part of a citizen. That is, Arendt's understanding of 'freedom', that allegedly universal desire and moral fact, 'is envisaged strictly from the perspective of the historical freemen: the original subjects of the American Revolution – white men augmented by white women and generations of white immigrants.' An important consequence follows from the critical reading offered by Grovogui: the 'civil rights movement' of black Americans should not be seen as a struggle to 'extend' civil rights to those who had not been brought within their purview, but rather is best seen as 'a practice of freedom aiming to redefine freedom itself within new moral, political and institutional political boundaries'. Grovogui's essay thus forwards a powerful argument for a recognition of the inescapabilty of historicity and culture to morality, with the conclusion that what we should be seeking is not a better universality, one which has fully purified itself of empirical/historical contaminants, but rather constantly self-critical, expansive notions of freedom and justice that are subject to negotiation and redefinition.

IR takes the nation-state as the constitutive and given unit of the discipline, but the nation is anything but given; it is not a brute ontological fact but rather an artefact, produced rather than found. It is an 'imagined community' in Benedict Anderson's influential description of it,[6] or in Sankaran Krishna's characterization, 'an emotive structure of belonging, a mental landscape as much as it is a demarcated territory on a physical planet'. The novel, Krishna observes, is more or less coeval with the nation, and has been one of the important forms through which nations have been imagined, represented and produced; conversely, the study of literature has the potential to 'enhance and enrich our understanding' of the nation. But more than this – because the nation is produced and not given, its unity is never assured and unproblematic. It is imagined in different ways, and thus approaching the given, unitary nation presumed by IR through the medium of literature may also 'enable us to stop regarding nations as things or entities that are already known to us, and instead regard them as fractal (in the sense of constantly changing and indeterminate) mindscapes.' Krishna wagers that a careful reading of literature will illuminate things about the nation that the discipline of IR, and indeed the social sciences more generally, cannot, and this wager forms the point of departure for a highly original and methodologically innovative essay.

'The postcolonial condition', writes Krishna, 'produces selves that are not satisfied and sovereign, but split and rest uneasily with themselves and their milieu. The postcolonial nation is a serrated – not smooth – space, led and represented by middle classes but not inclusive of vast numbers of society who are strangers to what one might call ... the "culture of imperialism".' That is, the postcolonial nation, because of the vast disparities which usually characterize it – disparities not only of wealth, but of culture, broadly conceived – is perhaps especially differentially imagined, and cleft. Krishna provides close and sensitive readings of three novels in English by the Indian authors Amitav Ghosh, Arundhati Roy and Kiran Desai, novels which in their different ways vividly capture, by representing and performing, the postcolonial nation as one that is 'alienated from itself, and [is] a site for the production of melancholic incompleteness'.

The point is not simply that there is a vast social and cultural gap between the middle class elites and the subaltern classes – a divide that the social sciences can more or less register and thematize – but that this divide serves to produce another, now *within* the middle class, national-citizen subject. The success of anti-colonial independence struggles gave the lie to the colonizer's claim that colonized peoples were not yet ready to be independent, that they required a period in the waiting room of history, under Western tutelage, until they could join the mainstream of history. These struggles were waged in the name of self-identical peoples, the sort of unified nation which IR presumes. However, the failure of the second of these claims, exemplified by the failure of the elites to establish hegemony over the subaltern classes and establish a unified culture, also meant a partial failure of the first claim; these elites remain painfully aware that political independence notwithstanding, they are still not fully part of the mainstream of history. The modernity they desire is still elsewhere, and far from inhabiting the modern and cosmopolitan, their lives involve a 'continuous negotiation between inside and outside, home and world, east and west, nation and international, provincial and cosmopolitan'; the characters in these novels are, in Krishna's elegiac description of them, 'injured selves oscillating between the home and the world, the national and the international, vainly looking for that moment when they could go through the looking-glass, and finally reunite with the split-self looking back at them.' These sensitive readings point to a more complicated and interesting understanding of the nation, less a given object or 'thing' than something produced by, and producing, certain modes of subjectivity, an understanding of which requires attention to the novel as much as it does to law and sovereignty.

The Afro-Asian conference, held in April 1955 in Bandung, Indonesia, brought together delegations from 29 states, most of these having recently achieved independence from colonial rule, and between them accounting for well over a billion people. The gathered delegates, despite the many differences between them, affirmed their opposition to colonialism and neocolonialism, declared their support of human rights and the principles of sovereignty and non-interference, urged increased economic and other exchanges between 'developing' countries, and began to articulate opposition to a bipolar world where relations between (and often within) states were often overdetermined by the Cold War: and in so doing, laid the foundations for what would later become the Non-Aligned Movement. At the time, this seemed to many, and not only the participants, to herald a 'revolt against the West' by those who until recently had been under its boot, and to inaugurate the possibilities of a new international order. Today all this seems very distant, and the meaning and significance of the Bandung Conference can easily be adjudged to be very limited: indeed, its rhetorical 'excesses' and rambunctiousness can easily be read as the bad manners of late entrants to the fraternity of civilized states, late entrants who have since been 'socialized' into the system they once sought to recast. And yet, it is intuitively clear to many, as Mustapha Pasha argues in his essay, that Bandung represented something much more than this: that any evaluation of its status as a historical event, to be judged by the consequences of which it was cause – even a generous evaluation – cannot do justice to its importance. Pasha's essay thus undertakes the important task of ascertaining and affirming the significance of Bandung. How to register this: how to capture the significance of the Bandung conference, a significance widely acknowledged because 'felt', by those who take colonialism and anti-colonialism seriously?

Pasha's answer is that as an 'event' in the flow of linear, historical time, Bandung is indeed of limited significance: the consequences to which it helped give rise, such as the non-aligned movement, Third Worldism, and talk of a 'New International Economic Order', are long gone. But its status as historical event does not exhaust the meaning of Bandung, which marked not simply a moment in the unfolding of history, but rather a 'discontinuous moment', a 'rupture' in the fabric of historical time. This can best be seen by counterposing 'memory' to 'history'. The abiding significance of Bandung, in Pasha's reading, lies not principally in its 'effects' as event, but in the fact that it 'is a reminder that decolonization is an impulse, not an event'; as an 'impulse' and an 'aspiration', a 'structure of feeling' containing a 'promise of perpetual decolonization', Bandung continues to signify 'a condition of active contestation and challenge to a normalized world order in which colonial rationality passes as civilization'. Bandung continues to haunt us as memory: and while memory, like history, conjures up something past, it does not represent a dead past that has efficacy only through causality and 'effects', but rather a living past, or as Pasha puts it, 'a part of the past which animates living aspirations'. Herein lies the importance of Bandung: 'Approaching Bandung outside historicist frames is to initially recognize that its salience depends not so much in its political achievements ... but rather in giving shape to a particular vision of inclusiveness and parity with durable affective and symbolic effects.' In its original and stimulating rereading of the Bandung conference, Pasha's essay shows, in a way that historicist readings cannot, why 'the memory of Bandung produces normative ideals that reappear in new global sites'.

The discipline of IR presupposes that the world is composed of nation-states that act in a self-interested fashion. Robbie Shilliam seeks to make sense of what does not square with the picture of the world produced by IR – generosity on a scale and in a form which exceeds being explained away in terms of national self-interest: such as the extraordinary aid donation given by the government of Guyana and the Guyanese people to Haiti, following the earthquake which devastated that nation in 2010. As a percentage of its GDP, Guyana gave 80 times as much as the US: but as important as the scale of the donations were the sentiments which inspired them, with politicians and activists giving voice to the sentiment that Guyanese were obligated and indebted to the people of Haiti, who in the late eighteenth century had been the first to rise in revolt, not simply against their own enslavement, but against the institution of slavery itself.

The social sciences have not altogether ignored gift-giving. Shilliam reminds us that American political science addressed this question under the rubric of 'exchange theory', which drew upon sociological and anthropological works on gift-giving, including the work that is the point of departure for virtually all discussions on this subject, Marcel Mauss's *The Gift*. However, whereas Mauss characterized the gift-giving of the Māori people of New Zealand as 'first and foremost a pattern of spiritual bonds between things which are to some extent parts of persons, and persons and groups that behave in some measure as if they were things', Mauss's successors in anthropology were troubled by his use of the notion of a spiritual bond, and in their different ways they all sought to 'despiritualize or make profane' his interpretation of the gift. For in anthropology, as in other social sciences, 'spiritual power cannot be allowed to hold any explanatory power in and of itself but must be consistently transmogrified into a profane form of power, whether symbolic, moral or ideological.' Spirituality can only function as a phenomenon to be explained, not as an element in an explanation:[7] to use it as such, as the native does, can only be treated as a sign of 'primitive thought'.

But to take this position is to disqualify, at the outset, the 'native's' explanation of her own actions and her own world. By what warrant do we disqualify such explanations and accord epistemic privilege to 'our' profane and secular understanding of the world? 'We should not', cautions Shilliam, 'assume that exploring the human condition as a profane condition produces a higher, more advanced truth about said condition.' Before we accord the social sciences such epistemic privilege, we need, at a minimum, to attend to the cosmologies and explanatory schemas of others, remaining open to the possibility that these exemplify a *different* way of understanding, ordering and inhabiting the world, rather than a *mistaken* way of doing so. Through a careful and respectful reading of aspects of Māori cosmology – it is a mark of how one's horizons expand when the normal boundaries of IR are challenged and breached, that a book on IR includes a serious discussion of Māori cosmology – Shilliam concludes that 'self-interest, realpolitik and soft power' are inadequate as explanations for the generosity of the Guyanese people, a generosity which is better understood as a form of giftgiving. He concludes that IR's treatment of all action as a species of rational self-interest is not a superior insight which reveals the real motives of actions, but is rather one of the dogmatic propositions by means of which IR consistently ignores or overwrites that which challenges its core presumptions.

International Relations is a discipline constantly in search of novelty, and while this betokens a certain open-mindedness, it also functions to incorporate and domesticate criticism; alternative ways of interpreting the international, and critiques of the discipline, often end up becoming a subset or school within it. The essays in this volume aspire to more than this: we invoke, and propose, postcolonial theory, not as one more strand or possibility in IR, but as a very different way of conceiving and studying the international. To radically rethink the international, and to think our way 'out of' IR, is of course a collective, and long-term, journey. This volume is intended as a first step on that road.

Notes

1 Introductions to the subject include Leela Gandhi, *Postcolonial Theory: A Critical Introduction* (Allen and Unwin 1998); Ania Loomba, *Colonialism/Postcolonialism* (Routledge; 2nd edition 2005); and Bart Moore-Gilbert, *Postcolonial Theory: Contexts, Practices, Politics* (Verso 1997).
2 Stuart Hall, 'When Was "The Post-Colonial": Thinking at the Limit', in I. Chambers and L. Curti (eds), *The Post-Colonial Question* (Routledge 1996), 252.
3 On this see Robert J.C. Young, *Postcolonialism: An Historical Introduction* (Wiley-Blackwell 2001).
4 One reason why terms/concepts such as 'hybridity' and 'diaspora' loom large in the postcolonial lexicon – on this see especially the essays by Homi Bhabha in his book *The Location of Culture* (Routledge: 2nd edition 2004).
5 Dipesh Chakrabarty, *Provincializing Europe: Postcolonial Thought and Historical Difference* (Princeton University Press 2000), 20.
6 Benedict Anderson, *Imagined Communities: on the Origin and Spread of Nationalism* (Verso, new edition, 2006).
7 On this point, see also Dipesh Chakrabarty, 'Minority Histories, Subaltern Pasts', *Postcolonial Studies*, 1: 1 (1998), 15–29 and Sanjay Seth, 'Reason or Reasoning? Clio or Siva?', *Social Text*, 78 (2004), 85–101.

Part I
Critique

1 Postcolonial theory and the critique of International Relations[1]

Sanjay Seth

This essay is a postcolonial critique of mainstream IR, in which I include the English School. There have been many critiques of IR – constructivist, feminist, poststructuralist and other; I draw freely from such critiques, and some of the issues raised, and points argued in this essay, have been highlighted by others, who do not write under the aegis of postcolonial theory. What is nonetheless distinctive about the critique offered here is that it seeks to systematically 'provincialize Europe', in a threefold sense: it challenges the centrality accorded to Europe as the historical source and origin of the international order; it queries the universality accorded to moral and legal perspectives which reflect and reproduce the power relations characteristic of the colonial encounter, and which are thus far from being universal; and it questions the epistemological privilege accorded to an understanding of knowledge which is blind to the constitutive, and not merely representational, role of knowledge.

In the first part of the essay I argue that mainstream IR, where it has been interested in history at all, has misdescribed the origins and character of the contemporary international order, and that an accurate understanding of the 'expansion of the international system' requires attention to its colonial origins. In the second part I suggest that mainstream IR is deeply Eurocentric, not only in its historical account of the emergence of the modern international order, but also in its account(s) of the nature and functioning of this order. The third part of the essay addresses the human sciences as heirs to a tradition of knowledge which defines knowledge as a relation between a cognizing, representing subject and an object, such that knowledge is always 'of' something out there, which exists independently of its apprehension. What this overlooks is that knowledges serve to constitute that which they purport to merely cognize or represent; in the case of IR theory, it serves to naturalize that which is historically produced. By the logic of my own argument, the same is true of other knowledges, such as liberal political theory; the difference is that whereas the unitary, rational individual of liberal political theory has almost assumed the status of an axiom, testifying to the success of historical processes, and of discourses (not least, liberal political theory itself), in naturalizing the individual, the naturalization of the nation-state and the world order is much less secure. This is precisely what makes 'the international' an interesting and revealing sphere of investigation, and one that can

16 *Critique*

and should be integrated into wider philosophical and ethical debates; but inasmuch as mainstream IR scholarship serves as the agent of such naturalization, it obscures rather than illuminates what is interesting about the international.

History

A great deal of IR displays little interest in history, for history is unimportant if the defining feature of the international order is considered to be the transhistorical fact of 'anarchy'. Kenneth Waltz writes that 'the enduring anarchic character of international politics accounts for the striking sameness in the quality of international life through the millennia...'.[2] Waltz recognizes that there have been differing international systems in the course of the millennia, differing according to whether their primarily political units were city-states, empires or nations, but different 'International-political systems, like economic markets, are individualist in origin, spontaneously generated, and unintentional.'[3] Thus not only is history not necessary, given that the fundamental nature of international life has changed little over 'millennia'; it would in any case be difficult to construct an *intelligible* account of historical change in the international arena. For Waltz, as for many other realists and neo-realists, reasoning

> starts from the premise that there *are* at any time a multiplicity of states and domestic societies, where the paradigmatic differences between ... domestic society and [international] anarchy are not questioned but simply assimilated as part of the premise ... analysts are [therefore] able to conclude that modern international politics exhibits a sameness that is basic to its history. International politics appears as no more and no less than an eternal struggle of multiple sovereign states in anarchy ...[4]

There are, however, those in the discipline who, even when they see anarchy as the defining feature of the international order, are nonetheless interested in how this historically evolved; and how an order which, in their account, first developed in Europe in the early modern period, came to encompass the globe. I refer of course to the 'English School', which has the considerable merit of enquiring into the historical origins of the contemporary international system.

However, as I argue below, the account of the 'expansion of international society' offered by the English School is Eurocentric and mistaken. And if even the historically sensitive elements in mainstream IR offer a mistakenly Eurocentric account of history, then one can begin to understand why the discipline is not of much help for those from other disciplines who seek its aid to better understand the origins and workings of the international order.

Adam Watson's detailed study of *The Evolution of International Society* partly grew out of the studies and papers of the British Committee on the Theory of International Politics, of which he had been a key member. It contains chapters on the state systems and empires of Sumer, Assyria, Persia, India, China and elsewhere, before arriving at an account of 'European international society'.

In Watson's account this began to emerge around the early sixteenth century, and was more or less formalized with the Westphalia settlement. It then spread beyond its original home, in an uncoordinated but orderly fashion: 'the members of the European society regulated their expansion between themselves, from the first orderly partition of the transatlantic world between Spain and Portugal down to the nineteenth-century arrangements for Africa, Oceania and Asia which avoided the colonial wars between Europeans that had previously marked their expansion.'[5] The spread was both necessitated and enabled by the Industrial Revolution, which gave Europe economic and technological superiority relative to other parts of the world, as well as a more general sense of superiority vis-à-vis these others. Europeans, Watson writes, 'wanted to use their superiority to Europeanize and modernize the non-European world, to bring "progress" to it';[6] whether non-Europeans welcomed or disliked the Europeans, they were deeply impressed, and 'found it difficult to resist what the Europeans had to offer'.[7] Increasing numbers of non-European rulers sought to join the European society of states, and while initially they were rebuffed, and the criteria of 'civilization' was used to exclude them, eventually Europe and the United States decided that 'all other independent states should be admitted to their international society on the same terms as themselves'.[8] Decolonization, according to Watson, brought the undisputed dominance of European powers to an end, and a new, non-discriminatory global society came into being, albeit one which 'inherited its organization and most of its concepts from its European predecessor'.[9]

Buzan and Little offer a similar, if more sophisticated (and less self-satisfied) account in *International Systems in World History*. Here they seek to document and explore the many non-European state systems that preceded the present one, a task that they see as necessary in order to avoid 'Eurocentricism',[10] something that they claim has been avoided by the English School,[11] on whose ideas they draw. They conclude that

> the standard model [of what they term 'American' IR] assumes that international systems are composed of a number of units amongst which contact is direct, and processes include diplomacy, war and trade ... Its Eurocentric vision underpins most of IR theory, and makes sense for most of the modern era. But its unconscious linkage to that particular patch of history means ... that it is incapable of dealing with both past and future international systems ...[12]

The Eurocentrism of IR mars its understanding of past international systems, and its capacity to comprehend changes that may lie in the future – but its Eurocentric assumptions 'make sense for most of the modern era' for there is no doubt that the existing international system, forged over the preceding few centuries, has its origins in Europe and must be understood with reference to a specifically European history. 'The European empires can ... be seen as the nursery, or mechanism, by which the political form of the modern state was transposed onto the rest of the world,' write Buzan and Little, and since 'the modern state is a quintessentially European phenomenon ... it is therefore to Europe's story that one has to look to explain it.'[13] Thus, while IR is admittedly Eurocentric in its understanding of the world, that Eurocentrism is warranted for the modern period – or as Hedley Bull and Watson had put it 16 years earlier,

> The present international political structure of the world – founded upon the division of mankind and of the earth into separate states, their acceptance of one another's sovereignty, of principles of law regulating their coexistence and co-operation, and of diplomatic conventions facilitating their intercourse – is, at least in its most basic features, the legacy of Europe's now vanished ascendancy. Because it was in fact Europe and not America, Asia, or Africa that first dominated and, in so doing, unified the world, it is not our perspective but the historical record itself that can be called Eurocentric.[14]

What the above accounts all offer is a rather sanitized version of 'expansion'. Watson's analysis, for instance, is one in which the violent and bloody conquest of the Americas appears as an orderly and regulated affair because it avoided colonial wars (between Europeans, that is); one in which Europeans subordinated and ruled over other peoples because they desired profit, but also because they sought to civilize non-Europeans, and bring progress to them; an account in which non-Europeans could not help but be impressed, such that they sought admission to the exclusive club of European powers; an account of how their importuning fell on deaf ears, until eventually Europe and the US relented and decided that they should be admitted as equal members; and the happy dénouement, one that saw a new international order come into being, but one which was an extension or expansion, rather than a departure from or repudiation, of the originally European society of states. An account of a period that includes the bloody conquest of the Americas, the transatlantic slave trade, the expropriation and sometimes genocide of indigenous peoples, wars of conquest, land grabs, exploitation and oppression, somehow manages to elide much of this history. It also elides the many mass struggles, violent and less violent, that constitute the history of decolonization – a history that here has only one powerful actor, the white man, who eventually comes to see that the very principles of his club mandate inclusion rather than exclusion.

But let us not dismiss Watson's account, or other similar if less egregious accounts of the 'expansion of international society', on 'polemical' grounds; for there are other grounds for doing so. This narrative of the expansion of political forms is modelled on the conventional account of the expansion of economic and social forms, that is, of the spread of capitalism (or modernity). This conventional account, which informs many disciplines, and is deeply ingrained in popular understandings, is one which presumes that capitalism began in Europe, and later radiated outwards through trade, armies and the like. The intellectual task is then by definition to identify what was (or came to be) distinctive about Europe[15] – what cluster of economic, or religious, or cultural or other characteristics, lacking in other parts of the world, enabled Europe to become, in Daniel Defert's phrase, 'a planetary process rather than a region of the world'.[16]

For some time now, there have been alternative accounts of the development of capitalist modernity, ones in which the development of capitalism and modernity is not a tale of endogenous development in Europe, but of structural interconnections between different parts of the world that long predated Europe's ascendance – and that, according to some accounts, provided the conditions for that ascendance.[17] Others, also dissenting from the conventional account, have not sought a grand alternative explanation, but have rather sought to show that the 'great divergence' between the West and the rest happened much later than the conventional narrative would have it, and due to historical exigencies rather than any trait or cluster of traits exceptional to Europe; once meaningful comparisons are made, the factors commonly thought to be unique to European history can be seen to have been present in parts of Asia.[18] What is significant for my purposes is not which, if any, of these accounts of the development and growth of capitalist modernity is accurate, but rather that the conventional account of the rise of capitalist modernity has been challenged by those who have noted that trade was not confined to inter-European trade, that the conquest of the Americas – and the influx of gold and silver which followed – played a part in the development of capitalism in Europe, and that the supply of raw materials from the colonies, and the existence of captive colonial markets for European manufactured goods, also played a part – in short, that Europe's relations with the world outside Europe may be relevant.

The 'expansion of international society' narrative, which in virtually all particulars follows the conventional account of the rise and spread of capitalist modernity – first the West, then the rest – has however not been seriously challenged or questioned. A rare exception within IR observes, 'At the same time that the "Westphalian system" of equally and mutually independent territorially sovereign states was taking shape, quite different colonial and imperial systems were being established beyond Europe';[19] 'the fundamental normative principles of the colonial and imperial systems beyond Europe' were not equality and sovereignty, but rather 'that sovereignty should be divided across national and territorial borders as required to develop commerce and to promote what Europeans and Americans saw as good government'.[20] Just as the period that saw the development of capitalism coincided with colonial conquest and trade, so too did the events and processes privileged in the conventional account of IR – the Peace of Augsburg and the settlement of Westphalia – roughly coincide with the subjugation and settlement of the Americas, the rise of the slave trade, the founding of the British East India Company and the Dutch East India Company, Macartney's mission to the Middle Kingdom, and so on. The nineteenth-century heyday of this European international system is also the period of the race for colonies, the carving up of Africa, of the development of political forms of rule such as mandates, paramountcy, concessions and franchises, spheres of interest and influence, protectorates and so on. Could it *really* be that all these processes did not significantly shape the development of the international order – that all these events were happening 'offstage' and did not shape the main dramatic narrative – or is this omission the result of bad staging?[21]

An example, or parallel, might help clarify what is at issue. For a generation, feminist scholars have been pointing out that the denial of rationality, suffrage and equality to women did not only mean that they were 'excluded': women were, after all, very much there. This denial of political rights was not simply an exclusion that was later remedied by inclusion; it rather shaped the nature of modern political thought and modern polities. The political orders being established in the eighteenth and nineteenth centuries were decisively shaped by the fact that they did extend political rights to women, and by the reasons why, and the mechanisms by which, such rights were denied. Or another example – the whites of urban South Africa were frequently ignorant about what happened in the black shanty towns of apartheid South Africa; indeed, were sometimes barely aware of their existence, even if their household labour was drawn from these areas. But the shanty towns were never the concern only of those who lived there, and those who policed them; their existence was closely tied up with, and served to shape (just as they were in turn shaped by) the prosperous white suburbs whose denizens were so blissfully unaware of the existence of the shanty towns and their inhabitants.

Analogously, it seems reasonable to presume, given that there was extensive contact between post-Westphalian Europe and the non-European world, and given that European colonialism operated through a diversity of often novel political forms, that all this was not unrelated to, and had some impact upon, the political forms and intrastate relations evolving in Europe. Thus any satisfactory account of the emergence of the modern international system cannot chart how an international society that developed in the West radiated outwards, but rather needs to explore the ways in which international society was shaped by the interaction between Europe and those it colonized. In this regard, any satisfactory account would be a postcolonial one.

The 'post' in postcolonialism, let it be noted, is not a periodization that signals the beginning of an era where colonialism is part of the past, but quite to the contrary, one that signifies the claim that conquest, colonialism and empire are not a footnote or episode in a larger story, such as that of capitalism, modernity or the expansion of international society, but are rather a central part of that story, and are constitutive of it. The 'post' does not mark the period after the colonial era, but rather the effects of this era in shaping the world that is ours. This world was not born out of the West having an impact upon and 'awakening' a dormant non-West, but of both of these being constituted in the course of multifarious (unequal, hierarchical and usually coercive) exchanges, such that neither was left untouched. As Stuart Hall puts it,

> Since the Sixteenth Century, these different temporalities and histories have been irrevocably and violently yoked together ... Their grossly unequal trajectories, which formed the very ground of political antagonism and cultural resistance, have nevertheless been impossible to disentangle,

conceptualise or narrate as discrete entities: though that is precisely what the dominant western historiographical tradition has often tried to do. No site, either 'here' or 'there', in its fantasied autonomy and in-difference, could develop without taking into account its significant and/or abjected others. The very notion of an autonomous, self-produced and self-identical cultural identity, like that of a self-sufficient economy or absolutely sovereign polity, had in fact to be discursively constructed in and through 'the Other'...The Other ceased to be a term fixed in place and time external to the system of identification and became, instead, a symbolically marked 'constitutive outside'...[22]

For some decades now, a burgeoning scholarship – some of it undertaken under the sign of postcolonial theory, some not – has sought to explore the ways in which literature, sexuality, politics and political theory, science and much else besides in the West, were affected, and sometimes decisively shaped, by colonialism and empire. The same, I suggest, needs to be done for any account of the emergence of international society.

Culture and theory

Stuart Hall, whom I quoted above, goes on to write,

> colonization so refigured the terrain that, ever since, the very idea of a world of separate identities, of isolated or separable and self-sufficient cultures and economies, has been obliged to yield to a variety of paradigms designed to capture these different but related forms of relationship, interconnection and discontinuity.[23]

Even if its historical account is suspect, IR, precisely as a function of the fact that it deals with the globe and with 'relations', is well placed to be one of those paradigms. In fact, as I argue in this section, it signally fails to be so.

IR realist and neo-realist strands of scholarship are not interested in questions of culture and culturally derived notions of what counts as morality. Since states simply exist, and by their nature pursue their interests, or else are compelled to do so by the systemic and structural circumstances of anarchy, the rules that govern state interaction are not seen to have anything to do with culture. Culture belongs to disciplines other than IR. In seeking to interrogate the place of culture and difference in mainstream IR, I therefore once again turn to those influenced by the English School, because the English School at least recognizes that the question of culture is central to, rather than peripheral to, international politics.

Robert Jackson's *The Global Covenant: Human Conduct in a World of States* makes an eloquent argument for the achievements of international society, which he characterizes as a covenant that recognizes and respects cultural and moral diversity, while avoiding many of its potentially unhappy effects. Like Bull, Watson, and Buzan and Little, Jackson regards the international order as originating in Europe, and gradually becoming globalized from the second half of the nineteenth century. In contrast to earlier systems which excluded many as 'barbarians', 'savages' and the like, this order 'is horizontal rather than hierarchical, inclusive rather than exclusive, and is based expressly on ... pluralist ethics ... the first bona fide normative discourse that communicates with and accommodates all the world's cultures and civilizations: human political diversity on a global scale.'[24] Here we have an account that, even if (in my terms) it gets its history wrong, is sensitive to difference, treating it as an inescapable fact, and even as something of ethical value. The question confronted by this new order, according to Jackson, was this: given the irreducible heterogeneity of the world's people, but given also that these peoples interact in numerous ways, they 'are going to have to find some mutually intelligible and mutually acceptable, or adequate, terms upon which they can conduct their relations ... These terms must go beyond existing cultures and civilizations.'[25] That is, the rules governing their interactions must be acceptable to all, without being those 'of' any constituent.

This is the problem to which equal state sovereignty, self-determination and non-intervention are the solution. These allow each constituent to choose and pursue its own 'domestic' way of life, while providing norms and rules for their interaction. These are procedural rules rather than substance, mere form rather than content. In Jackson's words, international law and diplomatic practice allow for interaction between 'the various political systems of a large and highly diverse planetary population', without 'require[ing] that statespeople must necessarily share deeper assumptions regarding social morality or political culture that are characteristic of particular civilizations, such as that of the West, or that of East Asia, or that of the Muslim world'.[26] 'Content' lies on the side of the state, each of which is different; 'procedure' governs their interactions, belongs to no one in particular, and thus can be accepted by all.

The problem Jackson poses for relations between states or peoples is a problem as old as the seventeenth and eighteenth centuries: once people were conceived of as free individuals, each possessed of his own property, religion, desires, goals and interests, how were they to interact with each other in a public domain, amicably if possible, but with principles to regulate their interaction and resolve conflict where it was not possible? The revolutions of 1776 and 1789 resolved this dilemma by means of a distinction between form and content, substance and procedure. As Marx brilliantly demonstrated in *On the Jewish Question*, the private now became the locus of particularity and content, while the public and political was constituted as a domain of formal and procedural rules regulating the interaction of individuals, but devoid of any content or particularity; blind to particularities such as religion and property, and partaking of none of them. Thus the modern political order was begun, and liberalism, the champion of this insurgent order, and its official face once it was triumphant, began its long career. But this answer or solution was beset by problems from the beginning, and so too is the international version of it.

In the realm of what IR calls 'domestic' political theory, one problem was that the purely 'procedural' was in fact highly substantive and normative; far from being neutral, as critics pointed out, the procedural norms adopted presupposed, and thus favoured, Christian values over other values, men over women, and so on.[27] The development of liberal political theory has in part been a process of seeking to 'purify' these procedures and norms of their content. Rawlsian liberalism famously invents the 'original position' and the 'veil of ignorance' to demonstrate, upon the foundation of a few minimal presuppositions, that rational individuals would choose procedural rules that favoured no one kind of individual, or substantive quality or attribute, such as race or wealth. Tellingly, in his later work Rawls finds that even this is not neutral or procedural enough; he abjures 'metaphysical' in favour of 'political' liberalism, an increasingly thin, spare or stripped-down liberalism which seeks to avoid presuming and thus privileging even the liberal values of individualism and autonomy: for 'so understood', writes Rawls, 'liberalism becomes but another sectarian doctrine.'[28] But this also, I would suggest, fails, and is bound to fail, for there simply *are* no 'neutral' procedural assumptions – all presumptions, including (perhaps especially) ones about what it means to be human, to be rational and desiring, are historically and culturally produced, and are thus 'particular' rather than universal.[29]

What is an insuperable problem for 'domestic' political theory is no less so for IR theory. Jackson is aware, of course, that the procedural rules he refers to do, in fact, arise from a particular historical and sociocultural setting. International law, he writes, 'although European in origin, has been adopted around the world'; and similarly the norms and practices of diplomacy are 'originally European but now universal'.[30] We have every reason, however, to doubt the 'universality' of international law, and to doubt that although originally European, it was cleansed of any cultural particularities, and became a neutral resource available to all. Antony Anghie finds instead that 'Over the centuries, international law developed a sophisticated series of technologies, doctrines, and disciplines that borrowed in important ways from the broader justifications of colonialism to address the problem of the governance of non-European peoples';[31] and James Gathii persuasively argues that this legacy continues to affect the workings of international law.[32] In any case, 'widespread', 'general' and even 'global' are not the same thing as 'universal'. The ubiquity of a practice or norm tells us nothing about its origins or the circumstances under which it was adopted (or imposed). 'Universal' suggests not just ubiquity, but some sort of transhistorical, transcultural, and/or transcendental warrant; it is no argument to suggest as Jackson does, and as Bull and Watson do, that the acceptance of these norms/procedures by non-Western states renders these norms/procedures universal, purging them of their particularistic, Western origins, any more than the adoption of the miniskirt (or, for that matter, the burqa) by all women would make these 'universal' features of womanhood.

As if recognizing this, immediately following the passages above, Jackson goes on to write,

> What statespeople also seem to possess is a common ability to recognize the limits imposed by the circumstances under which they must operate in their

conduct of foreign policy ... Statespeople can reasonably be expected to act with circumspection and prudence ... Prudence is not a European or Western virtue; it is a virtue of men and women everywhere.[33]

This is a rather revealing argument, for it is a last-ditch recourse to a sort of neo-realism – if the arguments regarding the neutral character of international law and diplomacy fail to persuade, the 'clincher' is that state interactions are shaped by the limits imposed by the way things are structured; limits which are known by prudential reasoning, which is a universal attribute – revealing, and also unconvincing. 'Prudence' *can* be thought to be a universal human attribute, just as marriage can be thought to be a universal feature of all societies, if you define it broadly enough. But in some cultures gift-giving is thought to be 'prudent', in others it is more prudent to receive than to give, and so on. Prudence is no more 'universal' than international law – it just sounds more universal because it is vague.

In short, the difficulties that political theory runs into when trying to equate the procedural with mere form, devoid of any particularistic content, are also encountered by international theory whenever it similarly seeks to acknowledge and yet disavow the importance of culture. In fact, this is even *more* of a problem for IR than for political theory. If the claimed universality of procedures or form is equally problematic for both, on the other side of the equation, the unit which is thought to be the source and bearer of content is especially problematic for IR. It seems intuitively obvious that humans are in some sense indivisible individuals, and therefore it is plausible to talk of them having desires, needs, interests and the like. In the next section of this paper I will suggest that even this is only seemingly obvious, and that it is a result of a historical process that has naturalized historically produced and therefore particularistic assumptions – but it clearly will not do to assume that 'cultures' and 'civilizations' are unitary beings possessed of 'a' need, interest, etc. And it is even more problematic to assume, as IR does when it tries to reconcile content with form, and substance with procedure, that cultures or civilizations are isomorphic with nation-states: to assume, in short, that the diversity which is here being characterized and valued is embodied or instantiated in and by the nation-state.

In *Imagined Communities*, Benedict Anderson argued that nationality was not a fact which inevitably led to the world being divided into so many nation-states, but rather that both nationality and nation were artefacts. It is a mark of the narrowing of the imaginations of us moderns that to a significant degree we have lost the capacity to imagine political community other than in the form of the nation and state.[34] Just as, for centuries after it was gone, the Roman Empire continued to dominate the European imagination, so for some centuries now our imagination has been dominated by the nation-state. That is why, when the colonized resisted, they often (though by no means always[35]) did so under the banner of nationalism, and sought their emancipation in the form of the sovereign nation-state. But since culture, civilization, language, or any of the other features which singly or in combination are invoked to define 'a people' never, in fact, corresponded to the nations which constitute the international order, then 'imagining' these in national form was always a creative, as well as a coercive, process. 'Creative' because a process of reimagining was required; Hindus and Muslim, Gujaratis and Bengalis, low and high castes – the many different ways in which the people of the subcontinent had conceived of themselves – had, for instance, to start imagining themselves as Indians. Nationalism was always a pedagogic process, one which had to posit as a fact (that the people in question were a nationality) what was in reality a project designed to produce that fact. It was also coercive: inattentive and unruly pupils had to be forced to learn, and to submit, so that peasants could be transformed into Frenchmen, Uighers into Chinese, Catalans into Spaniards. Precisely because the nation was not the political form that cultural community inevitably took in modern times, older forms of identity had now to be forced into the new container that was their alleged natural repository or form. In the case of some nation-states, this was largely successful; as some of the examples given above indicate, such imaginings continue to be contested, and are highly contingent and precarious.

With some exceptions, few scholars *actually* believe that nation-states instantiate and represent cultures and civilizations. This is less a characterization of how the world is, than an attempt to make it thus, or say that it must, at any rate, be assumed to be thus. It is one upheld, for the most part, by the UN, which continually performs the contradiction of enjoining the right to self-determination with the resolute defence of the territorial integrity and sovereignty of the existing nation-states, not only from 'external' challenges, but also from 'sub-nationalisms'.[36] But this does not in any way make nation-states isomorphic with 'peoples' or 'cultures', any more than the adoption of international law and diplomacy makes these 'neutral' procedures.

Knowing and being

In the preceding section I suggested that cultures/civilizations/peoples – the terms we use to connote collectivities whose constituent elements are held together by certain bonds – do not 'map onto' the nation-states of the world. In any case, we cannot treat collectivities, whether cultures or nations, *as if* they were like individuals, even by analogy. But this does not mean that individuals are natural, while cultures and nations are historical and constructed. We are accustomed to think that the social contract theorists of the seventeenth century awoke to the fact that men are born free, rational and equal, equipped with the capacity for willing, desiring and promising. In reality, there was often an anxiety underlying the seemingly self-assured pronouncements of these thinkers, an anxiety born of the recognition, or half-recognition, that this individual was less a premise that could be taken for granted and more something which had to be forged. In his close reading of Locke's work, Uday Mehta finds that the liberal citizen-subject capable of the free pursuit of self-interest was not a premise of Locke's thought, but rather something he thought had to be forged, through 'careful and detailed pedagogical crafting'.[37] Instead of seeing Locke and liberalism as articulating the framework and institutions through which a pent-up natural individuality finds expression, Mehta urges that we recognize that Locke and liberalism were 'involved in constructing a particular form and venue for individuality'.[38]

Others have also sought to show that the free, equal, rational and unitary individual presumed by the social sciences as an incontestable fact is no such thing; like the nation and state, s/he is a product of processes and discourses. The prime source for such 'sceptical' modes of thinking is of course Nietzsche, who in *On the Genealogy of Morals* and other writings argued that the individual capable of making promises, seeing in effects a consequence of the exercise of the will, and feeling guilt, was forged on the anvil of Greek philosophy, Christian morality and Roman law. Partly inspired by Nietzsche's work, Foucault's writings have in turn influenced those who have similarly sought to show how the individual was produced, including produced by the knowledges which posited him, rather than 'discovered' by a knowledge which finally recognized what had always been there, awaiting to be unveiled (as in Jacob Burckhardt's classic account, in which the 'veil' which made man 'conscious of himself only as a member of a race, people, party, family or corporation' finally lifted in Renaissance Italy, enabling man to recognize himself as a 'spiritual individual'[39]). In contrast and contestation with accounts which trace the emergence into sunlight of the individual subject who had once been shrouded in darkness (but who nonetheless had always been there, awaiting discovery), there are now accounts which trace the creation of this individual through various historical processes, including social, economic and discursive transformations.[40]

If Nietzsche, Freud, Foucault and others have offered critiques of some of the founding presumptions and basic categories of the human sciences, calling their seeming naturalness and incontestability into question, scholars working on the non-Western world have often simply encountered their 'empirical' inadequacy. In his recent, magisterial book on culture and power in pre-modern India, Sheldon Pollock argues that the social sciences

> have their origins in the West in capitalism and modernity and were devised to make sense of the behaviour of power and culture under Western capitalist modernity ... These are the particulars from which larger universalizations have typically been produced, in association with the universalization of Western power under colonialism and globalization.[41]

However, because it derives from

> a historically very peculiar, temporally very thin, and spatially very narrow slice of human history ... The theory developed from that history fails to help us understand, and even impedes us from seeing, what did happen elsewhere and how this might differ from what eventually produced the peculiar combination of culture and power in the modern world called the nation-state.[42]

In a similar vein, but reflecting upon the contemporary politics of the Third World, Sudipta Kaviraj observes:

> The language of modern politics is astonishingly and misleadingly universal. Wherever we go in the Third World, we meet socialists, liberals, a suspiciously high number of democrats of all kinds, nationalists of all varieties, federalists and centralists. Yet, much of the time, their actual behaviour is quite substantially different from what we are led to expect by the long-established meanings of these terms in Western political and social thought. In studying Third World politics, therefore, we face ... a serious mismatch between the language that describes this world, and the objects which inhabit it ... not [just] single isolated ideas but entire languages seem to be composed of systematically misleading expressions ...[43]

The conclusion to be drawn is neither that a recalcitrant reality must be forced into these categories, nor that these categories are 'merely' Western, and must be supplemented or replaced by an Indian social science, a Chinese one, and so on. Postcolonial writings, working at the junction of a keen awareness of this empirical mismatch on the one hand, and with a receptivity to the linguistic turn and to post-structuralist insights on the other, have been especially open to the idea that knowledges may serve to constitute the worlds that they purportedly 'represent', 'mirror', 'render' or 'portray'. Thus Timothy Mitchell argues that the distinction between real and representation, central to modern Western ways of apprehending and organizing the world, and thus central to how the French and British colonizers sought to make sense of Egypt and rule it, did not make much sense to the people of Egypt, who did not inhabit a world organized around this distinction.[44] In a similar vein, I have argued that many of the discourses that came to centre around the introduction of Western knowledge in colonial India – the complaint that Indian students were absorbing the new knowledge in their old ways, by rote learning, or the anxiety that educated Indians were in the throes of a moral crisis, 'torn' between their traditional beliefs and the new ideas they were exposed to at school and in university – should be read less as testifying to real problems, and more as indicating that certain foundational assumptions of modern knowledge could not, in fact, be assumed in India. I read these complaints and anxieties as indicating that the foundational assumptions that underlie them – that knowledge is a relation between a meaning-endowing subject and a world of disenchanted objects (which is why knowledge has to be made one's own, and rote learning is a failure of knowledge rather than a form of it), and that morality is a matter of 'beliefs' held in something called the 'mind' (hence why Western-educated Indians were assumed to be suffering moral crisis, even though most of them seemed blissfully unaware of this fact) – did not have purchase in India. However, as the institutions and practices of colonial administration and, not least, of modern knowledge itself, transformed life-worlds in India and Egypt, the social sciences became more adequate as tools for 'representing' that changed scene.

As the distinction between the real and representation became the grid organizing collective life, it assumed a certain reality, and now became meaningful in a way that it had not previously been; as the subject/object relation came to undergird not only pedagogy but the spatial layout of the city and the practices of the law court and the office, some Indians became subjects who did experience morality and religion as beliefs, and were now capable of being rent apart by the conflict between different beliefs.[45]

The free, equal, rational and unitary individual is not a fact of the world, the starting point of knowledge, but rather, a consequence or product which has been naturalized such that it can seem to be a fact. The elements which have produced it as a fact include those knowledges and discourses which purport to simply recognize and represent the fact that they have helped to produce. It is not that the individual is real and that culture and nation are cobbled together and contingent, but rather that the former has stabilized, and the marks of its manufacture have, over time, been erased; such is not the case with state and nation, which continue to be contingent and contested, with the struggles that went into their making often still inscribed on their bodies. Liberal political theory, one could say, has had more success in naturalizing the individual than mainstream IR theory has had in naturalizing state, nation and the international order.

Conclusion

These insights are the fruit of a variety of intellectual currents, and it is certainly not my intention to 'claim' these for postcolonial theory alone. The critique of mainstream IR takes many versions, and I have freely and gratefully drawn upon some of these in this essay. But postcolonial theory has been especially sensitive to the role of knowledge not simply as a 'mirror' which represents the 'real', but as a potent force for shaping what is 'out there' – and has been especially attentive to the many circumstances in which knowledges born in Europe are inadequate to their non-European object. In this, it should share a certain affinity with any discipline devoted to relationship, interconnection, diversity and discontinuity, such as IR. For 'the international' is a realm where endless and seemingly irresolvable contestations – over meanings and morals as much as resources and power – testify to the fact that few things have become so naturalized that they are not potentially subject to contestation, few presumptions so stabilized that they are not periodically destabilized. In this sense, there *is* something to the importance accorded to the sovereignty/anarchy distinction, even if not in the sense that mainstream IR usually draws it. In what is still one of the most illuminating texts on the subject, *Leviathan*, Hobbes shows that sovereignty is the name and form of a capacity to impose and stabilize meanings. It is always a function of strategies and tactics, struggles and conflicts, and to that degree, contingent and variable. This becomes especially apparent in the international realm, where no sovereignty has yet succeeded in imposing stable meanings.

It is precisely this – the fact that in the international realm meanings have not become stabilized, and the precarious and contested nature of modernity can be more readily seen – that makes 'the international' especially interesting. However, the discipline which makes the international the object of its enquiry is, for the most part, an obstacle to a recognition and exploration of this, rather than a guide to it. Mainstream IR seems content to naturalize what it could problematize, and to assume that which it should deconstruct: whence the need for its critique.

Notes

1 This chapter is a revised version of 'Postcolonial Theory and the Critique of International Relations', which appeared in *Millennium*, 40: 1 (August 2011).
2 Kenneth Waltz, *Theory of International Politics* (McGraw-Hill 1979), 66.
3 Waltz, op. cit., 91.
4 Richard Ashley, 'The Powers of Anarchy: Theory, Sovereignty, and the Domestication of Global Life', in James Der Derian (ed.), *International Theory: Critical Investigations* (Macmillan 1995), 115. Which is why where history does figure in IR texts, it is often little more than an illustrative device, for which purpose a paragraph or two on the Peloponnesian War, and a thumbnail sketch of the Peace of Augsburg and the Treaty of Westphalia take us rapidly to the modern world order. A similar history of political thought, usually featuring Thucydides, Machiavelli, Hobbes, Rousseau, Kant and sometimes others, provides a genealogy to a young discipline seeking distinguished forefathers – even if it requires readings so unfettered by any sense of historical context, and so unburdened by any textual evidence, that they should make any serious scholar blush. But as R.B.J. Walker observes, these are not *histories* of political thought, but rather accounts of 'an ahistorical repetition in which the struggles of these thinkers to make sense of the historical transformations in which they were caught are erased in favor of assertions that they all articulate essential truths about the same unchanging and usually tragic reality: the eternal game of relations between states' – R.B.J. Walker, 'History and Structure in the Theory of International Relations', in Der Derian, op. cit., 322.
5 Watson finds the collaboration of the great powers during the Boxer rebellion in China especially noteworthy. Admittedly, the great powers violated the independence of China, but they did so in the name of the international community, as the UN was later to do in other 'chaotic areas', *The Evolution of International Society* (Routledge 1992), 272–3.
6 Watson, op. cit., 268.
7 Watson, op. cit., 268–9.
8 Watson, op. cit., 258.
9 Watson, op. cit., 300.
10 Barry Buzan and Richard Little, *International Systems in World History: Remaking the Study of International Relations* (Oxford University Press 2000), 20–21.
11 Buzan and Little, op. cit., 30.
12 Buzan and Little, op. cit., 369.
13 Buzan and Little, op. cit., 246.
14 Hedley Bull and Adam Watson, 'Introduction', in Bull and Watson (eds), *The Expansion of International Society* (Oxford: Clarendon Press 1984), 2.
15 'Much of modern social science', as Kenneth Pomeranz observes, 'originated in efforts by late nineteenth and twentieth century Europeans to understand what made the economic development path of western Europe unique' – *The Great Divergence: China, Europe, and the Making of the Modern World Economy* (Princeton University Press 2000), 3.
16 Quoted in Mary L. Pratt, 'Scratches on the Face of the Country: or, What Mr Burrow saw in the Land of the Bushmen', *Critical Inquiry*, 12: 1 (autumn 1995), 125.

17 Andre Gunder Frank, for instance, writes that 'Europe did not pull itself up by its own economic bootstraps, and certainly not thanks to any kind of European "exceptionalism" of rationality, institutions, entrepreneurship, technology ... instead Europe used its American money to muscle in on and benefit from Asian production, markets, trade – in a word, to profit from the predominant position of Asia in the world economy' – Andre Gunder Frank, *ReOrient: Global Economy in the Asian Age* (University of California Press 1998), 4–5. See also John Hobson, *The Eastern Origins of Western Civilisation* (Cambridge University Press 2004); Jack Goody, *The East in the West* (Cambridge University Press 1996); J.M. Blaut, *The Colonizer's Model of the World: Geographical Diffusionism and Eurocentric History* (Guilford Press 1993); Gurminder Bhambra, *Rethinking Modernity: Postcolonialism and the Sociological Imagination* (Palgrave Macmillan 2007).

18 See, inter alia, Pomeranz, op. cit.; Roy Bin Wong, *China Transformed: Historical Change and the Limits of Western Experience* (Cornell University Press 1997); and various works by Sanjay Subrahmanyam, including 'Connected Histories – Notes towards a Reconfiguration of Early Modern Eurasia', *Modern Asian Studies*, 31: 3 (July 1997).

19 Edward Keene, *Beyond the Anarchical Society: Grotius, Colonialism and Order in World Politics* (Cambridge University Press 2002), 97.

20 Keene, op. cit., 98.

21 Keene makes a very similar point in his discussion of Hedley Bull's claim that the fact of European dominance means that any understanding of international society should concentrate on the emergence of a European society of states. Keene rejects this claim on grounds that it is a non sequitur. Since 'European dominance was primarily exercised through practices of colonialism and imperialism', if 'the fact of European dominance ought to dictate what our research program on order in modern world politics should be, it directs us *away* from the European states-system, not towards it.' Op. cit., 28.

22 Stuart Hall, 'When Was "The Post-Colonial": Thinking at the Limit', in I. Chambers and L. Curti (eds), *The Post-Colonial Question* (Routledge 1996), 252.

23 Hall, op. cit., 252–3.

24 Robert Jackson, *The Global Covenant: Human Conduct in a World of States* (Oxford University Press 2000), 14.

25 Jackson, op. cit., 14–15.

26 Jackson, op. cit., 24.

27 For a very influential example of this sort of argument, see Carole Pateman, *The Sexual Contract* (Stanford University Press, 1988).

28 John Rawls, 'Justice as Fairness: Political Not Metaphysical', *Philosophy and Public Affairs I*, 14: 3 (1985), 246. See also *Political Liberalism* (New York: Columbia University Press 1993), where the later position is developed and presented, and also *The Law of Peoples* (Harvard University Press 1999).

29 On this see Sanjay Seth, 'Liberalism and the Politics of (Multi)Culture: or, Plurality is not Difference', *Postcolonial Studies*, 4: 1 (2001).

30 Jackson, op. cit., 24.

31 Antony Anghie, 'Decolonizing the Concept of "Good Governance"', in Branwen Gruffydd Jones (ed.), *Decolonizing International Relations* (Rowman and Littlefield 2006), 123. See also his *Imperialism, Sovereignty and the Making of International Law* (Cambridge University Press 2005); and Siba Grovogui, *Sovereigns, Quasi Sovereigns and Africans: Race and Self-determination in International Law* (University of Minnesota Press 2006).

32 James Gathii, *War, Commerce, and International Law* (Oxford University Press 2009), and 'Dispossession through International Law: Iraq in Historical and Comparative Context', in Gruffydd Jones, op. cit.

33 Jackson, op. cit., 24.

34 On this see R.B.J. Walker's important *Inside/Outside: International Relations as Political Theory* (Cambridge University Press 1992). See also Sanjay Seth, 'A Postcolonial World?', in Greg Fry and J. O'Hagan (eds), *Contending Images of World Politics* (Macmillan 2000).
35 There were also anti-colonial movements that imagined a postcolonial future in terms other than those of the nation and state. See for instance, Michael Adas, *Prophets of Rebellion: Millenarian Protest Movements against the European Colonial Order* (University of North Carolina Press 1979); Ranajit Guha, *Elementary Aspects of Peasant Insurgency in Colonial India* (New Delhi: Oxford University Press 1986); Reynaldo Ileto, *Pasyon and revolution: popular movements in the Philippines, 1840–1910* (Quezon City: Ateneo de Manila University Press 1989); Sanjay Seth, 'Rewriting Histories of Nationalism: The Politics of "Moderate Nationalism" in Colonial India, 1870–1905', *American Historical Review*, 104: 1 (February 1999). That these have often been written out of the historical record, or else assimilated as precursors or variants of nationalism, is only further testimony to the grip the nation-state has acquired over us.
36 On this see James Mayall, *Nationalism and International Society* (Cambridge University Press 1990).
37 Uday Singh Mehta, *The Anxiety of Freedom: Imagination and Individuality in Locke's Political Thought* (Cornell University Press 1992), 13.
38 Mehta, op. cit., 169.
39 Jacob Burckhardt, *The Civilization of the Renaissance in Italy*, trans. by S.C.G. Middlemore (New York: Mentor 1960), 121.
40 See, for instance, Heller, Sosna and Wellbery (eds), *Reconstructing Individualism* (Stanford University Press 1986); Nikloas Rose, *Governing the Soul: Shaping of the Private Self* (Free Association Books, 2nd revised edition 1999) and 'Authority and the Genealogy of Subjectivity', in P. Heelas, S. Lash and P. Morris (eds) *Detraditionalization* (Wiley-Blackwell 1995); Roy Porter (ed.), *Rewriting the Self* (Routledge 1997).
41 Sheldon Pollock, *The Language of the Gods in the World of Men: Sanskrit, Culture, and Power in Premodern India* (University of California Press 2006), 33.
42 Pollock, op. cit., 564.
43 Sudipta Kaviraj, 'In search of civil society', in Sudipta Kaviraj and Sunil Khilnani (eds), *Civil Society: History and Possibilities* (Cambridge University Press 2001), 289.
44 Timothy Mitchell, *Colonising Egypt* (Cambridge University Press 1988).
45 Sanjay Seth, *Subject Lessons: The Western Education of Colonial India* (Duke University Press 2007).

2 The other side of the Westphalian frontier

John M. Hobson

It is an axiom of the discipline of International Relations (IR) that the modern era of world politics emerged with the birth of the sovereign state at Westphalia in 1648. Moreover, it is assumed that having been 'made in Europe', the sovereign state was exported across the world, in the process creating a 'globalized' system in the image of the European interstate system. This fundamental axiom is not merely problematic but betrays a deeper problem that haunts the discipline; that of its underlying Eurocentrism. In this chapter I aim to interrogate this standard understanding of the rise of the European sovereign state in order to reveal its underlying Eurocentrism, while simultaneously providing an alternative non-Eurocentric theoretical approach that could replace it.

In this chapter I argue that all the theories of the rise of the modern sovereign state share a remarkable consensus, insofar as they ascribe its origins to the *exceptional* properties of Europe. Of course, such a claim will appear as immediately counter-intuitive to most readers. Historical sociologists will think immediately of the ferocious debate that is conducted between Marxist/World-Systems theorists, liberals and neo-Weberians,[1] as much as IR scholars will think of the heated debate between liberals, realists, Marxists, constructivists and English School theorists.[2] But I argue that they all share in a Eurocentric consensus, which posits that the Europeans single-handedly created the sovereign state in the absence of any Eastern input.

To be more specific I argue that all these familiar theories of state-formation subscribe to what I call the *Eurocentric big bang theory* of world politics/globalization (BBT from henceforth). This discourse assumes a two-step narrative of the rise and spread of sovereignty. In the first step the big bang of modernity explodes within Europe in 1648 at Westphalia, having previously unfolded through an evolutionary process that is entirely endogenous to Europe, before the sovereign state is exported to the East through imperialism and proto-globalization. Critically, this discourse presupposes that Europe was, and still is for that matter, an *exceptional* civilization. That is, it exhibited advanced rational institutions, which ensured that the explosion of modernity was destined to occur only within Europe. For the logical corollary of this Eurocentric assumption is the belief that the Eastern Other was deemed to be either incapable of auto-generating or, if auto-generation was deemed to be possible, so this would inevitably follow the path that was trailblazed by the exceptional Europeans.[3] This in turn presupposes the twin Eurocentric moves of splitting apart East and West in the first instance by imputing an imaginary frontier or line of civilizational apartheid. And in a second move the West is inscribed with uniquely progressive properties that make its progress into modernity but a fait accompli, while the East is relegated to a backward ghetto that endures only regressive and barbaric institutions, and is thereby condemned (in the absence of the civilizing mission) to eke out an impoverished and stagnant existence in the shadowy recesses of the mainstream Western story. Accordingly, this means that the rise of political modernity would unfold through an endogenous Eurocentric 'logic of immanence', given that such an outcome was immanent within Europe's unique and exceptional social structure. Thus while the various theories of state-formation select out different features of the European social structure, nevertheless all are agreed that it is an autonomous and self-constituting Europe that we must exclusively focus upon if we are to tease out the origins of modern sovereignty.

The upshot, then, is that for all the heat of the various debates within IR and historical sociology, the fact is that when viewed through this particular non-Eurocentric lens they all appear as but minor variations on a consistent Eurocentric narrative. And while a very small minority of scholars have questioned the chronology or dating of the emergence of sovereignty, with some arguing that it appeared only in the nineteenth century,[4] and others predating it several centuries prior to 1648,[5] nevertheless all are agreed on the essential point that political modernity and sovereignty were pioneered by the exceptional Europeans and unfolded through the Eurocentric logic of immanence before they were subsequently exported to the East.

This chapter advances an alternative non-Eurocentric narrative for understanding the origins of sovereignty by peering at the Other side of the Westphalian–European frontier. While I shall take Westphalia as the very approximate moment when sovereignty was born – notwithstanding the point that it was only consolidated in the early twentieth century in the West and the late twentieth century in the East – nevertheless I want to argue that European political modernity was not purely 'Self-made' but was to an important extent 'Other-made'. While I shall certainly point to some of the autonomous inputs that the Europeans made, overall I seek to ontologically downgrade the monopoly of autonomy that Eurocentrism grants the Europeans while simultaneously upgrading the agency of the East that is lost within the Eurocentric narrative. Still, my purpose is not to invert Eurocentrism to thereby create a kind of Occidentalism, but to combine Eastern and Western agency in the account of the rise of sovereignty. This I do by introducing the context or crucible of inter-civilizational relations that comprises an agential East and an agential West within which sovereignty was forged.

More specifically I want to argue that this can best be understood through the 'dialogue of civilizations'. This comprises two core components. First, I discuss the dialogue in terms of the diffusion of Eastern 'resource portfolios' (ideas, institutions and technologies) that traversed across the Oriental global economy to be assimilated by the Europeans in the process of state-formation. This covers primarily the materialist side of state-formation, though I also include a discussion of the epistemic changes associated with the Renaissance and the Scientific Revolution. And second I refer to the imperial encounter between the Spanish and the indigenous 'Americans' after 1492. For this extra-European civilizational encounter was vital in constructing the *idea* of sovereignty. This, however, turned out to be much more of a monologue, even if this inter-civilizational encounter was a vital ingredient in the emergence of sovereignty within Europe. Overall, these inter-civilizational relations were bound up within what I call Oriental globalization; for it is my key claim that sovereignty was made possible by Eastern-led globalization or 'Oriental globalization'.

The upshot of my alternative narrative is to break with the linear Eurocentric narrative in four key ways. First, rather than assume that European sovereignty came first and then globalization second – as in the Eurocentric BBT – I suggest that globalization was a crucial *precondition* for the rise of sovereignty. Second, I argue that globalization between 1492–*c.*1800 was Eastern-led, thereby disturbing the Eurocentric assumption that globalization is essentially Westernization. Third, rather than imperialism following the rise of sovereignty I argue that the imperialist encounter with the Americas provided a constitutive element in the invention of sovereignty back in Europe. Fourth, I argue that state-formation did not unfold through a linear endogenous path within Europe but was significantly shaped by 'exogenous' factors that in aggregate produce a discontinuist picture of the process.

In turn, these four points, which highlight the dialogues of civilizations, serve to break down the imaginary frontier or line of civilizational apartheid between East and West, thereby revealing the Other in the Self. The chapter advances my narrative in three key sections; the first considers the bare outlines of the Oriental global economy after 1492, while the second section considers the Eastern input into the materialist side of the rise of sovereignty. And finally, the third section considers the inter-civilizational imperial encounter between the 'Europeans' and the Native 'Amerindians', within which the *idea* of sovereignty was partially forged.

The Oriental global backdrop to the rise of sovereignty

It is not my purpose to go into a full discussion of the presence of both Oriental globalization between 1492–1800 and 'Oriental regionalization' between *c.*500–1492. While I have discussed this in detail elsewhere,[6] my aim here is primarily to sketch the outlines in order to establish the point that there was a nascent global infrastructure along which Eastern 'resource portfolios' traversed before they were assimilated by the Europeans in the process of sovereign state-formation (the subject of the next section).

The period of Oriental globalization did not spring up out of nowhere in 1492 but was the accumulation of a set of near global connections that were forged under what could be called Oriental regionalization. This emerged gradually after about the sixth century CE and was made possible in large part by the formation of a series of interlinked regions or empires. These comprised T'ang China

(618–907), the Islamic Ummayad/Abbasid empire in West Asia (661–1258), the Ummayad polity in Spain (756–1031) and the Fatimids in North Africa (909–1171). These interlinked regions were vital in promoting an extensively pacified space that fostered not just growing inter-regional trade but, above all, constituted a kind of conveyor belt along which Eastern resource portfolios travelled both eastward and westward.

While a number of capitalist agents were important here – including Africans, Jews, Indians, Chinese and Javanese – the prime role in setting up the preconditions for the subsequent Oriental global economy was performed by the West Asian Muslims. Janet Abu-Lughod describes an interlinked Afro-Eurasian economy that peaked in the fourteenth century.[7] It comprised three prime routes, though the two most important ones were the Middle and Southern routes. Both these routes were presided over by the West Asian and North African Muslims. The Middle route had a land component that linked the Eastern Mediterranean with China and India, and a sea route that passed through the Persian Gulf. The Southern route linked the Alexandria–Cairo–Red Sea complex with the Arabian Sea and then, as with the Middle sea route, the Indian Ocean and beyond to South East Asia, China and Japan. These routes ensured that Europe was fundamentally connected to the Afro-Asian-led global economy after about the eighth century.

After 1000 this circuit intensified further preparing the groundwork for the subsequent Oriental globalization phase that emerged once the Americas had been brought into this system. The relatively brief appearance of the Mongol Empire, despite our popular image of Genghis Khan and his ruthless horsemen, enabled a pacified space particularly along the Northern route that in turn promoted inter-regional trade and the diffusion of Eastern resource portfolios. But when this route went into decline in the fourteenth century it was superseded by the Middle and Southern routes. Of course, Eurocentric world history assumes that it was the Venetians who dominated global trade. But with the 'Fall of Acre' in 1291 – the last outpost of the defeated Crusaders – the Venetians came to rely on the dominant Southern route which was presided over by the Egyptians. As Abu-Lughod claims, 'Whoever controlled the sea-route to Asia could set the terms of trade for a Europe now in retreat. From the thirteenth century and up to the sixteenth that power was Egypt.'[8] Moreover, Venetian trade did not dry up after 1291 but continued on, as I note later.

This Oriental regionalization process intensified further after 1492 as the Americas were inserted into it, thereby effecting the shift to a nascent Oriental *global* economy. Of course, Eurocentric world history views the entry of the Iberians and the European Age of Discovery as the key factor in establishing primitive or proto-globalization. That they played *a* role is undeniable. But such a role turned out to be schizophrenic. For in the Americas, the Spanish and Portuguese played an imperialist role, whereas in Asia they were confined to the role of dependent intermediary.[9] The former role will be analysed in the next section, the latter in the final section. But for the moment I want to note that in the Indian Ocean the Europeans functioned on the back of Asian superiority, with the Europeans being dependent upon Asian goodwill, capital, inter-country trading, and local knowledge right down to 1800, all of which guaranteed the Europeans but a very small slice of the Indian Ocean trade.[10]

Nevertheless, Eurocentrism claims that after 1492/1498 the Portuguese and Spanish initiated the process of proto-globalization, before the global baton of power was passed on to the Dutch and then the English. But in fact European trading connections intensified thanks largely to the role played by the Muslims and Indians and, above all, the Chinese who sat at or near the centre of the global economy between 1492 and 1800. And for a whole variety of reasons, the paradox here is that the official 1434 Chinese ban on foreign trade came just before Chinese trade escalated.[11] The conversion of the Chinese economy onto a silver standard in the mid–fifteenth century was the seminal moment. For as a result of the huge demand that the Chinese economy had for foreign silver, owing to its large trade surplus, global trade intensified rapidly.[12] Simultaneously it led to the opening up of a new trade route that went from South America to the Philippines via the Spanish Manila galleon and thence into China. Above all, it was this Chinese input that ultimately sucked Europe *directly* into the trading and financial global system (rather than vice versa as Eurocentrism posits), given that the Europeans had been only indirectly linked in previously. For it was the plundered Spanish bullion that not only enabled the Europeans to finance their trade deficit with Asia in general and China in particular, but also to finance their activities within the Indian Ocean in the first place.[13]

Nevertheless, the key point in all of this is that during the main period of European state-formation, the little Christian continent that constituted a small promontory off the edge of the Asian-led global economy, was linked directly into this nascent global system and received not just trade but all manner of Eastern resource portfolios that were subsequently assimilated in the sovereign state-formation process, to a consideration of which I now turn.

The dialogue of civilizations I: Eastern origins of sovereignty

This section counters the standard Eurocentric narrative of the rise of the modern sovereign state within Europe that works according to the Eurocentric *logic of immanence*. That Europe was partly self-made seems a reasonable proposition, but it should not be done to the exclusion of the formative role played by the East. Here I reveal how Eastern influences played an important role in shaping each of the manifold materialist sources of the sovereign state – mainly economic, geopolitical/military – though I also include various epistemic prerequisites associated with the Renaissance and Scientific Revolution. Here I accept that many of the sources that mainstream Eurocentric theories focus upon were important, but I argue that these in turn were significantly informed by Eastern influences.

War and the military revolution

Perhaps the single most important argument that is found right across the spectrum of state theory concerns the role played by warfare in general and the

Military Revolution (1550–1660) in particular. The centrepiece of this revolution lay in the deployment of guns, gunpowder and cannon, all of which were harnessed to scientific management procedures. But these crucial military technologies were in fact invented in China during what might be called the 'Chinese Military Revolution', c.850–c.1290. Gunpowder was invented around 850 after several centuries of prior experimentation. Nevertheless, to the extent that some Eurocentric historians concede this, they respond by claiming that it was deployed only in Chinese fireworks. But while it was used in Chinese flame-throwers around 969, by 1231 it was deployed in bombs, grenades and rockets, and by about 1275 the first metal-barrelled gun firing metal bullets was invented. Finally, by about 1290 a crude cannon, known as the 'eruptor', had been invented.[14] Of course, this might have all been coincidence were it not for the point that there is good circumstantial evidence to suggest that these inventions diffused across to be subsequently copied by the Europeans.

While Eurocentric historians sometimes attribute the discovery of gunpowder to Francis Bacon in 1267, it is noteworthy that the Chinese recipe for gunpowder was available in print form in 1044. Moreover, it was during the thirteenth century that numerous European friars were sojourning in China, such that some have claimed that it was William of Rubrick (Bacon's friend) who, having returned in 1257, could well have passed on the formula to Bacon.[15] Importantly, as Needham notes, Bacon's description of gunpowder bears an uncanny resemblance to Chinese firecrackers.[16] It is also noteworthy that the first English cannon of 1327, illustrated in a manuscript by Walter de Millemete, was an exact replica of the Chinese eruptor. Given that there is no evidence to support the claim that this cannon had been developed over a sufficient period of time in the English context prior to 1327, it seems extremely unlikely that this was an independent English invention. And it is possible that the Europeans finally, albeit belatedly, made the cannon and gun the centrepiece of their armies as they confronted the Ottoman Empire which was, as Marshall Hodgson originally pointed out, a 'gunpowder empire'.[17] Moreover, I note later that the Scientific Revolution was partly informed by imported Islamic ideas. This is significant because the European military revolution was also about applying scientific procedures to the practice of soldiery. Accordingly, I suggest that without these Eastern inventions and ideas there might never have been a European Military Revolution, which in turn constituted one factor in promoting the centralized sovereign state.

Nevertheless, it is noteworthy that there were obviously intra-European factors that conditioned or made the assimilation of Chinese military technologies attractive. For example, as rulers sought to transcend the centrifugal political power of the nobles, especially after 1450, so the adoption of modern military technologies effected a shift away from the feudal mode of warfare. And arguably it was only possible to begin this attack on noble/aristocratic power as a result of its progressive weakening following the impact of the Eurasian plague epidemic that hit Europe in 1347 (as I explain below). Ultimately the conclusion here is that while the Europeans did not come up with the major inventions themselves they did, however, succeed in putting all these Eastern influences together into what undoubtedly became a most potent and lethal mixture.

Economic aspects of state-formation

There are, of course, a variety of arguments that are important here. Some, including Marxists, emphasize the importance of the Renaissance Italian city-state system, within which the practice of extra-territoriality and diplomacy were initiated (at least within Europe).[18] This in turn links into the argument about the role of long-distance trade in underpinning state-formation.[19] And this in turn links back to the rise of the European commercial and financial revolution that first emerged within Italy in the eleventh century. It, therefore, makes sense to treat the arguments revolving around European trade and Italian capitalism together. While it is certainly the case that the Italian merchants played a primary role in the intra-European trading system, nevertheless this was only made possible by the fact that Italy was linked directly into the West Asian-led trading system. Indeed Italy was important within Europe because ultimately it constituted a vital trading bridgehead with Islamic West Asia. This continued on after 1291 as Italy benefited from its links with Egypt, and subsequently with the Ottoman Empire after 1517. Critically, Egypt was the central nodal point in the global economy between 1291–1517, with some 80 per cent of all global trade passing through it. Thus the Italian merchants were best understood as intermediaries rather than pioneers of global trade.

While Islamic West Asia contributed directly to the export of trade into Europe, its greater significance lay in its unique position within the global economy. Indeed West Asian and Levantine Islam constituted the 'bridge of the world' relaying trade from the Indian and Chinese economic powerhouses into Europe. In turn, Eastern trade was then pumped around Europe by the Italians as it flowed in from the Islamic world. Without this Eastern trading stream it is doubtful as to whether the Italians would have played the proactive role within Western Christendom (which in turn had nourished the French Champagne Fairs, the German Hansa and other localized markets). Moreover, it would be incorrect to assume that the Italians were the unique originators of the financial revolution for, once again, almost all of the institutions that the Italians became famous for originated in West Asia.

The famous *Commenda* partnership agreement (known as the *Collegantzia*), which was allegedly pioneered in Italy in the eleventh century, turns out to have been an Islamic invention – though it in turn had been developed from an earlier Persian institution.[20] Noteworthy too is that Muhammad had originally been a *Commenda* merchant. Moreover, banks, bills of exchange (*suftaja*), cheques (*hawāla*), credit institutions, and insurance originated in West Asia many centuries before they were disingenuously claimed as Italian inventions. And, last but not least, double-entry bookkeeping was not the monopolistic preserve of the Italians given that similar systems existed in China, West Asia and India. All in all, therefore, however important the Italian city-state system was in setting Europe on course for sovereignty, we should not treat it in isolation from the wider Eastern context. To do so is to give a weighting to Italian agency that it cannot bear. What then of European economic development after 1450?

Here I shall tackle this by considering another factor that is emphasized by materialist theories – notably the role of the Black Death. Some see this as an independent causal factor, leading to the enhancement of the relative bargaining power of the peasants vis-à-vis the nobles and the commutation of feudal dues into cash payments.[21] But others view it as an intervening variable, given that class struggles between landlords and peasants opened up the environment in which a Malthusian crisis coupled with the Black Death occurred.[22] Either way, though, whatever the exact ontological weighting should be, it seems fair to say that the Black Death played *a* role in preparing the groundwork for sovereign state formation.

It seems curious to discuss the Black Death without enquiring as to whence it originated. For this disease was a near-global phenomenon the impact of which was yet more devastating than the current AIDS epidemic. As William McNeill originally pointed out, the plague originated in China in 1331 and then spread across the Eurasian economy through the Oriental trade routes. It was carried along the caravan routes of the Mongol Empire, reaching the Crimea by 1346. It then penetrated the sea-trade routes to arrive in Western Christendom by 1347.[23] But the ramifications of this point are yet more far-reaching. For the Black Death brought an end to the Mongol Empire and with it the Northern route of the global economy.[24] This in turn served to isolate some of the Eastern parts of Christendom from the vital impulse that Eastern trade brought with it (most notably Russia). Nevertheless, the closing of the Northern route was ultimately significant not least because it brought the Middle and especially the Southern routes to the fore, both of which in turn nourished the European commercial recovery after 1450. And here I return to reconsider the pioneering role that the Italians allegedly played in stimulating capitalism, this time by examining the origins of the Renaissance and the subsequent scientific revolution.

Epistemic origins of sovereignty: the Renaissance and scientific revolution

If the Italians are wrongly credited with various economic institutional innovations that they did not in fact invent, and are wrongly treated as pioneers of global trade more generally, it might be replied that it is nonetheless incontrovertible that their intellectual genius was what lay at the heart of the Renaissance. And, of course, the Renaissance is thought to have been a rebirth of Ancient Greek ideas. That the Renaissance had major consequences for the rise of capitalism and the sovereign state in Europe seems a reasonable proposition. Problematic, though, is the Eurocentric claim that this was a pure European innovation. For the Europeans owe a large debt once more to the West Asian and North African

Muslims, in the absence of which there might never have been a European Renaissance or, equally, a Scientific Revolution.

Islamic breakthroughs in mathematics including algebra and trigonometry were vital. The former term was taken from the title of one of al-Khwārizmī's mathematical texts (as a result of the translation made by the Englishman Robert of Ketton in 1145). And by the beginning of the tenth century all six of the classical trigonometric functions had been defined and tabulated by Muslim mathematicians. This, in turn, presupposed the use of Indian numerals; a method that was introduced into Europe by the Muslims but relabelled 'Arabic numerals'. Developments in public health, hygiene and medicine were also notable. Al-Rāzī's medical works were translated and reprinted in Europe some 40 times between 1498 and 1866. And Ibn Sīnā's (or Avicenna's) *Canon of Medicine* became the founding text for European medical schools between the twelfth and fifteenth centuries. The Muslims developed numerous medicines and anaesthetics and pioneered the study of anatomy. Notable here is the Egyptian physician Ibn al-Nafis (d. 1288), whose work on the human body, which contradicted the traditional position of the Greek physician Galen, fully pre-empted the much-heralded work of William Harvey by 350 years. The Muslims were also keen cartographers, astrologers and astronomers and their ideas were avidly borrowed by the Europeans (see below). Notably, Ibn al-Shātir's mathematical models bore an uncanny resemblance to those used by Copernicus 150 years later. And as early as the ninth century, al-Khwārizmī calculated the circumference of the Earth to within 41 metres. Significantly, the Baconian idea that science should be based on the experimental method had already been pioneered by the Muslims (not the Greeks). Moreover, Ancient Egyptian Hermetic texts also featured in the Italian Renaissance, given that they were translated after 1460 by Marsilio Ficino at the Court of Cosimo de Medici. And last, but by no means least, it is of course true that single-point perspective art was an important feature of the Renaissance and, according to some, was a crucial idea that made sovereignty possible.[25] But while this idea is usually attributed to Filippo Bruneschelli around 1425, this necessarily obscures the key role played by Ibn Al-Haytham (Alhazen), who ushered in the optical revolution as early as the turn of the second millennium CE.[26]

Critically, the Eurocentric reply that the Muslims simply worked *within* the ideas of the Ancient Greeks misses the point that they were often critical of the ancient texts that they had translated and that they frequently took them in new directions. Moreover, there is a wealth of evidence to reveal how the Europeans accessed this Eastern knowledge.[27] Accordingly, the very phrase 'European Renaissance' is problematic since it exaggerates its Ancient Greek foundations and denies its substantial Eastern heritage. All in all, then, the appropriate conclusion would be that while the sovereign centralized state first emerged within Europe, it was only made possible by the role of extra-European Eastern inputs that flowed across the Oriental global economy after 1492, having previously diffused across the Afro-Eurasian regional economy between c.500–1492.

Imperial encounters and the dialogue of civilizations II: inventing 'America' and 'Europe', constructing sovereignty

Today, IR scholars acknowledge that IR theory and the idea of sovereignty rests to an important extent on the arguments laid out by the classical thinkers of political theory and international law. Most famously, these include Francisco di Vitoria, Hugo Grotius, Albert Gentili and Emerich de Vattel, as well as Thomas Hobbes and John Locke. The usual assumption is that what fundamentally motivated these scholars when developing their theories was the need to solve the problem of international conflict *within* Europe. But in the conventional historiography no attention is accorded to the extra-European context. This is problematic because the extra-European environment provided a vital impetus to political theory and international law, not to mention the whole process of modern European identity-formation and the construction of sovereignty.

Here I peer over the Eurocentric frontier or line of civilizational apartheid to resuscitate the imperial aspect of the rise of sovereignty. However, this will appear perplexing to some readers who are used to viewing sovereignty as the source of the bright light of order that streamed first across Europe in the aftermath of the Thirty Years' War and then lit up the world as it was subsequently exported as the 'gift of civilization' through Western imperialism (as in the BBT). But, reminiscent of the problem we encountered with respect to globalization in the last section, so we find here that the Eurocentric BBT places the sovereign cart before the Eurocentric imperialist horse. Imperialism did not merely follow sovereignty but also preceded it. For it was the imperial encounter with the Americas that retracked Christendom onto a new path that would culminate in a new Eurocentric European identity within which sovereignty was embedded.[28]

The 'discovery of America' is usually understood as a great opportunity for the expansion and consolidation of Europe. But this obscures the point that 'America' in the first instance constituted a massive epistemic threat to its so-called discoverers. The major aspect of this epistemic threat was that it frontally challenged the Catholic norms which framed European perceptions of non-European peoples and places. According to the biblical texts through which the world was read or imagined, there could be only three continents. For these were announced in Genesis wherein Noah's three sons were granted the three continents of the world – Japheth (Europe), Shem (Asia) and Ham (Africa). Accordingly, the discovery of a fourth continent unsettled this medieval geographical imaginary in no uncertain terms. No less problematic was the application of Catholic Christian norms to interpreting the Amerindians. Prevailing just war theory asserted that if a territory had once been Christian but had fallen into the hands of infidels, or if a people defined itself as an enemy of Christianity, so the Europeans had a right to conquer or reconquer the territory in question. But as Beate Jahn notes, the Amerindians had never been Christian and nor could they be described as enemies of Christianity since they had never known it, nor had they resisted it. 'The Spaniards simply had no legal category with which to capture [ie. read] the

Amerindians ... [Before 1492] Christians only knew of two types of people – Christians and anti-Christians. A third category could simply not exist because all peoples stemmed from Adam and all had to be preached to.'[29] Accordingly, the Spanish had to formulate *new* legal and social normative categories in order to be able to work out how to deal with the Amerindians. Critically, these new categories became the nascent ideas of 'European' international law within which sovereignty was embedded. And, at the same time, these new ideas formed the basis of an infant Eurocentrism.

For the purposes of this discussion I shall boil the impact of the 'invention of America' down to the creation of four key ideas: the emergence of a nascent Eurocentric 'standard of civilization' discourse; the emergence of the idea of the state of nature and with it the idea of sovereignty; the construction of what might be called the imperial *social efficiency argument*; and finally, a bipolar or schizophrenic conception of the international. I shall begin here by tracking these ideas in the thought of Francisco di Vitoria, before proceeding to outline how these ideas also found their place in the writings of other key political theorists and international lawyers, as they set about constructing the idea of sovereignty.

Francisco di Vitoria: The construction of infant imperialist Eurocentrism and sovereignty

In 1539 Francisco di Vitoria presented his now famous lecture 'De Indis et de Iure Belli Relectiones' ('On the American Indians'), which sought to read or interpret the American Indians so that the Spanish might formulate an appropriate policy towards them. This treatise was significant because it was the first stab at constructing international law.[30] Here it is important to recognize that international law was not already pre-formed such that it could readily prescribe 'legitimate' European conduct towards the 'Amerindians'. Rather it was forged initially as a result of the encounter between the Spanish and the Indians. Moreover, as Brett Bowden argues, in Vitoria's argument we have the first gleanings of a nascent conception of the 'standard of civilization'; a conceptual device which would become fully developed with the rise of mature Eurocentrism in the eighteenth and nineteenth centuries.[31]

In the second half of Vitoria's essay he sets out the infant Eurocentric categories that serve to legitimize Spanish imperialism in America. It is certainly true that in his justification of Spanish imperialism Vitoria initially insists that according to the law of nations (what Kant called 'cosmopolitan right') the Spaniards had the right to travel and live in the Indies as well as conduct trade with the Indians but only so long as they do no harm to them. In particular, the Spanish are justified in importing goods in order to trade them for the gold and silver which they would then export.[32] But crucially, unlike Kant, Vitoria smuggles in a particular notion of social efficiency/*terra nullius* that echoes the original Roman argument, when he asserts that 'in the law of nations ... a thing which does not belong to anyone (res nullius) becomes the property of the first

The other side of the Westphalian frontier 43

taker; [ie. the Spanish]... [I]f gold in the ground or pearls in the sea ... have not been appropriated [in this case by the Indians], they will belong by the law of nations to the first taker.'[33] And, of course, the first taker here is the Spanish interloper.

Having laid out these infant Eurocentric markers Vitoria then proceeds quickly towards an argument that justifies war and colonialism. For if the natives prevent all this commercial activity then the Spanish must in the first instance try and persuade them of their peaceful intentions. Should this fail then the Spanish have the right to 'defend' themselves through warfare. Crucially, he argues that this is a likely prospect, for

> the barbarians are by nature cowardly, foolish and ignorant ... [They may] be understandably fearful of men whose customs seem so strange, and who they can see armed and much stronger than themselves. If this fear moves them to mount an attack to drive the Spaniards away or kill them, it would indeed be lawful for the Spaniards to defend themselves.[34]

And he goes on to assert that if the barbarians continue to fight the Spanish then the latter may 'treat them no longer as innocent enemies, but as treacherous foes against whom all rights of war can be exercised, including plunder, enslavement, deposition of their former masters, and the institution of new ones'.[35]

Vitoria also insists that the Spanish have the right to preach to, and convert, the Indians to Christianity, and he argues that the pope can justifiably confine to the Spanish the right to trade with and to convert the barbarians, on the grounds that should other Christian – mainly Protestant – powers become involved, this could ultimately undermine the Catholic conversion process. It is reasonable to confine this right to the Spanish for a number of further reasons, including the point that they had gone to the trouble of discovering the New World and, therefore, deserve the fruits of that discovery,[36] thereby returning us to the 'first taker' legal justification. Vitoria insists that the Spanish '*may preach and work for the conversion of that people even against their will*, and may if necessary take up arms and declare war on them, insofar as this provides the safety and opportunity needed to preach the Gospel'.[37]

At the very end Vitoria produces a final eighth justification for war that is significant in terms of constructing a Eurocentric 'standard of civilization'. Nevertheless here we need to tread very carefully because he insists that such a justification is qualified: 'it may strike some as legitimate, though I myself do not dare either to affirm or condemn it out of hand.'[38] This justification asserts that while the Indians are not totally mad (ie. totally irrational), they are nevertheless very close to being mad and that, accordingly, they should be governed by the Spanish. And here he presents their institutions and norms as so inferior and irrational that they are ultimately unworthy of self-administration or self-determination – the very leitmotif of imperialist Eurocentrism.

All in all, there were several ideational components within which the idea of sovereignty emerged. First, 'America' was constructed as the example of the original *state of nature*, given that its inhabitants lacked rational institutions; by contrast, emergent Europe was said to comprise rational institutions (a key aspect of infant Eurocentrism). Second, if the Amerindians were to be denied sovereignty owing to their barbaric institutions, Europe's civilized institutions meant that European states were worthy of being awarded sovereignty. Third, within this infant Eurocentric approach it became axiomatic that the lack of sovereignty of the non-European world and the later emergence of European sovereign states enshrined imperialism as a natural and legitimate policy vis-à-vis the uncivilized societies (what I call the 'bipolar conception of the international' – see below). Thus while Vitoria launched this epistemic process, others subsequently took up the mantle when developing their ideas on sovereignty.

Imperialism, Eurocentrism and the construction of sovereignty beyond Vitoria

The social efficiency argument, which first emerged in Thomas More's *Utopia* (1516), was coupled by various thinkers with the idea of *terra nullius*. Albert Gentili played an important role in developing this idea further before it became widely adopted.[39] Gentili asserted that '"God did not create the world to be empty." And therefore the seizure of vacant places is regarded as a law of nature.'[40] From there Grotius and especially Locke extended this idea into one that became the imperial mantra that would be sung by many Western scholars right down to the twentieth century. In his *De Jure Belli ac Pacis* (1646), Grotius argued that the Americans lived in a *state of nature*. And because much of the land was either unoccupied or desert or 'waste-space' (ie. *terra nullius*) so the Europeans had a natural right to appropriate the land and develop it for productive purposes. As Grotius put it, the Spanish were entirely justified in waging war on the Aztecs under the following conditions: 'If they really were prevented from travelling or sojourning among those peoples, and were denied the right to share in those things which by the law of nations or by custom are common to all, and finally if they were debarred from trade'.[41]

Locke also believed that America constituted the original state of nature and that such a situation could not be tolerated. Thus he famously asserted that, 'in the beginning all the World was America'[42] and that '*America* ... is still a Pattern of the first Ages in *Asia* and *Europe*'.[43] Hobbes concurred, linking his famous claim that '"the life of man" is "solitary, poore, nasty, brutish, and short"' with the savage Natives of America. As he put it in Chapter 13 of *The Leviathan*: 'For the savage people in many places of America ... have no government at all, and live at this day in that brutish manner.'[44] This is significant not least because students today are generally taught that the notion of the 'state of nature' was used by classical political theorists as a heuristic device or 'thought experiment'.[45] But what is now becoming clear is that this concept, and its associated ideas of anarchy and sovereignty, emerged not through some abstract thought experiment but through the 'invention of America'.

Returning to Locke, we find him implicitly invoking the twin ideas of social efficiency and *terra nullius*, when he asks rhetorically

> whether in the wild woods and uncultivated wast [*sic*] of America left to Nature, without any improvement, tillage or husbandry, a thousand acres will yield the needy and wretched inhabitants as many conveniences of life as ten acres of equally fertile land doe [*sic*] in Devonshire where they are well cultivated?[46]

This was reinforced by his claim that 'God gave the World to Men in Common; but ... it cannot be supposed he meant it should always remain common and uncultivated. He gave it to the use of the Industrious and Rational.'[47] And, of course, 'industrious and rational' is equated with the behaviour of the Europeans. Congruent with social efficiency, only rational and industrious people deserve to be autonomous and self-determining. Thus, as Carole Pateman argues, by the mid-eighteenth century the concept of *terra nullius* was consolidated so that Native peoples would be denied ownership of the land they reside upon. Moreover, Locke argued that when savages failed to be productive so they violated natural law, which in turn required that the Europeans punish them accordingly. This argument was also articulated by Emerich de Vattel in his *The Law of Nations* (1758), where he asserts that the land 'of which savages stood in no particular need, and of which they made no actual and constant use' could legitimately be colonized and appropriated.[48]

The upshot of the construction of an imperialist infant Eurocentrism is the invention of the bipolar or schizophrenic image of the international. Because European international society was deemed to be comprised of civilized states, these deserved the trappings of sovereignty and the protection of international law. By contrast, in the extra-European world the civilized norms of international society should not apply, given that Eastern polities and societies were judged to be uncivilized. Accordingly, in this vision, Europe could treat the extra-European world as a site for colonial adventure, given that non-European states could not be accorded full sovereignty. In turn, the most backward, savage societies that were located initially within America (and later Australia and New Zealand), formed the basis for the idea of the state of nature. And having conceptualized the state of nature so the concept of sovereignty followed on in its wake, albeit one that was laced with Eurocentric imperial overtones, having been forged in the fire of the imperialist Amerindian crucible.

Conclusion

This chapter has sought to provide an alternative non-Eurocentric approach to understanding both the rise of the sovereign state and world politics more generally. In essence, its primary conceptual move is to transcend the imaginary line of civilizational apartheid that Eurocentric thinkers have constructed, thereby revealing the fundamental overlaps between East and West. Thus, in pointing up the 'dialogues of civilizations' in the making of the sovereign state, so we necessarily break with the twin ideas that the West is the pioneering subject of modernity and the East but its passive object. Rather, we can only properly understand world politics and the rise of sovereignty by granting agency not just to the West but also to the East. The second key move that this chapter makes is to problematize the Eurocentric big bang theory, which asserts that modernity was made in the West and was subsequently exported to the East through both proto-globalization and imperialism. Instead, this chapter has argued that Oriental globalization provided a crucible within which the rise of sovereignty was forged. Simultaneously, the last part argues that Spanish imperialism not merely preceded the rise of sovereignty but constituted an ideational crucible within which the concept of sovereignty was forged. In essence, then, only by bringing the wider global context and the relations between civilizations into focus can we properly understand the rise of the sovereign state in particular, and world politics in general.

Notes

1 For liberalism see D.C. North and R.P. Thomas, *The Rise of the Western World* (Cambridge: Cambridge University Press 1973); E.L. Jones, *The European Miracle* (Cambridge: Cambridge University Press 1981); J.R. Strayer, *On the Medieval Origins of the Modern State* (Princeton: Princeton University Press 2005). For Marxism see R. Brenner, 'The Agrarian Roots of Capitalism', in T.H. Ashton and C.H.E. Philpin (eds), *The Brenner Debate* (Cambridge: Cambridge University Press 1985), 213–327; I. Wallerstein, *The Modern World-System*, I (London: Academic Press 1974). And for neo-Weberianism see C. Tilly, *Coercion, Capital and European States, AD 990–1990* (Oxford: Blackwell 1990); A. Giddens, *The Nation State and Violence* (Cambridge: Polity 1985).
2 Cf. for neo-realism: R. Gilpin, *War and Change in World Politics* (Cambridge: Cambridge University Press 1981). For liberalism: H. Spruyt, *The Sovereign State and Its Competitors* (Princeton: Princeton University Press 1994). For Marxism: J. Rosenberg, *The Empire of Civil Society* (London: Verso 1994); B. Teschke, *The Myth of 1648* (London: Verso 2003). For constructivism: J. Ruggie, *Constructing the World Polity* (London: Routledge 1998), chs 5–7; C. Reus-Smit, *The Moral Purpose of the State* (Princeton: Princeton University Press 1999). For English School theory: A. Watson, *The Evolution of International Society* (London: Routledge 1992/2009).
3 This difference is discussed in J.M. Hobson, *The Eurocentric Conception of World Politics*. (Cambridge: Cambridge University Press, 2012).
4 A. Osiander, 'Sovereignty, International Relations and the Westphalian Myth', *International Organization*, 55: 2 (2001), 251–87; Reus-Smit, *Moral Purpose of the State*.
5 Teschke, *Myth of 1648*; Strayer, *Medieval Origins of the Modern State*.
6 See J.M. Hobson, *The Eastern Origins of Western Civilisation* (Cambridge: Cambridge University Press 2004), chs 2–4; J.M. Hobson, 'Orientalization in Globalization? Mapping the Promiscuous Architecture of Globalization, c.500–2010', in J.N. Pieterse and J. Kim (eds), *Globalization and Development in East Asia* (New York: Routledge 2012).
7 J.L. Abu-Lughod, *Before European Hegemony* (Oxford: Oxford University Press 1989).

8 Abu-Lughod, op. cit., 149.
9 See also E. Keene, *Beyond the Anarchical Society* (Cambridge: Cambridge University Press 2002).
10 Hobson, *Eastern Origins*, chs 4, 6–8.
11 Hobson, *Eastern Origins*, ch. 3.
12 D.O. Flynn and A. Giráldez, 'China and the Manila Galleons', in A.J.H. Latham and H. Kawakatsu (eds), *Japanese Industrialization and the Asian Economy* (London: Routledge 1994), 71–90; A.G. Frank, *ReOrient* (Berkeley: University of California Press 1998).
13 Frank, op. cit.; K. Pomeranz, *The Great Divergence* (Princeton: Princeton University Press 2000); Hobson, *Eastern Origins*, ch. 3.
14 J. Needham, P.Y. Ho, G. Lu and L. Wang, *Science and Civilisation in China*, V (7) (Cambridge: Cambridge University Press 1986).
15 A. Pacey, *Technology in World Civilization* (Cambridge, Mass.: MIT Press 1991), 45.
16 Needham et al., *Science and Civilisation*, 47–50, 570–2.
17 M.G.S. Hodgson, *Rethinking World History* (Cambridge: Cambridge University Press 1993).
18 Cf. Rosenberg, *Empire of Civil Society*; G. Mattingly, *Renaissance Diplomacy* (Harmondsworth: Penguin 1973).
19 E.g. North and Thomas, *Rise of the Western World*; Jones, *European Miracle*; Spruyt, *Sovereign State*; Strayer, *Medieval Origins of the Modern State*.
20 A.L. Udovitch, *Partnership and Profit in Medieval Islam* (Princeton: Princeton University Press 1970).
21 North and Thomas, *Rise of the Western World*.
22 Brenner, 'Agrarian Roots of Capitalism'.
23 W.H. McNeill, *Plagues and Peoples* (Garden City, NJ.: Anchor 1976).
24 Abu-Lughod, *Before European Hegemony*, ch. 5.
25 Ruggie, *Constructing the World Polity*, 186.
26 A. Bala, *The Dialogue of Civilizations in the Birth of Modern Science* (Houndmills: Palgrave Macmillan 2006), 85–94.
27 Hobson, *Eastern Origins*, ch. 8; J. Goody, *Islam in Europe* (Cambridge: Polity 2004), 56–83; Bala, op. cit.
28 See also B. Jahn, *The Cultural Construction of International Relations* (Houndmills: Palgrave 2000); N. Inayatullah and D.L. Blaney, *International Relations and the Problem of Difference* (London: Routledge 2004); B. Bowden, *The Empire of Civilization* (Chicago: Chicago University Press 2009).
29 Jahn, op. cit., 45.
30 A. Anghie, *Imperialism, Sovereignty and the Making of International Law* (Cambridge: Cambridge University Press 2005), ch. 2; Bowden, op. cit., 113.
31 Bowden, op. cit., 112–17.
32 F. di Vitoria, 'On the American Indians', in Vitoria, *Political Writings*, edited by A. Pagden and J. Lawrance (Cambridge: Cambridge University Press 1539/1991).
33 Vitoria, op. cit., §4, 280.
34 Vitoria, op. cit., §6, 282.
35 Vitoria, op. cit., §8, 283.
36 Vitoria, op. cit., §10, 284–5.
37 Vitoria, op. cit., §12, 285, emphasis in the original.
38 Vitoria, op. cit., §18, 290.
39 R. Tuck, *The Rights of War and Peace* (Oxford: Oxford University Press 1999), 47–50.
40 Gentili cited in Tuck, op. cit., 48.
41 Grotius cited in S. Grovogui, *Sovereigns, Quasi Sovereigns and Africans* (Minneapolis: University of Minnesota Press 1996), 58–9.

42 J. Locke, *Two Treatises of Government*, II, edited by P. Laslett (Cambridge: Cambridge University Press 1689/2005), §49, 301.
43 Locke, op. cit., §108, 339.
44 T. Hobbes, *The Leviathan*, ch. 13. Posted at: http://oregonstate.edu/instruct/phl302/texts/hobbes/leviathan-contents.html
45 C. Pateman and C.W. Mills, *Contract and Domination* (Cambridge: Polity 2007), 54.
46 Locke, op. cit., §37, 294.
47 Locke, op. cit., §34, 291.
48 Emerich de Vattel, cited in Pateman and Mills, op. cit., 53.

3 Slavery, finance and international political economy
Postcolonial reflections[1]

Branwen Gruffydd Jones

Why is a postcolonial perspective in international political economy necessary, and what might this entail? A postcolonial approach to social inquiry in general foregrounds the centrality of colonialism to the making of the modern world. This immediately raises the double burden of postcolonial critique. The claim that colonialism is central to and constitutive of modernity is both a historical, empirical claim, and a challenge to the dominant forms of knowledge which routinely and systematically marginalize colonialism in their theoretical and historical understanding of the modern world. A postcolonial approach is thus bound to contest the politics as well as the content of knowledge. It is bound to address the inadequacies in dominant forms of knowledge about the world not simply as gaps which can be filled in but, more fundamentally, as having in themselves played a necessary role in shaping historical developments.

In her exploration of the role of the Haitian revolution in the development of Hegel's political philosophy, Susan Buck-Morss observes that 'The history of philosophical scholarship is an example of how the colonial experience has been excluded from the stories Western thought tells about itself.'[2] Much the same could be said of the history of International Political Economy scholarship (IPE). Colonialism, slavery and race form a major gap in the canon of IPE, a set of issues which have been more or less effectively sidestepped.

Accordingly, two sets of questions arise: first, what is the historical relationship between slavery, colonialism, race and the political economy of capitalism? Second, what is the significance of this epistemological sidestepping? What is the relationship between the knowledge of political economy as it has been historically constituted and reproduced, and slavery/race/capital? The answer to the first question can be found *within* an expanded articulation of international or global political economy, while the very need for that expansion compels us to go beyond IPE. To explore the second question might mean to treat political economy as the object rather than means of enquiry, and to draw on other disciplinary traditions in order to generate a different set of insights into the relationships between forms of knowledge, race and slavery, and capitalist modernity.

This chapter begins to address these questions by exploring the role of transatlantic slavery in the history of capitalism, and the relationship between transatlantic slavery and political economy. The first section considers slavery and capitalism.

The foundational relationship between slavery and capitalism has been ignored or minimized by most historians of capitalism and is scarcely discussed within international political economy. There is however an important tradition of scholarship written by African-American, Caribbean and African scholars, from Du Bois to Inikori, which elaborates the centrality of transatlantic slavery to the development of modern capitalism. The second section considers the tradition of classical political economy, a body of scholarship born at the height of the era of transatlantic slavery, and reflects on the absence of colonialism and slavery in the theorization of capitalist economic accumulation. This is in part attributed to the philosophy of history, or historical imaginary, embedded within classical political economy, according to which individual societies move through distinct stages of historical progress from the savage to the civilized. The third section addresses the need for a different philosophy of history in order to adequately grasp the significance of transatlantic slavery to the global political economy of capital. The relationship between capitalism and slavery remains marginalized or minimized today, despite the major scholarship of Inikori and his predecessors, because it remains contained in the historical past. The final section turns to the argument of Ian Baucom to reveal new insights regarding the presence of slavery in the history of capital.

Slavery in the global political economy of capitalism

The dominant and enduring understanding of the historical development of capitalism is that capitalist social relations and processes of accumulation emerged in Europe from the contradictions of the feudal order, whether in towns and cities or in the countryside. Scholars have long debated the origins of capitalism, and most accounts centre largely or wholly on processes of social change which took place within Europe. Ellen Meiksins Wood has made a major contribution to these long-standing debates by focusing centrally on the historical method implicit within existing accounts.[3] She considers carefully the arguments of both Marxist and non-Marxist historians: Weber, Braudel, Pirenne, Polanyi, Mann, Hilton, Sweezy, Dobb, Anderson and others.[4] She highlights their many historical insights and contributions, but finds that in each case there is a tendency to 'beg the question': to assume rather than explain how and why capitalism developed from non-capitalist processes and forms. Central to Wood's approach is the refusal to take for granted the emergence of capitalist social relations and the institutional form of the market. Echoing Marx, she constructs her argument against all prevailing accounts of the origins of capitalism which assume as natural or universal precisely the distinct features which require historical explanation.

Wood's arguments about the historical specificity of capitalism and capitalist social relations are of enormous theoretical, methodological and political significance. She rightly insists on the need to fully recognize the importance and historical novelty of the social property relations emerging within English agriculture. Yet the ensuing argument that such processes constituted *the* most important set of conditions which made possible capitalist industrialization has the effect of marginalizing and, perhaps, taking for granted major global processes of political economy. Wood acknowledges the contribution of slavery and colonialism to the development of capitalism, but considers that while trade and empire were 'essential factors' in the development of industrial capitalism, 'they cannot be treated as primary causes':

> British imperialism also, of course, contributed to the development of the world's first industrial capitalism. But while industrialization did feed on the resources of empire, it is important to keep in mind that the logic of imperialism did not bring about industrial capitalism by itself. Imperial power in other European states did not produce the same effects, and on the eve of the Industrial Revolution, the domestic market was still more important in the British economy than was international trade. Agrarian capitalism was the root of British economic development.[5]

Industrial capitalism first arose in *Britain*, and not in other European powers such as France, Spain and Portugal, which had also amassed wealth from slavery and colonial trade. Therefore 'we have to look to the English domestic market, and to the agrarian capitalism in which it grew, to find the *differentia specifica* that harnessed commerce and empire to capitalist industry.'[6] This important insistence on the historical specificity of distinct processes of change seems to adamantly prioritize locale, and to attach cause to place, at the expense of exploring vital global connections, processes and relations.

Marx explicitly emphasized the centrality and necessity of the world market to capitalist development. He acknowledged that 'the expansion of foreign trade was the basis of capitalist production in its infancy' and becomes a continually reproduced product of capitalist accumulation.[7] He also explicitly acknowledged theoretically and historically that colonialism and slavery constituted the necessary foundation for the development of capitalism:

> The discovery of gold and silver in America, the extirpation, enslavement and entombment in mines of the indigenous population of that continent, the beginnings of the conquest and plunder of India, and the conversion of Africa into a preserve for the commercial hunting of blackskins, are all things which characterize the dawn of the era of capitalist production. These idyllic proceedings are the chief moments of primitive accumulation.[8]

Marx conceived of the relationship between slavery and capitalism in terms of original or 'so-called primitive accumulation'[9]: the form of accumulation which has to have occurred already in order to make possible the development of capitalist accumulation. He is explicit about the character of this process: 'In actual history it is notorious that conquest, enslavement, robbery, murder, briefly force, play the great part.'[10] He recognized the importance of slavery to England: 'Liverpool grew fat on the basis of the slave trade. This was its method of primitive accumulation.'[11]

The historical expropriation of rural populations in Europe was *one* pole of primitive accumulation; slave trade, slavery and colonial expropriation was the other: 'the veiled slavery of the wage-labourers in Europe needed the unqualified slavery of the New World as its pedestal.'[12] Nevertheless, these historical insights are not elaborated in any great length. While emphasizing a theoretical and historical relationship, in Marx's work slavery remains effectively confined to the question of the historical origins of capitalism.

There is however an important body of scholarship which has brought the relationship between slavery and capitalism onto centre stage. This literature would rarely be found in a course or textbook on theories of International Political Economy as such, though perhaps might find a way into specialist courses on the Third World. Yet what such scholarship provides is precisely a historical and theoretical elaboration of the role of slavery in the global political economy of capitalism.

The necessity and significance of transatlantic slavery for the development of Europe was first emphasized and seriously examined by black scholars from the Caribbean and America. The centrality of the transatlantic slave system to Europe's economy was highlighted by C.L.R. James, scholar and revolutionary from Trinidad, in the opening pages of his book *The Black Jacobins,* published in 1938:

> In 1789 the French West Indian colony of San Domingo supplied two thirds of the overseas trade of France and was the greatest individual market for the European slave-trade. It was an integral part of the economic life of the age, the greatest colony in the world, the pride of France, and the envy of every other imperialist nation. The whole structure rested on the labour of half a million slaves.[13]

James's aim in *The Black Jacobins* was not to elaborate this fundamental insight of political economy, however, but to examine the radical political agency of the slaves in the Haitian revolution. His work influenced another historian from Trinidad, Eric Williams, whose seminal book *Capitalism and Slavery*, published in 1944, focused on precisely these relations of political economy.[14] Williams developed two related strands of argument. First, he revealed the centrality of the triangular trade to Britain's commercial expansion and prosperity in the seventeenth and eighteenth centuries, and the development of industry:

> The triangular trade ... gave a triple stimulus to British industry. The Negroes were purchased with British manufactures; transported to the plantations, they produced sugar, cotton, indigo, molasses and other tropical products, the processing of which created new industries in England; while the maintenance of the Negroes and their owners on the plantations provided another market for British industry, New England agriculture and the Newfoundland fisheries. By 1750 there was hardly a trading or a manufacturing town in England which was not in some way connected with the triangular or direct

colonial trade. The profits obtained provided one of the main streams of that accumulation of capital in England which financed the Industrial Revolution.[15]

Second, he argued that it was the economic logics and interests of industrialization which were the primary reasons for Britain moving to abolish the slave trade in 1807. The humanitarian abolitionists certainly played a part: indeed they were 'the spearhead of the onslaught which destroyed the West Indian system and freed the Negro. But their importance has been seriously misrepresented and grossly exaggerated by men who have sacrificed scholarship to sentimentality.'[16]

Two years later, in 1946, W.E.B. Du Bois incorporated Williams's argument into a broader analysis of the role of Africa in world history, written against the 'consistent effort to rationalize Negro slavery by omitting Africa from world history, so that today it is almost universally assumed that history can be truly written without reference to Negroid peoples.'[17] Part of his work focuses on slavery and the slave trade: 'that extraordinary movement which made investment in human flesh the first experiment in organized modern capitalism; which indeed made capitalism possible.'[18] The twin burden of postcolonial critique is central to Du Bois's writings. He has a clear consciousness that his task is not one of filling the gaps in existing historical knowledge: the politics of knowledge is ever present in his work. While detailing the many sources consulted in writing his account, he emphasizes, 'I still labor under the difficulty of the persistent lack of interest in Africa so long characteristic of modern history and sociology.'[19] And despite his many sources, he knows that he will be challenged: 'I feel now as though I were approaching a crowd of friends and enemies, who ask a bit breathlessly, whose and whence is the testimony on which I rely for something that even resembles Authority?' To this he responds: 'I am challenging Authority.'[20]

The question of the role of transatlantic slavery in the development of industrial capitalism in Europe has since been confirmed and further elaborated by others, above all in the major work of Nigerian historian Joseph Inikori.[21] On the basis of decades of meticulous and rigorous research, Inikori has demonstrated the major significance of overseas trade with the slave-based economies of the Atlantic to the development of capitalism and industry in England and the rest of Europe. His work emphasizes the emergence of the Atlantic world as a connected totality in which the histories of Western Europe, the Americas and Africa are necessarily connected by three and a half centuries of slave-based production and commerce.

The colonization of the Americas by Spain and Portugal in the sixteenth century, and later by France, Britain and the Netherlands in the seventeenth century, led to the emergence of a new Atlantic economic system in which export production in the Americas was central. The goods acquired or produced for export included gold and silver, cocoa, cotton, coffee, leather, tobacco, rubber and sugar, with sugar becoming the central product by the seventeenth century. Having effectively decimated the populations of the Americas within a few generations, and after attempts to employ white indentured servants from Europe proved unsustainable, the European colonists turned to Africa to meet their demand for labour: 'Negroes therefore were stolen in Africa to work the lands stolen from the Indians in America.'[22] Slave-based production in the Americas expanded explosively during the eighteenth and early nineteenth centuries. The expanding transatlantic commerce centred on slave-based production was integrally related to the growth of intra-European trade, the commercialization of social life and the development of industry in Western Europe from the sixteenth to the nineteenth centuries. This commerce rested on the violent capture and transport across the Atlantic ocean of more than thirteen million Africans.[23]

A major theme in Eric Williams's book is the role of profits from the plantation economies in providing the conditions for the development of technological innovation, manufacturing and industry in Britain. Inikori has built on Williams's original work to develop an elaborate and intricate account of the multiple ways in which industrial development in Britain was made possible by and directly related to the transatlantic slave economy in its many dimensions.[24] The participation of British merchants in buying, transporting and selling slaves from Africa to the Americas stimulated the production of export commodities required by the trade, and the development of shipping services and the shipbuilding industry, both of which stimulated the development of coal and iron production, iron smelting and metal industries, in particular the production of iron nails, guns, and special copper and brass goods for the slave trade and slave vessels. The expansion and industrialization of textile manufacturing, which was at the centre of the industrial revolution, rested on overseas trade for the raw materials – raw cotton, wool, silk, flax, gums, indigo and other dyestuffs – the majority of which came from the Americas. The expanding Atlantic markets were the major stimulus for the growth of the main sectors of Britain's manufacturing in the industrial revolution. The industrial development of Western Europe and North America was thus integrally linked to and enabled by the enormous growth in international trade centred on African slavery in the Americas and the transatlantic slave trade.

One of the many dimensions Inikori has examined is the role of financial institutions.[25] Inikori acknowledges that financial institutions were not especially important in providing funds for fixed capital investment during the industrial revolution, but he underlines their fundamental role in enabling the circulation of capital: 'the financial institutions performed one of the major functions without which an industrial revolution in the private enterprise English economy of the period would be inconceivable.'[26] From the eighteenth century Britain emerged as the world's leading financial centre. The development of banking, the stock exchange, and insurance services flourished in Britain during the eighteenth and nineteenth centuries. This was primarily because of the significance of the transatlantic slave economy to Britain, not only in terms of the profits generated from the slave economy which were available for investment, as Eric Williams emphasized, but also because of the specific and peculiar financial needs of the transatlantic slave economy.

First was the demand for credit. The various operations of the transatlantic slave economy were heavily reliant on the extension of credit, more so than other forms of international trade.[27] One reason was the length of time that the various sections of the transatlantic slave economy required for completion. In the eighteenth century it would take a ship several weeks to travel from British ports to Africa. There the ship would remain for several months, while the business of selling the cargo of British manufactured goods to European and African traders at the coast, and buying a shipload of captive slaves, was completed. The voyage to the Americas, the offloading and sale of the cargo of slaves, and the acquisition and loading of a cargo of plantation goods, took some months more, before the final return journey to Britain.[28] Because of this long transatlantic, transcontinental scope of the trade and the complex inter-relations between the various component parts, credit needed to be extended for considerable periods of time before repayments could be made.

A further major demand for credit arose from the plantation economy itself.[29] For a plantation owner, the purchase of slaves was a very significant lump cost – the equivalent essentially of modern factories investing in machinery.[30] Precisely because the labour on plantations was slave labour, the cost to the plantation owner had to be paid upfront, while the returns to the plantation owner from the use of the slave labour would then accrue as a gradual stream of income over a period of ten to fifteen years or so.[31] So this specific and essential characteristic of the slave plantation economy generated major demands for credit.

A second feature of the transatlantic economy was the development of joint-stock companies. Some of the first joint-stock companies, such as the South Sea Company and the Royal African Company, were trading companies involved in various sections of the transatlantic slave economy.[32] The various and significant requirements for credit, and for services managing investment and exchange of stock on trading companies, gave rise in Britain from the eighteenth century to the significant growth – in terms of numbers, size and complexity – of financial institutions and services: banking houses, discount houses, and the stock exchange.

Third, a further, specific form of financial service which grew in and because of the needs of the slave economy was marine insurance.[33] Basic forms of marine insurance had long existed since the middle ages, and the first dominant centres of marine insurance were Italy and Holland. But prior to the slave trade, only a small proportion of overseas trade was actually insured; insurance wasn't a specialized activity and it really only consisted of a basic loan. If the ship returned successfully, the insurers would be repaid, with an additional sum; but if the ship was lost, the insurers would lose their investment. It was the specific requirements of the slave trade which generated a transformation in the form of marine insurance and the significant growth in insurance provision, and during the eighteenth century Britain became the dominant centre for marine insurance.[34] The high risks entailed in the slave trade because of the complexity of the system, the length of voyages, the risks of piracy, attack, insurrection or shipwreck, as well as the large sums needed to be invested at the outset of a slave venture, made insurance much more important for the traders and investors. This led to the development of insurance as a specialized and increasingly complex activity, and the growth of specialized financial institutions undertaking insurance, in various British cities – Edinburgh, Liverpool, Bristol and, above all, London.

The absence of slavery in the history of political economy

We have seen that the transatlantic economic system centred on the slave trade and slave-based production was foundational to the development of capitalism in Europe; and yet this fundamental relationship has remained largely excluded from the historiography of the origins of capitalism. To what extent has transatlantic slavery been incorporated in the theoretical knowledge of political economy? The traditions of political economy as a body of knowledge, from classical political economy to contemporary International Political Economy, have had little to say about slavery in their theoretical examinations of capitalism. The discipline of IPE is of recent origins, commonly understood to have emerged as a distinct area of inquiry in the 1970s.[35] With few exceptions,[36] the IPE literature has said virtually nothing about transatlantic slavery. Contemporary IPE traces its roots to the works of classical political economy.[37] Indeed Burch has argued that 'IPE, liberalism and modernity share the same ontological framework to such a degree that IPE exemplifies the liberal-modern worldview. In this sense, IPE is a cultural artifact of modernity.'[38] Classical political economy developed during the eighteenth century, in Scotland, England and France. As the theoretical analysis of 'the economy' and economic accumulation developed in the works of classical political economy, the focus was not a global economic system but rather, the national economy. Thus, when the very idea of 'the economy' was first explicitly articulated and theoretically developed, it was articulated in terms of a *national* economy. Yet the eighteenth century, the historical moment of the birth of political economy as a branch of knowledge, was also the historical moment when the economies of Britain and France were fundamentally enmeshed in the transatlantic economic system based on the slave trade and slave-labour.

How should we make sense of this quite striking point – that the very idea of 'the economy' was first conceived as the *national* economy in a historical period of major global or transnational, transcontinental economic relations, structures and processes? We could consider the necessary fictive or ideological relationships between the economy and the idea of the 'nation' itself. If practices related to the economy were central to the definition and historical forging of 'the nation' then it is understandable that economic consciousness would first emerge as consciousness of the *national* economy. This set of historical and constitutive relationships between the national state, the economy and fictional constructs has been explored by Patrick Brantlinger, who foregrounds the central role of money and public credit in the historical development of the nation-state:

> Public credit is at once tied to state legitimacy, and hence to national debts, and to the political category of public opinion as an aspect of the democratic

public spheres emergent during the Enlightenment. Money and its corollary public credit (or public debt), which is all that legitimates money to begin with, are thus even more fundamental to the fictional or ideological creation and maintenance of the imagined communities of modern nation-states than are more explicitly nationalistic cultural forms including both literary canons and competing political ideologies.[39]

Many scholars have emphasized and explored the historical relationships between state formation, war, and modern finance.[40] But we need also to consider the broader epistemological context in order to appreciate how and why a specific conception of the economy was inscribed in the knowledge of political economy from the outset.

The classical political economists, Hutcheson, Hume, Steuart, Smith, Quesnay, Mirabeau, Turgot and others, were the first to conceive, in any systematic way, of 'the economy' as a specific entity or realm of social world, as a separate or analytically separable institutional reality.[41] Their approach to the economy was shaped by broader epistemological transformations in Europe during the eighteenth century. The project of political economy was to develop systematic knowledge of the economy, and to identify rational, secular explanations, in the form of natural or quasi-natural laws, which would account for the dynamics of the economy and the accumulation of wealth.[42] The French Physiocrats envisaged the economy as a quasi-natural system, with its own properties and laws.[43] Political economy was understood as a science of the economy which, by means of gathering of data, systematic analysis and theoretical reasoning, could generate knowledge of the way the economy works, its natural properties and functioning.[44] The Physiocrats sought to uncover the physiology of economic society, and they located the source of wealth in agriculture.[45] They were the first to seek to systematically quantify and measure economic processes, in terms of flows or movements of value between different groups and sections of society and different areas or sectors of activity, over specified periods of time.[46] In what Eric Roll called the most spectacular part of the physiocrat doctrine, the flow and circulation of value within the national economy was depicted in an abstract, quantified manner in the form of tables, in Quesnay's *Tableau Économique*.[47] Quesnay's tables gave graphic, objective and numeric form to the idea of the national economy.[48]

The Scottish scholar Adam Smith spent some time touring and studying in France and Switzerland during 1764–6. He met, admired and was undoubtedly influenced by the Physiocrats and shared many of their concerns, though he had developed his own economic ideas prior to his stay in France.[49] Smith sought to explain the basis of national economic growth as an outcome of secular rather than divine processes. He proposed an understanding of the functioning of the economy as essentially rooted in human nature. Human beings have a number of contrasting qualities and capacities, and while sympathy and intimate knowledge are important for social interaction among friends, the practices of production and exchange among anonymous others in the market are governed by different impulses of self-interest and self-preservation.⁵⁰ And yet, the combined result of the actions of each individual privately pursuing his or her own interests is the increase of wealth, prosperity, culture and civilization for society as a whole. For Smith it is the division of labour within society and the mechanism of competition operating in the market which explain why individuals pursuing their own interests spontaneously generate, through no intention of their own, socially beneficial outcomes.⁵¹

Thus for Adam Smith it is the activities of exchange in the market, which themselves are rooted in human nature, which account for the generation of wealth. The expansion of the market allows for greater specialization, division of labour and efficiency; foreign trade stimulates production, specialization of knowledge and technology, division of labour, and the accumulation of wealth in society.⁵² The expansion of trade and markets is both evidence of civilization, and a means to civilization. Adam Smith shared the general historical understanding of the Scottish (and, more broadly, European) Enlightenment: that history took the form of progressive change through successive stages.⁵³ Societies develop at different rates, or exist at different stages of historical development. Smith identified four stages of historical development which corresponded to different types of economic activity within one society. The most basic was the hunter-gatherer form; next, a society sustained by the economy of shepherds or pastoralists; then an agricultural economy; and finally, the society, economy and civilization of commerce.⁵⁴ David Hume, Smith's friend and contemporary, likewise consistently contrasted the situation of a primitive or savage economy with the more sophisticated, complex, civilized economy of commerce, as did James Steuart.⁵⁵ This understanding of history in terms of distinct societies undergoing evolutionary change through successive stages, with the civilization of commercial society at the historical apex, was an integral strand of enlightenment thought and infused classical political economy, especially the Scottish school.⁵⁶ For Smith, the division of labour is one of the keys to civilization, accounting for why the accommodation of an 'industrious and frugal peasant' in Europe 'exceeds that of many an African king, the absolute master of the lives and liberties of ten thousand naked savages'.⁵⁷

Adam Smith and his contemporaries were very much concerned with the colonial economy of the Americas, but not in terms of a causal element in their explanation of wealth and accumulation. Their concern was to criticize the colonial monopoly system, which hampered the growth of prosperity and productive power of both England and the colonies.⁵⁸ Eric Williams situates the historical coordinates of Adam Smith's political economy: '*The Wealth of Nations* was the philosophical antecedent of the American Revolution. Both were twin products of the same cause, the brake applied by the mercantile system on the development of the productive power of England and her colonies.'⁵⁹ Smith and other political economists of the eighteenth century were critical of the colonial economy because of the inefficiency of the monopoly system, and they were critical of slavery as an inefficient form of economy which provided no incentive for the slave to maximize his effort.⁶⁰ But their theorization of the economy and economic growth centred explicitly on the national economy, and the processes and conditions generating wealth and surplus were located within the national economy, whether springing ultimately from land and agriculture, or from the activities of labour and exchange. Their analyses examined the national economy and national accumulation by measuring and tabulating economic activities and flows of rent, wages and profit, between different groups within society (labourers, owners of land, labour and capital) within or across specified periods of time, usually a year.[61] A sense of economic institutions and processes of accumulation as consisting of or embedded in globally structured relations and globally extended conditions of possibility was not incorporated in any systematic way in their theoretical or historical conception of the economy and accumulation.

Thus, aside from the concern with the restrictions of colonial monopolies, slavery and the slave trade were largely absent from the theoretical origins of political economy, while the *national* economy emerged from the beginning as the basic unit of analysis. It is often emphasized that later, with Ricardo, Mill and their successors, political economy became more narrowly economic, abandoning the ethical and moral concerns which animated the original political economists of the eighteenth century, and moving from historical induction to logical deduction.[62] Yet from the very beginning, even in its more historical and moral phase, political economy was shaped by deeper strands of Enlightenment thought in its focus on the national economy and society and its imagination of stages of historical development, progress and civilization. These underlying features help to account for the striking absence or marginalization of transatlantic slavery from the first systematic theorization of the economy, born as it was at the height of the slave-based transatlantic economy. The methods of analytical abstraction employed at the beginning of political economy, alongside a stadial, evolutionary conception of historical progress, issued in a conception of a generic national economy, abstracted from history and global context.

The presence of slavery in the history of finance capital

If modes and techniques of analytical abstraction were inscribed in political economy from the moment of its birth in the eighteenth century, they have reached extreme proportions today in the remarkable and utterly mystifying acrobatics of econometrics – which, for many, remains central to the contemporary *science* of political economy. Within IPE, however, this positivist strand is by no means dominant, and rich traditions of critical IPE are firmly established.[63] Nevertheless other features which might be traced back to classical political economy have remained far more broadly influential. The assumption of the *national economy* as the basic unit of analysis continues implicitly to inform much IPE, and arguably underpins the entire discipline of Development Studies. Critical scholars of *global* political economy therefore insist on the need for a different ontology which foregrounds the global political economy as a complex, integrated entity and thus the global and historical constitution of all 'economies', and rejects any model of *a* general economy.[64] This, certainly, is consistent with

Inikori's argument that the long era of transatlantic slavery gave rise to a transatlantic economic system which was a complex, differentiated and structured totality causally linking the very different patterns of social change in Africa, the Americas and Europe over three centuries. Accordingly, the economic development of Europe cannot be understood outside of its insertion in this transatlantic system.

Thus the expansion of political economy which is necessary to reveal the fundamental historical significance of slavery operates in part at the level of ontology. Even so, this remains consistent with an understanding which situates transatlantic slavery, as important as it was, in the pre- or early history of modern capitalism. But if we go beyond even an expanded political economy and global ontology, we find arguments defending a different philosophy of history, one which would locate the transatlantic slave economy not prior to but *within* the same historical contemporaneity as our own capitalist present.

As we've seen, classical political economy emerged with an underlying historical imagination. The political economists of the eighteenth century assumed a stadial, evolutionary development of societies from savagery to civilization. This entails a linear conception of historical time as a path of progression and advance. And it entails an atomistic social ontology informing the conception of both the individual and the economy. The individual is a rational being pursuing his or her own interests, and the national economy is a bounded, identifiable realm of society whose rhythms and cycles can be measured, quantified and depicted in numerical form in tables, with the source of wealth and accumulation springing from internal conditions of land, agriculture and behaviours rooted in human nature. One of Marx's fundamental criticisms of classical political economy was its abstraction from history. The classical political economists took as given the existence of capitalist social relations, the capitalist economy, and attendant behaviours and cultural forms – none of these phenomena needed historical explanation. The economic individual is the point of departure for Adam Smith and Ricardo: 'they saw this individual not as an historical result, but as the starting point of history; not as something evolving in the course of history, but posited by nature, because for them this individual was in conformity with nature, in keeping with their idea of human nature.'[65]

Marx's writings were not entirely free from the influence of evolutionary and stadial theories of historical progress, however, and a basic conception of history as the forward-moving passage of time and events in some kind of linear fashion still retains an unacknowledged grip on the imagination of much contemporary social scientific inquiry. Thus, however important transatlantic slavery was to the origins of capitalism, those origins are now long surpassed, and therefore only of 'historical' interest.

Du Bois, however, recalls the history of Africa precisely because of its contemporary importance: 'I want to appeal to the past in order to explain the present. I know how unpopular this method is. What have we moderns, we wisest of the wise, to do with the dead past?'[66] He recounts an experience of an editor asking him to 'leave out the history and come to the present', to which Du Bois wanted

Slavery, finance and international political economy 61

to respond: 'Dear, dear jackass! Don't you understand that the past *is* the present; that without what *was,* nothing *is*? That, of the infinite dead, the living are but unimportant bits?'[67]

That without what *was,* nothing *is.* In this sharp phrase, Du Bois encapsulates an entirely different understanding of historical time, of the relationship between past and present, an entirely different philosophy of history. In his recent examination of the era of transatlantic slavery and finance capital, Ian Baucom has elaborated the philosophy of history which was, perhaps, intimated in these words of Du Bois.[68] Drawing on a breadth of scholarship – including the work of Benjamin, Arrighi, Jameson, Pocock, Spivak and Derrida – Baucom sets out a distinct, non-linear understanding of historical process, the relationships between past, present and future, and a distinct understanding of the ways in which historical processes and tendencies are manifest in events and conjunctures. First, the future is contained within the present, and the present is the future which was contained in the past. The present might embody in a stronger, more concentrated, developed or intensified form, features identifiable in the past. Thus to study the past is to learn about the present. This entails, second, a cumulative rather than a linear sense of historical time and process. Features, processes, relations, practices do not pass by but remain and grow stronger into the present and future: 'Time does not pass … it accumulates'.[69] Third, a specific event can encapsulate, even in its singularity, features which are essential to and defining of the historical era.[70]

Baucom employs and elaborates this distinct philosophy of history and critical inquiry in a concentrated analysis of a particular event of the eighteenth century. His analysis reveals defining, essential features of the historical era of transatlantic slavery and finance capital. These features do not belong simply to the historical past; they have not been superseded by the march of historical time. Rather, they constitute forms which have continued to develop, which remain embedded ever more strongly in our own present.

The event, or set of events, begins with the voyage of a slave ship, the *Zong,* which set sail from Africa in 1781. The *Zong* (originally *Zorg*) was a Dutch vessel which had been captured in February 1781 off the coast of the Gold Coast by a Bristol privateer, and then purchased by a syndicate of investors based in Liverpool.[71] Remaining on the coast of West Africa for several months purchasing slaves, food and water, on 6 September the *Zong* finally set sail from São Tomé for the long voyage, the 'middle passage', to Jamaica with a crew of seventeen men and a cargo of four hundred and forty slaves. Historical records tell us that during the latter part of the eighteenth century, between 1761 and 1790, mortality rates in the English slave trade averaged between 8.5–9.6 per cent, mainly due to disease and malnutrition.[72] Several weeks later, towards the end of November, the ship was approaching the coast of Jamaica. By this time seven crew members and over sixty slaves had perished from disease, and many remaining were in ill health. The stores of fresh water on the ship were running low. On 27 November the Captain of the ship, Luke Collingwood, had a meeting with his crew, and decided that they would throw overboard some of the remaining slaves.

Their reasoning was that it was necessary to get rid of some of the slaves, so as to be able to keep alive and in reasonable health the remaining slaves to be sold on arrival in Jamaica. Over the following three days, one hundred and twenty-three slaves were brought up from the hold, shackled, and thrown overboard to their death. A further ten who had been rounded up for this fate broke free and voluntarily jumped overboard instead of being thrown. In total, one hundred and thirty-three men were deliberately sent to their death in the Atlantic.[73]

Collingwood died shortly after arrival in Jamaica. When the ship eventually arrived back in England in 1782, the new captain, Edward Howard, gave his report to the shipowners and advised them to make an insurance claim – to claim the full, insured value of the slaves who had been essentially murdered in this manner. The owners did precisely this; the insurance company objected, and the case went to court. The court found in favour of the shipowners – the insurance claimants. The insurers, supported by prominent abolitionists, appealed; the appeal case was again resolved in favour of the claimants.[74]

The case was tried not as a murder case, but as a dispute over property arising from an insurance claim. Baucom recounts and examines this specific case in detail because of what it reveals as essentially defining of the age of finance capital.[75] The argument of the captain and shipowners rested on demonstrating that it was necessary to forcibly abandon some of the slaves in order to save the rest – not 'save' as in save their lives, but as in save their *value* as commodities to be sold on arrival in Jamaica, as valuable cargo. Further, that the one hundred and thirty-three slaves who had necessarily to be jettisoned constituted a part of the cargo, and therefore carried specific value – a proportion of the value of the ship's cargo as a whole, which had been insured according to the contractual agreement between the shipowners and insurance providers at the outset. According to prevailing marine insurance law, if a ship was compelled of necessity to jettison part of its cargo in order to safeguard the rest of the cargo and the ship as a whole, then insurance was liable to be paid on the jettisoned goods.[76] So the case made in court was essentially that the shipowners had the right to recover the monetary value of their insured goods, even though the actual goods had perished.

Baucom argues that what this reveals is not only that the transatlantic slave trade rested on the legal treatment of African people as property that could be bought, sold and owned – as a basic commodity, which in terms of legal status was the same as any other tradable commodity; but that, as a cargo, slaves were constituted as the subjects of *insurance*. This exposes the historically novel and peculiar feature of the theories, practices and techniques of value specific to *finance capital*, which see value not only as entirely abstract, but also as completely detachable from the material entity which is the original bearer of value. The financial practices born of transatlantic slavery are so historically significant not simply because, as slaves, human beings were bought and sold for a price – thus reducing a person to a monetary value in exchange. More fundamental is that the practice of insuring a cargo of slaves in principle detaches the monetary value from the very bodily existence of those people, so that even after they have been deliberately murdered, their *value* still exists in the form of a financial sum which can be claimed from an insurance house:

> Licensed by insurance to utterly detach value from the material existence of objects ... finance capital is free to speculate in and profit from its imaginary valuations, to exchange both use-values and exchange-values for the indestructible money-form.[77]

Although the *Zong* case, even on appeal, was found in favour of the claimants, the case brought the horrors of the slave trade to wide attention in Britain. Indeed the appeal case wrestled with the question of whether the event in question constituted the necessary jettisoning of cargo, or the barbaric murder of human beings. The case became a key focus for the British abolitionist movement. Nevertheless, Baucom argues, its significance in terms of what it reveals about defining practices and imaginaries of finance capital locates this event firmly in the history of our own 'exorbitantly financialized present'.[78] It is this form and practice of value, as imagining, treating and realizing the detachment of monetary value from having any actual relation with the entities in which value is originally embodied, which remains, all the more so, a central feature of finance capital in our own times: 'our time ... is a present time which ... inherits its nonimmediate past by intensifying it, by "perfecting" its capital protocols.'[79]

If it was insurance which first liberated value from its bodily form, today it is derivatives which continue that process in ever greater ways: 'in one respect, derivatives can be seen as the massive extension of insurance to a wide and increasing range of "exposures."'[80] Derivatives and securities, some of the defining features of global finance in the current era,[81] manifest more complex, developed and intensified forms of this initial, essential process of finance capital: the detachment of monetary value from its material object, its bodily form:[82]

> Technologically driven derivatives detach the value, cost, and price of money – manifest in exchange and interest rates – from the fundamentals of the economy, particularly the state of production, the social welfare of the producers, and the political needs of citizens.[83]

While ever increasing in complexity, the array of derivatives and securities at the heart of global finance today take the detachment of value, and the social implications of this detachment, to vastly new scales. And, just as financial investors in Liverpool had scant interest in or direct experience of the brutalities and atrocities of the actual slave trade, but were concerned only with the magnitude and security of the returns on their financial investments, so today financial investors in the world's stock, securities and derivatives exchanges have little interest in or direct experience of the underlying material and lived realities and tragedies upon which their speculative activities ultimately depend.

Conclusion

This chapter has explored several related lines of inquiry in an effort to confront the challenge that postcolonial theory poses to International Political Economy. The first point of entry might be considered the most basic: to consider important aspects of world history and experience which have been overlooked or marginalized by IPE. While the contemporary discipline or sub-discipline of IPE is generally understood to have emerged recently, in the 1970s, a branch of inquiry so-named must surely address, both theoretically and historically, the origins, character and development of the modern international capitalist system and economy. In this regard, contemporary IPE has had very little to say about the foundational importance of transatlantic slavery to the development and structure of global capitalism. There is, of course, a major body of scholarship about transatlantic slavery, including its dynamics of political economy, but this literature is found in history or specialist slavery studies and not, for the most part, in the realm of IPE. Many scholars have wrestled with this subject but it is pioneering African American, Caribbean and African scholars who have done so with most persistence. This raises an important element of the postcolonial challenge to social inquiry, especially the disciplinary traditions of International Relations and International Political Economy. Addressing the postcolonial challenge can never be considered simply as a process of filling in the gaps in an otherwise adequate body of knowledge. To acknowledge and take seriously the centrality of colonialism to world history and the modern condition is to question the underlying assumptions, imaginations and epistemologies of disciplinary forms which have ignored, overlooked or forgotten colonialism; it is to question the politics of social inquiry and disciplinary formation.

The postcolonial challenge demands that the politics of knowledge be placed centre stage, and the historical and necessary relationship between academic knowledge and colonialism be taken seriously. Accordingly, the next step in the chapter was to turn to IPE's canonical origins in classical Political Economy. Classical Political Economy was born in England, Scotland and France in the eighteenth century, more or less at the height of the era of transatlantic slavery. Yet this transcontinental system of economic relations and processes – of production, exchange and consumption; of theft, war, racial violence and dehumanization; of the systematic capture, trade, enslavement and death of African people on a massive, modern scale – this vast economic system hardly figured in the theoretical analysis of the wealth of nations. Rather, the economy was conceived as a nationally delimited sphere of flows and actors. The classical political economists were very well aware of, and concerned about, the colonial economy, but the subject hardly entered their theoretical conceptualization of the economy and accumulation. This, perhaps, can be partly accounted for by considering the distinct historical imagination inscribed in political economy from the outset. Classical political economy shared and developed the historical imagination of the European enlightenment: an imagination of societal progress through successive stages of advance, from the savage to the civilized. In this imagination the wealth of nations is the product of civilized economies, while slavery is located in earlier phases and distant historical origins.

Modern political economy has long moved on from the vocabulary of civilization, primitivism and savagery. However, the essential imagination of history in terms of a linear path of progress along which different countries travel at different speeds (advanced, developing, less developed) remains an implicit, sometimes explicit assumption of much contemporary social science. The final section of the chapter therefore confronted a further element of the postcolonial challenge: the need for a different philosophy of history. This responds to Du Bois's question: 'What have we moderns, we wisest of the wise, to do with the dead past?' A linear conception of history can admit the importance of transatlantic slavery while containing its significance safely in the past – to an earlier, and long superseded phase of global capitalism and world history. Ian Baucom has proposed a very different philosophy of history which is cumulative rather than linear. The present, then, contains and is structured by the past; the present exhibits an accumulation and intensification of the past. A defining feature of our global capitalist present is the profound dominance of finance. Critical IPE produces excellent analyses of the complexities, politics and recent origins of global finance, but has not paused to consider the relationship between modern finance and transatlantic slavery. The work of Inikori and Baucom reveals that the modernity of capitalist finance cannot be fully accounted for unless its origins in the modern practices of transatlantic slave-based trade and accumulation are examined. It was the peculiar features of the transatlantic slave economy which first gave rise to specialized forms and techniques of finance, especially the detachment of monetary value from bodily form at the heart of insurance; and it is these very features of finance which, in ever more developed and complex forms, remain central to global capitalism today. This locates transatlantic slavery not in the distant past, the prehistory of capitalism, but firmly within the history of our own present global condition. This set of related reflections about slavery and political economy elaborates the necessity and ramifications of a postcolonial sensibility, which cannot be reduced to another approach within, or an expansion of, existing disciplinary traditions left more or less intact.

Notes

1 This chapter was presented at the workshop *Re-imagining International Political Economy: thinking beyond states, markets and globalisation* organised by the departing students of the MA in IPE at the University of Manchester, August 2010. Many thanks to Matthias Ebenau for the invitation, and to all participants for stimulating discussion and comments. Thanks also to Robbie Shilliam, Sanjay Seth and Alison Ayers for helpful discussions.
2 Susan Buck-Morss, *Hegel, Haiti, and Universal History* (Pittsburgh, PA: University of Pittsburgh Press 2009), 16.
3 Ellen Meiksins Wood, *Democracy Against Capitalism: renewing historical materialism* (Cambridge: Cambridge University Press 1995); Ellen Meiksins Wood, *The Origins of Capitalism* (New York: Monthly Review Press 1999).
4 Wood, *The Origins of Capitalism*.

5 Wood, *The Origins of Capitalism*, 101.
6 Wood, *The Origins of Capitalism*, 101.
7 Karl Marx, *Capital, Vol. 3* (London: Penguin 1991, 1894), 344.
8 Karl Marx, *Capital, Vol. 1* (London: Penguin 1990, 1867), 915.
9 Marx, *Capital, Vol. 1*, part eight.
10 Marx, *Capital, Vol. 1*, 836.
11 Marx, *Capital, Vol. 1*, 932.
12 Marx, *Capital, Vol. 1*, 933.
13 C.L.R. James, *The Black Jacobins: Toussaint L'Ouverture and the San Domingo Revolution*, first published 1938 (London: Penguin 2001), xviii.
14 Eric Williams, *Capitalism and Slavery* (London: André Deutsch (first published Chapel Hill: University of North Carolina Press 1944) 1987). See also Barbara L. Solow and Stanley L. Engerman (eds), *British Capitalism and Caribbean Slavery: the Legacy of Eric Williams* (Cambridge: Cambridge University Press 1987).
15 Williams, *Capitalism and Slavery*, 52.
16 Williams, *Capitalism and Slavery*, 178.
17 William Edward Burghardt Du Bois, *The World and Africa: An Inquiry into the Part Which Africa has Played in World History* (New York: International Publishers 1996, 1946), vii.
18 Du Bois, *The World and Africa*, 68.
19 Du Bois, *The World and Africa*, viii.
20 Du Bois, *The World and Africa*, viii.
21 Joseph E. Inikori, *Africans and the Industrial Revolution in England: A study in international trade and economic development* (Cambridge: Cambridge University Press 2002); Joseph E. Inikori, 'Africa in world history: the export slave trade from Africa and the emergence of the Atlantic economic order', in Bethwell A. Ogot (ed.), *Africa from the Sixteenth to the Eighteenth Century* (Heinemann/ UNESCO/ University of California Press 1992); Joseph E. Inikori, 'Slavery and the Development of Industrial Capitalism in England', *Journal of Interdisciplinary History*, 17: 4 (1987), 771–93; Joseph E. Inikori, 'Market Structure and the Profits of the British African Trade in the Late Eighteenth Century', *Journal of Economic History*, 41: 4 (1981), 745–76; Joseph E. Inikori, 'The slave trade and the Atlantic economies 1451–1870', in UNESCO (ed.), *The African Slave Trade from the Fifteenth to the Nineteenth Century* (Paris: United Nations Educational, Scientific and Cultural Organization 1979).
22 Williams, *Capitalism and Slavery*, 9.
23 Joseph E. Inikori, 'Africa and the Trans-Atlantic Slave Trade', in Toyin Falola (ed.), *Africa, vol.1: African History before 1885* (Carolina: Carolina Academic Press 2000).
24 Inikori, *Africans and the Industrial Revolution*, 406.
25 Inikori, *Africans and the Industrial Revolution*, 314–61.
26 Inikori, *Africans and the Industrial Revolution*, 314.
27 Inikori, *Africans and the Industrial Revolution*, 322–38; Joseph E. Inikori, 'The credit needs of the African trade and the development of the credit economy in England', *Explorations in Economic History*, 27 (1990), 197–231.
28 Inikori, *Africans and the Industrial Revolution*, 323.
29 Inikori, *Africans and the Industrial Revolution*, 325–8.
30 Inikori, *Africans and the Industrial Revolution*, 325.
31 The mortality rates of slaves in the plantation regime were high. Blackburn records that in the seventeenth century, 'The sugar plantations on which over three-quarters of all Caribbean slaves worked consumed the lives of slaves almost as voraciously as the mills ground the mounds of cut cane. Planters estimated that the young African brought to their estates had an average life expectancy of little more than seven years.' Robin Blackburn, *The Making of New World Slavery: From the Baroque to the Modern, 1492–1800* (London and New York: Verso 1997), 339.

32 The development of joint-stock companies was a feature of overseas colonial trade as such, and was not specific to the slave trade. In 1717 the total share capital of joint-stock companies amounted to more than £20 million, of which the South Sea Company had £10 million, and the East India Company £3,194,000. Inikori, *Africans and the Industrial Revolution*, 320–22.
33 Inikori, *Africans and the Industrial Revolution*, 338–60; Michael Lobban, 'Slavery, Insurance and Law', *Journal of Legal History*, 28: 3 (2007), 319–28.
34 Inikori, *Africans and the Industrial Revolution*, 338–60.
35 Robert O'Brien, 'International Political Economy and International Relations: apprentice or teacher?', in J. Macmillan and Andrew Linklater (eds), *Boundaries in Question: New Directions in International Relations* (London: Pinter Publishers 1995).
36 Such as Robert O'Brien and Marc Williams, *Global Political Economy: Evolution and Dynamics* (Basingstoke: Palgrave Macmillan 2010).
37 Matthew Watson, *Foundations of International Political Economy* (Basingstoke: Palgrave 2005); Raymond C. Miller (ed.), *International Political Economy: Contrasting World Views* (London: Routledge 2008).
38 Kurt Burch, 'Constituting IPE and modernity', in Kurt Burch and Robert Allen Denemark (eds), *Constituting International Political Economy* (Boulder, Colo.: Lynne Rienner. International Political Economy Yearbook vol. 10 1997), 21.
39 Patrick Brantlinger, *Fictions of State: Culture and Credit in Britain, 1694–1994* (Ithaca, N.Y.: Cornell University Press 1996), 22.
40 Benno Teschke, *The Myth of 1648: Class, Geopolitics and the Making of Modern International Relations* (London: Verso 2003); John Brewer, *The Sinews of Power: War, Money and the English State 1688–1783* (New York: Knopf 1989).
41 James A. Caporaso and David P. Levine, *Theories of Political Economy* (Cambridge: Cambridge University Press 1992); Susan Buck-Morss, 'Envisioning Capital: Political Economy on Display', *Critical Inquiry*, 21 (1995), 434–67; Michel Foucault, *Security, Territory, Population. Lectures at the Collège de France 1977–1978* (Basingstoke: Palgrave Macmillan 2007).
42 Andrew S. Skinner, 'Economic Theory', in Alexander Broadie (ed.), *The Cambridge Companion to the Scottish Enlightenment* (Cambridge: Cambridge University Press 2003); Maurice Dobb, *Theories of Value and Distribution Since Adam Smith: Ideology and Economic Theory* (Cambridge: Cambridge University Press 1973); Craig Smith, *Adam Smith's Political Philosophy: The Invisible Hand and Spontaneous Order* (London: Routledge 2006), 82; Iain McLean, *Adam Smith, radical and egalitarian: an interpretation for the twenty-first century* (Edinburgh: Edinburgh University Press 2006), 87. McLean situates the epistemological transformations of the Scottish Enlightenment in relation to historical changes. He argues, specifically, that it was the existence of a 'weak state and weak church' in Scotland during the first half of the eighteenth century which made politically possible the circulation of secular ideas of Hutcheson, Smith, Hume, Ferguson and other scholars of the Scottish enlightenment. See Samuel Hollander, 'Adam Smith and the Self-Interest Axiom', *Journal of Law and Economics*, 20: 1 (1977), 133–52 for Smith's scientific method.
43 P. T. Manicas, *A History and Philosophy of the Social Sciences* (Oxford: Blackwell 1987), 39.
44 Skinner, 'Economic Theory', 192–4.
45 Dobb, *Theories of Value*, 40.
46 Eric Roll, *A History of Economic Thought* (London: Faber and Faber 1992), 112–14.
47 Roll, *A History*, 114.
48 Buck-Morss, 'Envisioning Capital', 440–43.
49 Dobb, *Theories of Value*, 41; Roll, *A History*, 127; McLean, *Adam Smith, radical and egalitarian*, 82; Skinner, 'Economic Theory',192.
50 These ideas are developed in *Theory of Moral Sentiments*. See also Craig Smith, *Adam Smith's Political Philosophy*, 69–75.

68 *Critique*

51 Adam Smith, *The Wealth of Nations* (Harmondsworth: Penguin Books 1979 [1776]), 109–17; Craig Smith, *Adam Smith's Political Philosophy*, 80–82.
52 Dobb, *Theories of Value*, 56; Craig Smith, *Adam Smith's Political Philosophy*, 74–6.
53 Craig Smith, *Adam Smith's Political Philosophy*, 79; Ronald L. Meek, *Smith, Marx, and after: ten essays in the development of economic thought* (London: Chapman and Hall 1977); Ronald L. Meek, 'Smith, Turgot and the four stages "theory"', *History of Political Economy*, 3: 1 (1971), 9–27.
54 McLean, *Adam Smith, radical and egalitarian*, 67–8.
55 Skinner, 'Economic Theory', 181–5.
56 Skinner, 'Economic Theory', 185; Maureen Harkin, 'Adam Smith's missing history: primitives, progress and problems of genre', *ELH*, 72 (2005), 429–51. See especially the work of Blaney and Inayatullah for an extended development of this theme. David L. Blaney and Naeem Inayatullah, 'The savage Smith and the temporal walls of capitalism', in Beate Jahn (ed.), *Classical Theory in International Relations* (Cambridge: Cambridge University Press 2006) and *Savage Economics: Wealth, Poverty and the Temporal Walls of Capitalism* (London: Routledge 2009).
57 Adam Smith, *The Wealth of Nations*, 117.
58 Bernard Semmel, *The Liberal Ideal and the Demons of Empire: Theories of Imperialism from Adam Smith to Lenin* (New York: Johns Hopkins University Press 1993), 18–21; Dobb, *Theories of Value*, 55; McLean, *Adam Smith, radical and egalitarian*, 73–5, 79. See *The Wealth of Nations*, Book IV, Chapter vii.
59 Williams, *Capitalism and Slavery*, 107.
60 Adam Smith, *The Wealth of Nations*, 488–90; Craig Smith, *Adam Smith's Political Philosophy*, 78.
61 Skinner, 'Economic Theory', 194.
62 Neville Morley, 'Political Economy and Classical Antiquity', *Journal of the History of Ideas*, 59: 1 (1998), 95–114.
63 See, for example, Jason P. Abbott (ed.), *Critical Perspectives on International Political Economy* (Basingstoke: Palgrave Macmillan 2002); Nicola Phillips (ed.), *Globalizing International Political Economy* (London: Palgrave Macmillan 2005); Mary Ann Tétreault, Robert A. Denemark, Kurt Burch and Kenneth P. Thomas (eds), *Rethinking Global Political Economy: Emerging Issues, Unfolding Odysseys* (London: Routledge 2003); V. Spike Peterson, *A Critical Rewriting of Global Political Economy: Integrating Reproductive, Productive and Virtual Economies* (London: Routledge 2003); Ronnie D. Lipschutz, 'Because People Matter: Studying Global Political Economy', *International Studies Perspectives*, 2: 4 (2003), 321–39.
64 Stephen Gill and David Law, *The Global Political Economy: Perspectives, Problems and Policies* (London: Harvester Wheatsheaf 1988); John MacLean, 'Philosophical Roots of Globalization and Philosophical Routes to Globalization', in Randall D. Germain (ed.), *Globalization and its Critics: Perspectives from Political Economy* (Basingstoke: Macmillan 2000); Sandra Halperin, 'Re-Envisioning Global Development: Conceptual and Methodological Issues', *Globalizations*, 4: 4 (2007), 547–61.
65 Karl Marx, *A Contribution to the Critique of Political Economy* (Moscow: Progress Publishers 1970, 1859), 188.
66 Du Bois, *The World and Africa*, 80.
67 Du Bois, *The World and Africa*, 80.
68 Ian Baucom, *Specters of the Atlantic: finance capital, slavery, and the philosophy of history* (Durham, NC: Duke University Press 2005).
69 Baucom, *Specters of the Atlantic*, 34, 311.
70 Baucom, *Specters of the Atlantic*, 3–34.
71 Jane Webster, 'The *Zong* in the context of the eighteenth-century slave trade', *Journal of Legal History*, 28: 3 (2007), 287–8.
72 Blackburn, *The Making of New World Slavery*, 392.

73 Baucom, *Specters of the Atlantic*; Webster, 'The *Zong*'. The *Zong* massacre has long been the subject of reflections on transatlantic slavery in literature, poetry and art. Turner's painting *Slavers throwing overboard the dead and dying – Typhoon coming on*, painted in 1840, is understood to have been based on the *Zong*. Novelists and poets who have reflected on the *Zong* include Fred D'Aguiar, *Feeding the Ghosts* (London: Chatto and Windus 1997) and Derek Walcott, 'The sea is history' in *Collected Poems: 1948–1984* (New York: Farrar, Straus and Giroux 1986); see Ian Baucom, 'Specters of the Atlantic', *The South Atlantic Quarterly*, 100: 1 (2001), 61–82. Most recently the Otolith Group, shortlisted for the Turner Prize in 2010, have developed work, *Hydra Decapita*, in response to Baucom's argument. See Gil Leung, 'What form would that extraction take now? The Otolith Group in Conversation with Gil Leung', *Lux*, 2010, available at: http://lux.org.uk/blog/what-form-would-abstraction-take-now-otolith-group-conversation-gil-leung-part-1-3 (accessed 2 January 2011).
74 Baucom, *Specters of the Atlantic*; Webster, 'The *Zong*'.
75 Baucom, *Specters of the Atlantic*, 80–112; Ian Baucom, '"Signum rememorativum, demonstrativum, prognostikon": Slavery and Finance Capital', in Nancy Henry and Cannon Schmitt (eds), *Victorian Investments: New Perspectives on Finance and Culture* (Bloomington and Indianapolis: Indiana University Press 2009).
76 In addition to Baucom, see James Oldham, 'Insurance Litigation Involving the *Zong* and Other British Slave Ships, 1780–1807', *Journal of Legal History*, 28: 3 (2007), 299–318 and Tim Armstrong, 'Slavery, insurance and sacrifice in the Black Atlantic', in Bernhard Klein and Gesa Mackenthun (eds), *Sea Changes: Historicizing the Ocean* (New York: Routledge 2003) for detailed analyses.
77 Baucom, *Specters of the Atlantic*, 96.
78 Baucom, *Specters of the Atlantic*, 26.
79 Baucom, *Specters of the Atlantic*, 29.
80 Dick Bryan and Michael Rafferty, *Capitalism With Derivatives: A Political Economy of Financial Derivatives, Capital and Class* (Basingstoke: Palgrave Macmillan 2005), 1.
81 Derivatives are financial contracts whose value is related to or based on the value of an underlying asset, set of assets or conditions (commodity derivatives are based on wheat, cotton, etc; financial derivatives are based on exchange rates, interest rates and stock indexes). Securities are financial instruments providing returns whose value arises from an underlying asset or debt obligation. The trading of derivatives based on underlying material commodities such as wheat dates to the early twentieth century, and was largely restricted to specific realms of trade in agricultural and mineral commodities. Financial derivatives represent a qualitatively new level of complexity and abstraction: the 'underlying' basis of value is itself an aspect of finance – an interest rate, exchange rate, or stock index, for example. Financial derivatives based on interest rates and currencies began to develop in the aftermath of the collapse of the Bretton Woods monetary regime in the early 1970s. Since the 1980s, the use of financial derivatives has expanded massively, to occupy a central place in global finance.
82 See Bryan and Rafferty, *Capitalism With Derivatives*; Edward LiPuma and Benjamin Lee, *Financial Derivatives and the Globalisation of Risk* (Durham, NC: Duke University Press 2004); Benjamin Lee and Edward LiPuma, 'Cultures of circulation: the imaginations of modernity', *Public Culture*, 14 (2002), 191–214.
83 LiPuma and Lee, *Financial Derivatives*, 2.

4 Time and the others

Christine Helliwell and Barry Hindess

> The Oriental doesn't put the same high price on life as does a Westerner. Life is plentiful. Life is cheap in the Orient.[1]

The documentary in which the above quote appears gives us few clues as to how to interpret Westmoreland's statement. Is it part of a larger speech – perhaps the conclusion to be drawn from an (unrecorded) argument he had presented earlier – or is he simply throwing out a rationalization for the view that those making the documentary are making an unnecessary fuss over a few (million) dead gooks? Either way, it seems likely that his comments should be read as reflecting, not a perception of Orientals in general, but rather a kind of received military wisdom based on a number of wars against Eastern militaries – those of Japan, North Korea, China and, in this case, North Vietnam – which suggests that the leaders of these militaries do not hesitate to throw large numbers of their own soldiers into the grinder. In this context, Westmoreland's comment could be paraphrased as: they don't appear to have been concerned about the size of their butcher's bill, so why should we be? Yet the second part of the statement complicates this dubious logic. There are millions of people living in New York City, a fact that, along with Westmoreland's association of quantity with low value, might lead the unwary to suspect that nobody would make a fuss about the killing of a few thousand New York workers. Yet, few people in the US are likely to read this fact or to have read it in 1974, at least in public, as suggesting that life is so cheap in New York and other major Western cities that thousands can be slaughtered in the pursuit of greater ends. There is clearly something more complicated going on here than can be accounted for via a simple equation between plenitude and cheapness.

However much we may puzzle over these remarks, their basic import is clear enough. Westmoreland's view at the time of this interview, which we take to be an extreme formulation of a widespread Western perception, was that Oriental (in this case Vietnamese) lives should not be accorded the same value as Western ones, at least when it comes to war. This chapter focuses on this differential valuation, arguing that it is in large part a function of what Johannes Fabian calls 'allochronism' or 'the denial of coevalness'.

Writing of the denial of coevalness within anthropology, Fabian describes it as the 'persistent and systematic tendency to place the referent(s) of anthropology in a Time other than the present of the producer of anthropological discourse'.[2] Fabian argues that within anthropology the temporal has always been subordinated to the visual-spatial, resulting in the tendency to treat travel to different places as if it were travel to different (earlier) times.[3] As a result, in anthropological accounts of other societies, physical/geographical difference is equated with temporal difference, and there is a denial of coevalness – that is, a denial that those being studied exist in the same time period as the anthropologist. Instead, the contemporary Other is transmuted into our past/primitive ancestor. In this respect, anthropological practice simply reflects a deep-seated view found, since at least the Enlightenment era, in Western societies more generally.[4] Thus Joseph Conrad could memorably write in *Heart of Darkness*, describing Marlow's trip up a river in Africa:

> We penetrated deeper and deeper into the heart of darkness .... We were wanderers on prehistoric earth, on an earth that wore the aspect of an unknown planet .... But suddenly, as we struggled round a bend, there would be a glimpse of rush walls, of peaked grass-roofs, a burst of yells, a whirl of black limbs, a mass of hands clapping, of feet stamping, of bodies swaying, of eyes rolling .... The prehistoric man was cursing us, praying to us, welcoming us – who could tell? We were cut off from the comprehension of our surroundings; we glided past like phantoms, wondering and secretly appalled, as sane men would be before an enthusiastic outbreak in a madhouse. We could not understand because we were too far and could not remember, because we were traveling in the night of first ages, of those ages that are gone, leaving hardly a sign – and no memories.[5]

Arland Thornton describes the practice of reading the relations between contemporaneous peoples in historical terms as 'reading history sideways', and argues that scholars have engaged in such reading for several centuries 'to construct histories of virtually every dimension of human life'.[6] As he points out, this practice explicitly underpins the popular system of categorization whereby populations are described as 'modern', 'traditional', 'developed', 'developing' and so on;[7] this system is used by governments and international organizations such as the World Bank, as well as throughout academia, most particularly in the social sciences.[8] The denial of coevalness, then, features no less in politics, international relations and the other social sciences than it does in anthropology.[9] It appears, most obviously perhaps, in discourses of modernity, modernization and development, all of which divide the contemporary world into societies that are fully of our time, and others – pre-modern, modernizing or developing societies – that remain at greater or lesser distances behind; but Thornton shows that it also pervades other, apparently more 'neutral' academic discourses – in his case, those relating to family life. Outside academia, influential versions of the denial of coevalness inform the work of major development agencies and the international human rights regime, and figure in other aspects of the West's interactions with the non-Western world. To take a simple example, Susan Rose-Ackerman, an economist who has worked closely with the World Bank, notes that what counts as corruption often depends on context: 'one person's bribe is another person's gift.' Yet at the same time she believes that it is important to show 'when the legacy of the past no longer fits modern conditions'.[10]

Both Fabian's title, *Time and the Other* – which we have adapted for the title of this paper – and his focus on the anthropologist's fieldwork report, suggest a narrow view of the problem, as if it concerned anthropology's treatment of a singular Other. In part this is because his book focuses on the specific relationship between the anthropologist and the singular society that he or she is studying: his or her Other. He argues that while the anthropologist and those being studied are equally present in the moment of fieldwork, the written fieldwork report produced after the anthropologist has travelled home often represents those being studied as living in the anthropologist's past. However, in the broader field of contemporary social thought, and even in anthropology itself, we find evidence of scholars dealing with a distance not only between observer and observed, but also between observer and a plurality of Others – a multiplicity of distinct groups of people, all of them located somewhere behind the time of the 'modern' observer. An early example comes from the well-known letter from Edmund Burke to the historian William Robertson written in 1777. In the letter, Burke comments that 'the Great Map of Mankind is unrolled at once; and there is no state or Gradation of barbarism, and no mode of refinement which we have not at the same time instantly under our View.'[11] Here Burke represents many of his contemporaries in other parts of the world as living in conditions of barbarism that, in this case, he imagines can be found in the distant European past. Just a few years later we find Kant and Schiller expressing similar views about their own contemporaries.[12]

In an important article on the discourse of 'the native' as used within anthropology, Appadurai notes that while non-native observers are regarded as quintessentially mobile – movers, seers, knowers – 'natives' are understood as immobile through their belonging to a place.[13] In a similar vein, and picking up on Fabian's account of the relationship between (distant) place and (distant) time in anthropological work, our contention is that all such literatures suggest that, scattered across the realm of the present, there is an archipelago of deprived temporal gulags that serve as detention centres or rudimentary training camps for contemporaries who have been condemned to the more or less distant past.[14]

The plurality of others whose membership of the present is both denied and affirmed by contemporary social thought is, in fact, made clear in Fabian's own discussion. For instance, he notes that

> Anthropology ... gave to politics and economics ... a firm belief in 'natural', i.e., evolutionary Time. It promoted a scheme in terms of which not only past cultures, but all living societies were irrevocably placed on a temporal slope, a stream of Time – some upstream, others downstream.[15]

However, this plurality has a more general significance. Following Edward Said's seminal discussion of the West's construction of its oriental *Other*,[16] One's relationship with the *Other* became a popular theme in late twentieth century humanities discourses and in some areas of the social sciences. The result is that Fabian is far from being alone in his apparent homogenization of the others he would prefer us to write about differently.[17]

At this point, some of our readers might be wondering what is so problematic about the denial of coevalness. Why should we be so concerned to dispute it? Surely, it might be said, the denial of coevalness can itself be seen as a recognition of others' otherness, and as therefore not necessarily disparaging: equivalent to saying that some person or group is old-fashioned or quaint, a characteristic that in certain contexts (for example, with respect to manners or morality) might be viewed as positive. But as Abu-Lughod makes clear in her critique of the anthropological notion of culture, discourses of difference of this kind are rarely disinterested. She argues that culture is 'the essential tool for making other';[18] in a slightly different vein, we argue for the importance of temporality.

This brings us back to the central concern of this chapter: the disproportion in conventional Western perceptions of the relative values of Western (or American) and non-Western lives, as suggested by the quotation with which we began. How, we might ask, is it that, within the contemporary West, Western lives are widely assumed to be so much more important than the lives of others? In our view, there is more to this assumption than the ethnocentrism commonly associated with cultural difference: an important part of the answer to our question is to be found in the contemporary denial of coevalness.[19] More specifically, we suggest that, in contemporary Western social thought, those who are seen as belonging to the present assume a greater moral and political significance than those who are seen as belonging to the past.

This is not an easy claim to establish. Most contemporary social or political theorists would not dare assert or knowingly imply in their writings that Western lives are more valuable than the lives of others, and dead theorists, like Herbert Spencer, who appear to have suggested something to this effect, are widely regarded as extremists.[20] The cosmopolitan pretensions of so much Western social thought appear to entail a positive, inclusive perception of non-Western others that militates against any undervaluation of their lives.[21] Consequently we are forced to work largely with circumstantial evidence.

Our argument proceeds through discussion, first, of the conventional distinction between past and present and, second, of the cult of the individual. We argue that the association of individualism with the post-Reformation West is the link between the denial of coevalness and the differential valuation of Western and non-Western lives. The latter are seen as less important than Western lives to the extent that they are seen as less than fully individualized.

I Past and present

Most readers of this chapter will have learned, like its authors, to think of the past as remote and unalterable and to see the present as discontinuous with the past. On the one hand, the present is perceived as an open field of human action and much of what happens within it is seen as resulting from the choices and actions of its inhabitants. On the other, the past is seen as a field in which action has already taken place with results that are able to be known, at least in principle. However much we may disagree in the present about what these results are and how they might be evaluated, we believe that our debates and choices now can do nothing to change them. The way 'they do [did] things ... there [then]'[22] is seen as unalterable.

This perception of an unbridgeable break between past and present is crucial to the process by which those who are seen to live at earlier stages of Western history come to be devalued. Because they are identified with the past, it is difficult to see them as of the present: they are in a separate and distinct place from us. It also means that they are anachronistic, somewhere they should not be, since the past is somewhere that we (should) have moved on from, somewhere we (should) have left behind.

We should note that this belief in the radical difference between the past and the present is not a product of untutored experience, and has not always been part of the conventional Western view. In a fine polemic at the beginning of *The Limits of History*,[23] Constantin Fasolt maintains that our current view of the difference between past and present is the most important continuing result of a revolt by sixteenth-century protestant 'historians' against the Papacy and the Holy Roman Empire at a time when they both claimed to be eternal and based their claims to legitimacy on a continuity with the past. They thus maintained that certain decisions made in the past should continue to hold in the present. The historians, in Fasolt's view, insisted that the Papacy and the Empire misrepresented the past and that the past had no dominion over the present.

As Fasolt describes it, the historians' revolt was a declaration of independence (DoI) of the present from determination by the past, and had several major social and political consequences. First, Fasolt suggests, the DoI laid the foundation for subsequent understandings of state sovereignty and citizenship:

> No state could be sovereign if its inhabitants lacked the ability to change a course of action adopted ... in the past... No citizen could be a full member of the community so long as she was tied to ancestral traditions ... – the problem of Antigone in Sophocles' tragedy.[24]

Second, this DoI establishes two fundamental principles of historical inquiry: one, that every action must be placed in the context of its time and should not be judged with the benefit of hindsight; and the other, a methodological assertion of individual agency, which insists that the evidence, documentary or otherwise, that we have about the past should always be seen as resulting from choices made by some person or persons acting in their own present.

Third, the idea of an historical DoI identifies a fundamental break with the past. It suggests that there was a time in which people were dominated by the past, and in which they allowed themselves to be ruled by custom and tradition and should thus be seen as irrational. States will therefore be tempted to produce damning historical representations of the pre-DoI past from which they commonly claim to have emerged.

Having briefly presented Fasolt's argument, we should register a number of partial reservations. We might begin by noting that Fasolt's argument reads like a minor variation on the all-too-familiar Western tale of the fresh start, in which something happens to overturn existing ideas and/or arrangements, with the West subsequently heading off in an entirely new direction. Second, as happens in many good polemics, several of Fasolt's claims are overstated. On the issues of sovereignty and citizenship, for example, readers familiar with the role of the constitution in American political and legal debate may feel that contemporary notions of sovereignty are less hostile to determination by the past than he suggests.[25] Nor would it be difficult to argue that, far from being incompatible with full membership of a political community, problems of the kind faced by Antigone are precisely what one should expect of such membership.[26]

Nevertheless, Fasolt's discussion highlights an important feature of the current distinction between past and present: that those who seem to live in the present are perceived as free agents in a way that those who seem to live in the past are not. The former act on the basis of individualized free will, while the latter are ruled by custom and tradition: they are, in effect, ruled by the past itself.

To see the force of this distinction, and how it is used in social/political analysis, it is worth looking at Tsevan Todorov's impressive *The Conquest of America*, in which he provides an explanation for the Spanish victory over the Aztecs in the early sixteenth century (1519–21). Todorov tells us in the book that at the time of the Spanish invasion of what is now Mexico, 'reference to the past is essential for the Aztec mentality of the period' (1984: 81–2), and that 'submission of the present to the past ... remains a significant characteristic of the Indian society of the period...'[27] As a result, 'no-one's life is ever [perceived by the Aztecs as] an open and indeterminate field, to be shaped by an individual free will, but [as] the realization of an order always pre-ordained... [28] Since they perceived others in this way, the Indians neglected "the interhuman dimension" of communication and had difficulty predicting, and responding creatively to, the behaviour of the Spanish: "the Indians" distorted image of the Spaniards during the first encounters, and notably... [their] paralyzing belief that the Spaniards are gods ... can be explained only by an incapacity to perceive the other's human identity – ie., to recognize him both as equal and as different.'[29] In effect, Todorov suggests that the Indians were living in the past and could only treat others as living there too. In contrast, he treats the difference between Columbus's and Cortes's perceptions of the Americans – recorded roughly thirty years apart – as showing that the Spanish of this period were learning to live in the present. This involved developing a 'capacity to understand the other'[30] – that is, to see other people as free agents, and to react to them accordingly.[31] When the contest is presented in these terms, it is not surprising that the Spanish are seen as having overwhelmed the Aztecs. [32]

In *The Order of Things*, Michel Foucault describes the emergence of the 'figure of man' around the start of the nineteenth century as an 'absolutely singular event' in Western cultural history.[33] His use of the term 'figure', rather than 'concept' or 'understanding' is significant, since it does not refer to any one conception of the human individual – of the kind that might be elaborated by some particular school of psychology or philosophy, for instance. 'Man' is simply that which functions in modern – which, in the context of the book, means little more than post-Kantian – discourses both 'as an object of knowledge and as a subject that knows'.[34] In our view, the post-Reformation division between past and present maps neatly onto the parts of this Kantian figure: those who exist in the present are seen as knowing *subjects* with whom we may interact, while our contemporaries who are thought to belong to the past are seen, in part, as subjects of this kind, but mostly as objects submerged in their own communities, and thus as not entirely individualized. Because they belong to the past, their actions are seen as determined by the cultures and traditions to which they are in thrall. We can see this distinction at work in Todorov's discussion. We 'moderns' (represented here by the Spanish invaders) can know them, but they cannot know us.

II The importance of the individual

There is nothing in this mapping of subject/object onto present/past that necessarily requires us to regard the lives of contemporaries who are thought to live in the past as any less significant than the lives of those who belong unequivocally in the present. We may nevertheless note an important objectifying mode in which contemporary people who are thought to live in the past are often perceived: the mode of preservation. When the past – which, as we have seen is regarded as generally inaccessible – can nevertheless be seen as persisting in the present, there may be both the modernizing temptation to clear it out of the way and a countervailing desire to preserve it for the future.

Readers may recall campaigns to save endangered 'hunter-gatherer'[35] communities living in the Amazonian rainforest, the Kalahari Desert or elsewhere, some of whom are said to have deliberately avoided contact with civilization. For example, an article on indigenous peoples tells us that when

> people refer to threatened or endangered species, they likely think of plants and animals …. However, as with endangered plants and animals, there are areas of the world that harbor aboriginal peoples who are in risk of losing centuries of evolved customs and even their ability to exist as a culture. After thousands of years of total isolation, these native bastions have managed to avoid the vagaries of the industrialized world.[36]

This apparently well-meaning account draws a revealing parallel between aboriginal peoples and endangered animal species. Like campaigns to save animal species – the snow leopard, the whale, the great white shark, the giant panda or the orangutan – campaigns to save endangered tribes focus less on the survival of individuals – other than exceptional cases like that of the well-known Yanomami activist, Davi Kopenawa – than on that of the way of life/culture to which those individuals are said to belong. [37]

This neglect of the individual is highly significant. As sociologists and others have noted, one of the distinctive characteristics of many contemporary Western societies is the ideology of individualism, according to which, as Durkheim famously put it,

> the human person ... is considered as sacred .... Nowhere are the rights of man affirmed more energetically, since the individual is here placed on the level of sacrosanct objects; nowhere is he more jealously protected from external encroachments, whatever their source.[38]

Since organizations such as Human Rights Watch, Survival International and so on largely originate in Western individualistic societies, it seems odd that they should be neglecting individuals – and promoting the rights of whole societies – in this way.

Yet we find a closely related disdain for the individual running throughout the history of Western thought, suggesting that this neglect mirrors a more widespread tendency. By way of example, let us turn to the work of John Stuart Mill, who at first sight seems a most unlikely perpetrator of this misdemeanour, since his *On Liberty* is well-known for its insistence on the principle of individual liberty:

> the only purpose for which power can be rightfully exercised over any *member of a civilized community*, against his will, is to prevent harm to others. His own good ... is not a sufficient warrant.[39]

We will return shortly to the qualification highlighted here. In the meantime, we should note that an important part of Mill's argument in *Considerations on Representative Government*, published only a couple of years later, appears to undermine this principle. He describes representative government there as

> the ideal type of the most perfect polity, for which, in consequence, any portion of mankind are better adapted in proportion to their degree of general improvement. As they range lower and lower in development, that form of government will be, generally speaking, less suitable to them.[40]

Unfortunately, he laments, in many cases the people of a less advanced country

> must be governed by the dominant country, or by persons delegated for that purpose by it. This mode of government is as legitimate as any other if it is the one which in the existing state of civilization of the subject people most facilitates their transition to a higher stage of improvement. There are ... conditions of society in which *a vigorous despotism* is in itself *the best mode of government* for training the people in what is specifically wanting *to render them capable of a higher civilization*.[41]

78 *Critique*

Earlier in the same book, Mill gives a forceful example of the kind of vigorous despotism he has in mind:

> Even personal slavery, by giving a commencement to industrial life, and enforcing it as an exclusive occupation of the most numerous portion of the community, may accelerate the transition to a better freedom than that of fighting and rapine.[42]

Mill's point here is not to endorse slavery, but rather to emphasize the difficulty of preparing uncivilized peoples – those who are located 'lower and lower' down the timescale – for free government. However, there is another feature of this passage that we should note, since Mill was an opponent of slavery and was well aware of its consequences for the individuals caught up in it.[43] In view of this awareness, it is significant that Mill nevertheless finds even slavery defensible when its implementation will accelerate social development. In a sense, he is making an argument similar to that which Westmoreland attributes to Oriental military leaders: that it is acceptable to sacrifice individuals under certain conditions. But as for Westmoreland, only certain kinds of individuals are able to be sacrificed in this way: those from societies that range 'lower and lower in development', that is, further and further in the past.

Our point here is less to accuse Mill of flagrant inconsistency than it is to show how temporality figures in his commitment to the value of the individual. Returning to the passage from *On Liberty* cited at the beginning of this discussion of Mill, we highlighted there his insistence on the importance of the principle of individual liberty as applying specifically to that minority of people who were members '*of a civilized community*'. It seems that, in Mill's view, peoples from less developed (past) societies do not qualify for the right to individual liberty because they lack the mental freedom and individuality (conditions he emphasizes in Chapters Two and Three of *On Liberty*) required to exercise it properly.[44] As one of us has pointed out elsewhere, liberalism has always been prepared to judge that there may be individuals who have not (yet) achieved a condition in which they can be governed through freedom.[45]

Lacking such mental freedom and individuality, the peoples of our past are instead governed by group custom and, as such, live in an unhappy state.

> It is desirable, in short, that in things which do not primarily concern others, individuality should assert itself. Where, not the person's own character, but the traditions or customs of other people are the rule of conduct, there is wanting one of the principal ingredients of human happiness, and quite the chief ingredient of individual and social progress.

And again:

> The despotism of custom is everywhere the standing hindrance to human advancement, being in unceasing antagonism to that disposition to aim at

something better than customary, which is called, according to circumstances, the spirit of liberty, or that of progress or improvement.[46]

We find in Mill, then, an equation of individualism – regarded as being in opposition to rule by tradition or customs – with 'the spirit of progress or development'. Without making the claim quite so bluntly, Mill seems to believe that in the absence of the spirit of individuality, people will be submerged into the traditions and customs of the group and will therefore be unable to express their own judgment and individual character. In this regard, he was little different from many of his contemporaries. This view of less developed societies as characterized by a lack of individuality, and dominated by group tradition, was handed down to contemporary social science via such thinkers as Maine, Tönnies, Durkheim and Le Bon among others.[47] We see clearly here a mapping of the two dimensions of Foucault's figure of man onto two different types of society: present (individualistic) and past (non-individualistic). Lacking individuals, the latter are also seen to lack self-knowledge and the imaginative capability required to know others. They, then, can only be the objects of knowledge, in contrast to the members of more advanced societies who are able to know them, and therefore also to know what is best for them.

While some of the effects of this for contemporary social and political thought have been sketched out in our discussion earlier of Todorov's book, this conflation has other more sinister consequences. As we have seen in our discussion of Mill, it is easy to ignore the rights of individuals when they belong to societies seen as characterized by a lack of the individuality deemed sacred by many in the West. Such individuals are believed to be not (yet) able to understand and appreciate those rights, and thus not (yet) able to be governed through them. It is no surprise, then, that lacking such a suitably developed spirit of liberty and individuality, Mill regarded the peoples of India as not sufficiently advanced 'to be fitted for representative government'.[48] Nor that not too long after *On Liberty* was published, we find British colonial officials arguing that peoples who have yet to develop the idea of individual liberty are not to be trusted with self-government. Thus Lord Cromer, one-time British Consul General – in effect, Viceroy – in Egypt, writing on the government of subject peoples, insists that 'the fatally simple idea of despotic rule' – the obverse of individual liberty – will not readily 'give way to the far more complex conception of ordered liberty. The transformation, if it ever takes place at all, will probably be the work, not of generations, but of centuries.'[49]

Armed with such a conceit, it was not difficult to argue that subject peoples could be expected to benefit from being governed by agents of the imperial power. But nor was it difficult to imagine that the lives of those people – unindividuated as they were seen to be – counted for little compared with those of real individuals in the West. To the extent that we are living with the residues of such imperial fancies, we should expect perceived temporal backwardness to be associated with a perceived lack of real individuality and thus to be accorded a lower value. As General Westmoreland makes clear, the lives that continue to matter are those of real individuals, who are to be found, for the most part, in the prosperous societies of the contemporary West.

Notes

1 US General William Westmoreland, quoted in the documentary film *Hearts and Minds* (1974).
2 Johannes Fabian, *Time and the Other. How Anthropology Makes its Object* (New York: Columbia University Press 1983), 31.
3 François Hartog in *The Mirror of Herodotus. The Representation of the Other in the Writing of History* (Berkeley and Los Angeles: University of California Press 1988) has argued that this association between distance in space and distance in time is a feature of Western thought more generally.
4 See Christine Helliwell and Barry Hindess, 'The temporalizing of difference', *Ethnicities*, 5: 3 (2005), 414–18; Bernard McGrane, *Beyond Anthropology: Society and the Other* (New York: Columbia University Press 1989).
5 Joseph Conrad, *Heart of Darkness* (Harmondsworth: Penguin 1973 [1902]), 51.
6 Arland Thornton, *Reading History Sideways. The Fallacy and Enduring Impact of the Developmental Paradigm on Family Life* (Chicago: University of Chicago Press 2005), 4.
7 Ibid., 104.
8 See Thornton, op. cit.; J.M. Blaut, *The Colonizer's Model of the World* (New York and London: The Guilford Press 1993); Susan Greenhalgh, 'The social construction of population science: an intellectual, institutional, and political history of twentieth-century demography', *Comparative Studies in Society and History*, 38: 1(1996), 26–66.
9 Naeem Inayatullah and David Blaney, *International Relations and the Problem of Difference* (New York: Routledge 2004).
10 Susan Rose-Ackerman, *Corruption and Government: Causes, Consequences and Reform* (Cambridge and New York: Cambridge University Press 1999), 5.
11 Edmund Burke, 'Letter to William Robertson, 9 June 1777', in T.W. Copeland (ed.), *Edmund Burke: Correspondence, Volume 3* (Cambridge: Cambridge University Press 1961), 351.
12 Immanuel Kant, 'Idea for a Universal History', in H. Reiss (ed.), *Kant's Political Writings* (Cambridge: Cambridge University Press 1970 [1784]), 41–53; Friedrich von Schiller, 'The Nature and Value of Universal History', *History and Theory*, 11: 3 (1972[1789]), 321–34.
13 Arjun Appadurai, 'Putting hierarchy in its place', *Cultural Anthropology*, 3: 1 (1988), 36–49 at p.37.
14 See Barry Hindess, 'Been there, done that', *Postcolonial Studies*, 11: 2 (2008), 201–13.
15 Fabian, op. cit., 17.
16 Edward Said, *Orientalism* (London: Pantheon 1978). Said's invocation of a singular Other has been criticized – albeit from slightly different perspectives – by a number of scholars. See e.g. Lisa Lowe, *Critical Terrains: French and British Orientalisms* (Ithaca, NY: Cornell University Press 1991); Homi Bhabha, *The Location of Culture* (London: Routledge 1994); Valerie Kennedy, *Edward Said: A Critical Introduction* (Cambridge: Polity 2000); John M. MacKenzie, *Orientalism: History, Theory and the Arts* (Manchester: Manchester University Press 1995).
17 There are too many examples to list, but see Tsevan Todorov's well-known *The Conquest of America* (New York: Harper & Row 1984). Todorov begins by announcing the subject of the book – 'the discovery *self* makes of the *other*' – which he

proposes to investigate by questioning the narrative 'of the [European] discovery and conquest of America' (3, 4). Yet, later in the book Todorov notes that 'Mexico at the time, is not a homogeneous state, but a conglomerate of populations ...' (ibid.). There was, in other words, no singular *other* waiting to be discovered in America by the European invaders, any more than there was a singular European self waiting to find them, but rather a plurality of both. See also Inga Clendinnen's critical discussion of Todorov in her '"Fierce and unnatural cruelty": Cortes and the conquest of Mexico', *Representations*, 33(1991), 65–100.

18 Lila Abu-Lughod, 'Writing against culture', in Henrietta L. Moore and Todd Sanders (eds), *Anthropology in Theory: Issues in Epistemology* (Oxford: Blackwell 2006 [1991]), 466–79 at p.470.

19 We refer to the 'contemporary' denial of coevalness here because an earlier denial can be found in Greek and Roman antiquity. While this paper focuses on the denial of coevalness in post-Reformation Western social thought, it will be the task of a later paper to argue that this is radically different, in both character and effect, from earlier forms of denial.

20 In his *Principles of Biology*, Spencer affirms the idea that the 'survival of the fittest, which I have here sought to express in mechanical terms, is that which Mr. Darwin has called "natural selection", or the preservation of favoured races in the struggle for life' ((London: Williams and Norgate 1864), 444.

21 We argue elsewhere that this cosmopolitan inclusiveness comes at an unpleasant price (see Christine Helliwell and Barry Hindess, 'Kantian cosmopolitanism and its limits', forthcoming).

22 Cf. the opening line of L. P. Hartley's *The Go-Between*: 'The past is a foreign country; they do things differently there' ((London: Penguin 1958), 7. This and the following paragraphs are based on Barry Hindess, 'The past is another culture', *International Political Sociology*, 1: 4 (2007), 325–38.

23 Constatin Fasolt, *The Limits of History* (Chicago: University of Chicago Press 2004).

24 Ibid., 7.

25 Cf. Michael I. Meyerson, *Liberty's Blueprint* (New York: Basic Books 2008).

26 Cf. Peter Nyers (ed.), *Securitizations of Citizenship* (London: Routledge 2008); Engin Isin and Greg Nielsen, *Acts of Citizenship* (London: Zed Books 2008).

27 Todorov, op. cit., 83.

28 Ibid., 69.

29 Ibid., 75–6.

30 Ibid., 248.

31 Todorov associates this last capacity with the development of writing by identifying the absence of writing in the one case and its presence in the other as the chief reason for the Europeans' 'extraordinary success' (ibid.). See Matthew Restall, *Seven Myths of the Spanish Conquest* (Oxford: Oxford University Press 2003), 90–99 for a critique of this argument.

32 Clendinnen (op. cit.) argues that the conflict was much closer than Todorov suggests, and that there is little sense in searching for what Todorov calls the 'chief reason'. Paul Hirst offers a more sympathetic account of Todorov's argument in 'The evolution of consciousness', *Economy & Society*, 23: 1(1994), 47–65).

33 Michel Foucault, *The Order of Things* (London: Tavistock 1970), xxii.

34 Ibid., 312.

35 This problematic category invokes its own denial of coevalness. Cf. Mark Pluciennik, *Social Evolution* (London: Duckworth 2005).

36 Bob Jones, 'Endangered Humans – Human Rights Watch – Indigenous peoples', *Humanist* (July–August 2003), available at: http://findarticles.com/p/articles/mi_m1374/is_4_63/ai_104971401 (accessed 7 June 2008).

37 Survival International, an NGO that describes itself as 'the movement for tribal peoples' and as focusing on tribal peoples who have the most to lose (usually those most recently in contact with the outside world) reported on 16 November 2007 that a Brazilian rancher had threatened to kill Davi Kopenawa.

38 Emile Durkheim, 'Individualism and the intellectuals', in W. F. S. Pickering (ed.), *Durkheim on Religion* (London and Boston: Routledge and Kegan Paul 1975 [1898]), 59–73 at p.62. For a recent discussion of individualism see Steven Lukes, *Individualism* (Colchester: ECPR Press 2006). See also Louis Dumont, *Homo Hierarchicus: the Caste System and its Implications* (Chicago: University of Chicago Press 1970) and *Essays on Individualism* (Chicago: University of Chicago Press 1986 [1983]) for perhaps the most well-known account of the difference between 'individualist' and what he terms 'holistic' societies. While Dumont has (rightly) been heavily criticized for, among other things, essentializing this distinction, nevertheless, as Appadurai puts it, 'most scholars working on the caste systems of South Asia (even the most obdurately empiricist critics of Dumont) will grant that Dumont's idea of hierarchy captures the distance between the value-assumptions of India and post-Enlightenment Europe like no previous characterization' (Appadurai, op. cit., 42).

39 John Stuart Mill, 'On Liberty', in John M. Robson (ed.), *Collected Works of John Stuart Mill, Volume xviii* (Toronto: University of Toronto Press and London: Routledge 1977 [1859]), 213–310 at p.223 (emphasis ours).

40 John Stuart Mill, 'Considerations on Representative Government', in John M. Robson (ed.), *Collected Works of John Stuart Mill, Volume xix* (Toronto: University of Toronto Press and London: Routledge 1977 [1861]), 371–570 at p.413.

41 Ibid., 567 (emphasis ours).

42 Ibid., 394–5.

43 Mill's view of slavery is made abundantly clear in his rebuttal of Thomas Carlyle's 'Occasional Discourse on the Negro Question':

> There are, Heaven knows, vicious and tyrannical institutions in ample abundance on the earth. But this institution is the only one of them all which requires, to keep it going, that human beings should be burnt alive. And not [of] negroes only; the Edinburgh Review, in a recent number, gave the hideous details of the burning alive of an unfortunate Northern huckster by Lynch law, on mere suspicion of having aided in the escape of a slave. What must American slavery be, if deeds like these are necessary under it? – and if they are not necessary and are yet done, is not the evidence against slavery still more damning? The South are in rebellion not for simple slavery; they are in rebellion for the right of burning human creatures alive.
> *The Contest in America* (Boston, Mass.: Little Brown and Co. 1862), 20

Note how Mill uses the fate of the unfortunate, but presumably white, Northern huckster to bolster his case.

44 'It is possible that he might be guided in some good path, and kept out of harm's way, without any of these things [i.e. his own judgment and feelings]. But what would be his comparative worth as a human being?' (Mill, 'Liberty', 263).

45 Barry Hindess 2001, 'The liberal government of unfreedom', *Alternatives*, 26: 2 (2001), 93–111.

46 Mill, 'Liberty', 261.

47 Sir Henry Sumner Maine, *Ancient Law* (London: John Murray 1861); Ferdinand Tönnies, *Gemeinschaft und Gesellschaft* (Leipzig: Fues's Verlag 1887); Emile Durkheim, *The Division of Labour in Society* (Basingstoke: Macmillan 1984 [1893]); Gustave LeBon, *The Crowd* (New York: Viking 1960). Cf. Vincent Crapanzano, 'The moment of prestidigitation: magic, illusion, and mana in the thought of Emile Durkheim and Marcel Mauss', in Elazar Bakan and Ronald Bush (eds), *Prehistories*

of the Future: The Primitivist Project and the Culture of Modernism (Stanford, CA: Stanford University Press 1995), 95–113; Robert Nye, 'Savage crowds, modernism and modern politics', in Elazar Bakan and Ronald Bush (eds), *Prehistories of the Future: The Primitivist Project and the Culture of Modernism* (Stanford, CA: Stanford University Press 1995, 42–55).
48 Mill, 'Representative Government', 567.
49 Lord Cromer, 'The government of subject races', *Edinburgh Review*, 207 (1908), 1–27 at p. 13.

Part II
Performance

5 War, armed forces and society in postcolonial perspective[1]

Tarak Barkawi

International Relations (IR) imagines that it takes questions of war and peace very seriously, more so than any other social science. As traditionally rendered, the discipline originates in competing accounts of the causes of the Second World War and of the sources of interstate peace. During the Cold War, the 'American social science' focused on the national security problematic facing the United States, devoting resources to bipolarity, nuclear strategy and low-intensity conflict.[2] The 'democratic peace' was the discipline's distinctive contribution to the age of globalization, while security studies today focus on counter-terrorism and counter-insurgency, or the critique of the War on Terror and the new era of surveillance and governance of populations it entails. It would seem that the discipline, mainstream and critical, has been and continues to be centrally focused on questions of force and war and their implications for world politics.

Elsewhere Mark Laffey and I have shown that the premises of security studies are profoundly Eurocentric, that world politics are conceived from the point of view of the major Western powers, and that this Eurocentrism fatally compromises security studies as a social science.[3] In this chapter, I take up the slippage between 'security' and 'war', and argue firstly that in fact IR does not study war per se, but rather strategy and security. In so doing, IR protects its nation-state ontology of the world – a world composed of discrete units – for it is by and large states that have security policies and pursue strategies. War, surprisingly, given its significance, is not the central object of any social science, but were it to become so, it would necessarily entail a relational ontology. Such an ontology is at the heart of the postcolonial, which envisions a world jointly produced out of the experience of imperialism and colonialism. What then does the intersection of war and the postcolonial reveal about the making of the modern world? What would the research agenda of a postcolonial war studies look like?

One point of contact between war, armed forces and the postcolonial concerns modernity, which, as postcolonial critics point out, has been predominantly conceived in Eurocentric terms, as a self-generated property of the West which was exported to the rest of the world. The postcolonial critics, however, largely leave war out of *their* accounts of modernity.[4] Yet warfare made possible and sustained not only colonialism, but the modern world orders we seek to understand.

War and the military also play important but underacknowledged roles in Eurocentric constructions of modernity. Modern, regular armed forces are conceived as embodying nationalism, rationality and high technology, and are sharply distinguished from pre-modern, non-Western 'warriors' and indigenous military traditions. Conceived as organically connected to the nation on the one hand, and as the epitome of modern social organization on the other, unexamined assumptions about the military help secure the core construct of IR: the modern and national Western state. The nation-state also serves, implicitly or explicitly, as the framework for most other social, historical and political inquiry.

A postcolonial critique can reveal what drops out in the reduction of war and the military to the modern nation-state. The military is refigured as a *cosmopolitan* institution – at home anywhere in the world, one with a heritage that predates modernity and its nations and states, and which cannot be properly understood by beginning with geographic units, whether 'the West' or territorial states. Such a critique helps broach fundamental questions about the nature and character of the human potential for violent conflict, that is, for the very questions IR is concerned with.

Taken together, postcolonial reformulations of war and armed forces demonstrate the significance of postcoloniality not only for IR but for the reorganization of the social sciences more generally. In a variety of ways, the social sciences are based upon geographic compartmentalizations of the world, presuming and reproducing boundaries between the 'inside' and 'outside' of states, societies, economies, regions and cultures. In its insistence that the modern world was formed in and through imperial encounters, and in keeping colonizer and colonized in the same analytic frame, as jointly shaping one another, postcoloniality draws attention not so much to boundary crossings as to the international processes by which a world apparently composed of discrete units was formed. War and the military figure importantly in these processes, but analytically have been reduced to the nation-state and to the international system of states. Postcolonial critique helps us see war and armed forces anew, phenomena whose meaning and significance both traditional and critical scholars have all too often taken for granted.

The strange absence of war studies

In a widely cited article published in 1991, Stephen Walt found it 'easy to identify' the main focus of security studies: 'the phenomenon of war'.[5] In fact, specifically speaking, neither security studies nor IR more generally inquire into, much less theorize, war as a set of social relations and processes. War is only conceived through the prism of IR theory, not in its own terms. Consequently, IR and security studies research topics such as the incidence of war in the international system, the causes of war, crisis decision-making, the dynamics of alliances, the advantages and disadvantages of strategies and military doctrines, and so on, none of which are the same object of analysis as 'war'. In inquiry based on the 'wider agenda' of security, including critical security studies, there has been a decisive and substantive move away from war and armed forces as topics of study.[6] Perhaps surprisingly, given its self-identity, IR is part and parcel of the decentring of war in the organization of social scientific knowledge inspired by the European Enlightenments.

Strategic studies offers a prime example of this decentring. Strategy concerns how to prevail in war, and more broadly how to use military force among other instrumentalities to achieve political ends. The study of strategy is not the study of war per se, nor does it amount to a social science adequate to the 'phenomenon of war' as a totality, however essential an understanding of strategic thought would be to such a science. More generally, the problem is that no social science discipline takes war as its central object of analysis, as in the case of politics, society, economy or culture, each of which have their own cognate discipline. In the absence of a discipline, war itself is not centred as the object of analysis and debate, as itself the focus of a continuing scholarly conversation. At issue are the concerns of *some other* scholarly conversation, such as the relationship between war and state building, the effects of war on public opinion and elections, the war proneness of the international system, the legality or ethics of war, or the consequences of war for society.

Of course we learn much of war through studies of these and other kinds. Historians, sociologists, peace and conflict studies and feminist scholars have all made seminal contributions to the study of war, however conceived, but the point here is that such studies have not developed into and are not conceived as a body of inquiry oriented to the problematic of war as the central object of inquiry.[7] What war consists of is most often taken for granted, usually as the clash of arms, and is addressed only in and through the terms of a discipline or scholarly project principally devoted to some other subject. In other words, war is reduced to another social domain. War appears as a builder of states in historical sociology, a pattern of public opinion in political science, an effect of the international system in international relations scholarship, or a disrupter of personalities in literature and psychology. War is strangely decentred and fragmented as an object of inquiry, in ways intensified by the institutional diversity of the sites where war is studied.

In many ways, the absence of war studies is a consequence of larger currents in modern social and political thought favouring peace over war, and in particular the pacific and rational presuppositions of the Enlightenment thinking that shaped the universities and disciplines. These worked to displace both the classical tradition of antiquity, in which war figures prominently, and the historical weight of war, its presence in the societies scholars lived in and thought about. As Michael Mann observes, 'From the Enlightenment to Durkheim most major sociologists omitted war from their central problematic', believing 'future society would be pacific and transnational'.[8] Proceeding in this manner was possible even as wars raged inside and outside Europe because many Enlightenment thinkers understood civilization as a teleological process through which violence – barbarous, rude, uncivil – was being removed from society.[9] Alternatively, as for some eighteenth-century theorists, war was a pathology generated by the politics of commercial competition between states, one to be avoided by restructuring commerce.[10] Before the Cold War, the study of war, armed forces and strategy had little university presence in the Western academy. Even in history, military history was not part of the professionalization of the discipline from the late nineteenth century, either in Germany or in the Anglo-American academy.[11]

The lack of a postcolonial war studies is therefore only part of a more general problem. Walt moves from the idea of the 'phenomenon of war' to this definition of security studies: 'the study of the threat, use, and control of military force'.[12] What is the difference between 'war' as a central object of systematic inquiry and this definition? The definition is what might be called a strategic appropriation of war, of a kind that happens when Carl von Clausewitz is taken to have 'defined war' as the 'continuation of policy by other means'.[13] Although he can be quoted in this way, Clausewitz's conception of war vastly exceeds such an instrumental approach. At a minimum there is the matter of the 'variable relations' between his 'trinities' of people, government and army with their attendant characteristics of passion, reason and technique.[14] For Clausewitz, and many of the thin line of major thinkers who have tackled war as their centrepiece, a key dimension of war is its socially generative properties.[15] War consumes and reworks social and political orders. As a strategist and staff officer, Clausewitz enjoins leadership to think carefully about ends and means in war, for war is a resistant medium for instrumental action. As a philosopher of war, he is attentive to the ways in which war undermines and even reverses the relations between ends and means, as in his ideas of 'total' and 'true' or 'absolute' war. He repeatedly emphasizes war's capacity to unmake certainties, in chaotic and unpredictable ways.[16] This was in part a reflection of his own experience of a period of violent social transformation occasioned by the Napoleonic way of war and its impact on a profoundly conservative Prussian military and society.[17]

These larger themes, which Clausewitz would take to be central to any notion of war, are offset in Walt's definition, which invokes the 'use' and 'control' of force, and the idea of a threat – an intentional action which can be made and responded to in a more or less rational fashion. War does not appear as a force that might rework and operate upon these intentions, their bearers and the social formations of which they are a part. Instead Walt emphasizes the strategic, instrumentally rational element, while embedding security studies in IR, the central object of analysis of which is a system of sovereign states, not war.[18] That is, Walt goes from strategy to international politics, whereas Clausewitz takes up strategy as a route into an account of the fundamental character and nature of war. In broad and initial strokes, and with the postcolonial in mind, what might we take away from Clausewitz's efforts?

The first point is that the ontology of war is inherently relational, something soldiers capture with the idea that 'the enemy always has a vote'. This is true in a larger sense, addressed below, that of polities and societies in relations of war, in which the fates of the combatant become bound up together in unpredictable ways. But it is also true of war's essential activity, *fighting*, the reciprocal organized violence that Clausewitz understood to be war's inescapable means.[19] It is fighting that generates the vortex that pulls in combatant societies, their leaderships and populations. Fighting is an engagement with the enemy the nature and outcome of which lies outside of either side's control but which is jointly shaped by their interaction and context. At this most basic, 'tactical' level war's main characteristic is evident: its ability to draw people into a violent embrace from which no one ever emerges the same. The study of war must therefore keep the clash of arms in central focus. But at the same time, the significance and implications of fighting, of battles and campaigns and other wartime events, are far from straightforward and vastly exceed specifically 'military' matters. Much of what passes for war studies and military history remains focused only on the conduct of military operations and not the wider implications, while 'war and society' literature typically focuses on the social consequences of war alone. The relations that comprise war are thus severed and compartmentalized into different areas of study.[20]

A second area that Clausewitz points us towards concerns the relations between war, power and knowledge. Bowdlerizing Max Weber, IR and political science define the state by its territorial monopoly on the legitimate use of force. A key aspect of this legitimacy, however, is the state's claim to the *knowledges* required for the efficacious constitution, organization and command of force. This may take the form of a state's claim to high technology, or to the superior qualities of its aristocratic officers, or those of particular weapons systems or operational techniques, the English longbow or blitzkrieg for example. The claim to the authoritative command of force is intimately wrapped up in the narratives that underpin the more general legitimacy of a political order. Ideas surrounding the military indispensability of the Prussian *Junkers*, for example, helped constitute an order of public reason in pre-Napoleonic Prussia that both informed the organization of armed forces and legitimated political authority more generally. The problem that actual experience of war poses for these knowledges and authoritative claims is that war has a strong tendency to recurrently undermine them. For both winners and losers, war can disrupt and transform orders of public reason and the political identities they define. The troops generally do not come home by Christmas, and crisis ensues.

One implication of this pervasive tendency of war to destroy expectations and truths is that war and armed forces are the site of a key power/knowledge complex. Political authority takes a direct interest in knowledges related to the governance and use of force, as for example in the US 'military-academic complex' that developed during the Second World War. Directly or indirectly, from military staffs in the nineteenth century to university departments in the Cold War, the state shapes a great deal of inquiry related to war and armed forces, much of it of course done in the register of strategy. Despite such intellectual resources, war retains its power to surprise those leaders who would wage it, and to undermine their claims to the efficacious command of force. As war so often underwrites the narratives that sustain legitimacy, here is one of the sources of war's power to consume and rework political and social orders: war's ability to destroy truths. Note that these relations only emerge when fighting – the site at which claims to military efficaciousness face the 'test of the real' – is kept in the same analytic frame with the wider social and political context.

The third and summative major area Clausewitz points to is the socially generative powers of war. As he observed of his own time: 'Since [Napoleon], all campaigns have produced such comet like vibrations that they can scarcely be thought of as only military because they involve the whole of society.'[21] War entwines armed forces and their social formations in mutually constitutive relations. '[W]ar must be seen as a social activity related to the whole complex of social life and organisation.'[22] War is shaped by, and shapes, social context. A central implication here is that war, as it were, exceeds 'war' as the clash of arms and is related to a whole range of social phenomena on and off the battlefield. War's excess – its powers to shape social and political orders – breaks down conventional distinctions between 'peace' and 'war'. 'Peacetime' social orders are profoundly informed by war, as for example in the economy, in gender relations, in rituals of state, and in popular entertainment. In order to understand these connections between 'war' and 'peace', one cannot study *only* the social effects of war, as in much 'war and society' literature and other disciplinary engagements with war. Rather, war must be kept analytically centred while at the same time placed in broader context.

From world wars to small wars

Some of the points made above can be illustrated with the example of the Second World War in IR scholarship. The core debate between realists and liberals regarding the amelioration of great power conflict – *realpolitik* versus international institutions – rests upon competing accounts of its origins and aftermath. Work on the war proneness of different regime types – the so-called 'Democratic Peace' – grew out of these debates. Normative orientations across a range of positions in IR and security studies draw sustenance from Eurocentric tales of the 'good war'. More fundamental if less remarked upon in disciplinary literature is the international system before the war – one largely composed of European great powers and their empires – and that after the war, in which the sovereign state system rapidly went global and imperialism reverted to more informal modes. However one wishes to characterize them, the Second World War marks basic shifts in the character of world politics.

Yet note that in this overview the social, political and cultural processes of the *war itself* remain a black box. It is taken for granted that the war changed everything, but just how it did so is left unaddressed in the discipline concerned with 'war and peace' and the sub-discipline supposedly focused on 'the phenomenon of war'. It is also more or less taken for granted that we know what the war consisted of and when it began and ended. But just how is it that the war consumed one world order and spat out another? Notably absent – on the major conflagration of the twentieth century – are efforts to theorize and understand the war itself as a set of reciprocal processes and relations.[23] While the social science disciplines largely defined by the nation state – history, sociology, political science – have literatures addressing various processes and effects of the war on their objects of analysis, the only discipline concerned with the 'international' does not address the war as a combined set of international social relations, a set of relations all are agreed transformed the world.

If we accept that war is a socially generative force, we cannot take for granted the identities of the entities which engage in it and emerge from it. Nor can we make easy assumptions about the geographic and temporal scope of a war, as in the Correlates of War (CoW) database, used extensively in IR scholarship, which conceptualizes war by reference to numbers of battle deaths and to sovereign territorial criteria.[24] This is especially so in the case of a 'world war' that played out in interconnected ways across different regions, articulating various peoples and their diverse struggles, transforming political entities and producing new ones. The dates we take to mark off the Second World War, 1939–1945, reflect Eurocentric assumptions. For example, for the Chinese and the Japanese, the war began much earlier, ending for the former in 1950, only to spill over directly into the Korean War as Korean communist forces fighting with their Chinese allies returned home to make possible the invasion of South Korea, which became a founding event of the global Cold War.

There are other connections between the war itself and the forces in the colonized world it shaped and unleashed. Western prestige in Asia never recovered from the daring and well-executed campaigns by which the Japanese toppled the Europeans in the Far East in the six months from December 1941. A racial order in which only the white man authoritatively and efficaciously commanded force was put to an end on the field of battle. Due in large part to the social and political energies let loose by these campaigns, which took down colonial orders built over three centuries, a whole series of struggles across the Asian rim ensued well exceeding the putative 'end' of the war.[25] CoW tries heroically to disentangle these conflicts into separate wars that fit within its categories, such as interstate or civil war. But these wars, their processes and effects, were globally interconnected, generating new political entities while disassembling others. For CoW a 'new' war started in August 1945 in the former Dutch colony of Indonesia, when Indonesian nationalists, who had been fighting the Japanese occupation forces, declared independence. They faced off first against British Indian troops sent to take the Japanese surrender and then against Dutch forces trying to reclaim their prize possession. Lacking any grip on the international relations that comprise empire, much less the social and political processes of war, CoW is left carving out 'wars' by reference to formal sovereign criteria and observable indicators like battle deaths.[26] This is not so much to study war as it is to conceive it in the analytic and methodological terms of IR theory and positivism.

Because there is no war studies which delves into and theorizes these processes, we tend to reduce the war's effects to other social processes. Constructivist security studies cites changing 'norms' towards self-rule as an important source of decolonization, not the exhaustion of the imperial powers in war, or the ways in which Japanese victories provided public lessons in the collapse of the imperial world's racial hierarchy and of the venality of the whites once they were on the run.[27] The world wars played central roles in the course and character of the Indian nationalist movement. The break-up of the Raj and the successor states created, their identities and conflicts, were intimately bound up with the death throes of the British Empire at war. During the Second World War, for example, India moved from having a debtor to a creditor relationship with London, a decisive switch in imperial relations occasioned by the expense of war.[28] These and other effects of the Second World War are vast and continuing, in more ways than can be surveyed here, and they have something to do with what happened in the war itself.

Like imperialism, war is a 'full spectrum' social phenomenon, reworking economies, cultures and polities through diverse agencies in interconnected ways across time and space. Having tried to outline and open up this space for inquiry in a preliminary way, I turn now to highlighting two areas of specific postcolonial interest, world wars and small wars, although many others can be imagined, before moving on in the remaining substantive section of the chapter to consider armed forces. Conventional historiography admits of two 'world wars', while more specialist scholarship identifies other conflicts that combined the fates of the European and non-European worlds, as for example in the globally interconnected operations of the Seven Years War (1756–1763). But such interconnections tend to fall away in scholarship compartmentalized by geography. For example, while there is a rich military history of the many major wars by which the Europeans and ultimately Britain's East India Company conquered the Indian subcontinent, relatively little of it places it in global context. Indeed, the 'new military history of South Asia' focuses on the local encounter between European and indigenous military forms, and their consequences for politics and society on the subcontinent.[29] Even Fred Anderson's magisterial *Crucible of War*, closely attentive to the political, cultural and economic interconnections – local, regional, international – occasioned by the Seven Years Wars, focuses primarily on relations between London and North America, and on the implications of the conflict for the American Revolution.[30] There have been some efforts to think through the Eurocentrism of military history and map out global military histories.[31] But the category of world war has been left strangely unexamined and untheorized, yet is richly suggestive from a postcolonial perspective of the ways in which warfare and other military relations tie together and mutually shape Europe and non-Europe.

In the broad terms of a 'full spectrum' war studies favoured here, there is scope for new scholarship on the global relations and interconnections generated and shaped by war and armed force, for wars we might consider 'worldwide' and for the global interconnections forged by other kinds of warfare. This is especially so when the paucity of war studies is considered against the theoretic and empirical density of scholarship on imperial and global connections in respect of society, economy, culture and politics. All of these 'pacific' relations and connections rested on a framework carved out and maintained by force and war.

Indeed, relations of war and force have had the same worldwide character as everything else has had since 1492, entwined with all the other dimensions of the social. And so here is one area for a vibrant postcolonial war studies to develop, one which among other things reconceives what we have taken to be *European* military histories and relations. A second step in this direction, which also illustrates the potential of keeping 'war front' and 'home front' in the same analytic frame, concerns the study and significance of so-called 'small wars', those between imperial powers and indigenous often 'irregular' opponents. Much of the literature concerning them is of the 'how to' variety, whether the military manuals and strategic reflections of the powerful concerning the problem of putting down the revolting natives of any given era, or guides to 'people's war', such as Mao's.[32] Small wars also show up in the histories of nation-states and their formation, particularly of course as anti-colonial struggles that gave birth to new states.

Other scholarship, however, suggests new departures. The impact of the Vietnam War on American society, culture and politics, and to a lesser extent the Korean War, has generated wide-ranging literatures tracing these effects.[33] Mary Renda has looked at the interconnections between US society and culture and the experience and representation of the occupation of Haiti, while Paul Kramer plays out the imbrications of conquering and governing the Philippines for US politics and gender and race relations.[34] There are also studies of global interconnection between and among resistance struggles themselves, as in Rebecca Karl's *Staging the World* or Matthew Clavin's study of representations of the Haitian Revolution and Toussaint Louverture in the pre-Civil War US.[35] Peter Linebaugh and Marcus Rediker's *Many-Headed Hydra* draws out the connections between resistance struggles in the metropole and those on the peripheries of empire.[36] In these kinds of ways and others, 'small war' begins to take on not only interregional and global significance, but a more general role in shaping modern world orders in all their dimensions.

Amid the expansive research agenda such work begins to entail, there is space for the study of individual small wars. In addition to its relational character, war has a historicity to it that resists too much generalization. Specific wars work profound and continuing effects at home and abroad, which must be addressed in their own terms of analysis. To have such effects, wars need not be 'world wars', or even existential wars to preserve political independence. In modern times, Western powers have repeatedly encountered severe political and cultural crises as a consequence of untoward events and defeat in 'small wars', from regime change in France and Portugal occasioned by wars of decolonization to the US's debacle in Vietnam. These wars changed metropolitan histories and societies and set them on new courses.

Why should relatively small wars in military terms have these effects? One possibility relates to the Orientalist and colonialist constructs through which the non-European world is viewed and its peoples engaged in warfare. Such constructs are often not the most realistic basis for wartime operations, shot through as they are with demeaning stereotypes of the Other and overestimations of the Self, but are intimately bound up in the identities and cultures of Western powers. Even in small wars, the West risks the undoing of these identities on the battlefield, engendering cultural and political crisis back home. Effort to recoup these crises, such as the rewriting of the history and meaning of the Vietnam War in public discourse during the Reagan era must also be conceived as part of a war's continuing effects during 'peace'. All of this cultural work in and around small wars takes place in a dense social and historical context interconnected with faraway events and places. Taken together, there is great scope for the study of the international and wartime constitution of states and societies amid imperial war, with ramifications for our understandings of modern histories and world orders.

Armies of the West?

The study of war entails the study of those who fight war. But here too Eurocentrism warps inquiry, as does the relative lack of interest of the main disciplines in soldiers and other combatants *in their roles as fighters*. Soldiers and the military more generally are bound up in the self-conception of the West as modern. Western superiority is registered in the supposed brute fact of military dominance over the non-European world. As with the railroad, the steamship and electronic communications, advanced military forces are a principal symbol of Western modernity. Western soldiers, with their capacity for disciplined self-regulation, are quintessential modern subjects. A powerful mass army of such soldiers marks the moment at which European nations come of age. The willingness of soldiers to serve their country is central to the definition of democratic citizenship and the modern political institutions through which it is realized.[37] As John Keegan writes in his introduction to Victor Davis Hanson's *The Western Way of War*, 'A free man ... has mortgaged his life to his liberty, and must be ready to risk his life on the battlefield if the mortgage is to be redeemed.'[38] Ironically, these modern Western militaries with their officer/other ranks hierarchies were organized around 'a remnant of a now lost social class distinction dating from the Middle Ages.'[39]

Positive images of Western military modernity have their contrasting others in the Orient. While the West fields soldiers, the Orient deploys savages and barbarians who violate the rules of civilized warfare. At the same time, unlike Western men, most of whom can be made into proper soldiers if need be, Oriental males were generally considered effeminate and unsuitable for military service. The exceptions were certain 'martial races' which, while brave, lack intelligence and require European leadership and training.[40] The West fights wars rationally, and for a purpose, while the Orient engages in passionate, unreasoning violence when it is not languishing in sensuality. These divergent images of the military, combat and modernity are protean and adaptable to different times and places, not least the War on Terror of our own day.

Military sociology and other studies of soldiers are informed by Eurocentrism. In debates about why and how soldiers fight, the major positions available reflect different aspects of modernity and Western self-understanding. For example, military sociology's dominant approach concerns the design and quality of military organizations and their capacity to produce tightly knit 'primary groups' of soldiers.⁴¹ Here is modernity as rational organization with the power to govern the behaviour of humans, who are conceived as bundles of psychological and affective impulses which can be directed and manipulated. Married with cognitive psychology and survey research, this approach identifies organizational processes, such as training, the replacement of casualties and the like, and how they contribute or not to the formation and maintenance of primary groups as well as shape their behaviour. The dark side of modernity, as amoral bureaucratic machine, is also found here. Organizational routines, the disposition to obey, and group dynamics can discourage self-regard and ethical reflection by individual soldiers, impelling them towards battle and even atrocity, as in Christopher Browning's seminal study of how 'ordinary men' came to participate in the Holocaust.⁴²

Elsewhere the focus is on the national social context of soldiers and armies. Modernity appears as the nation-state, mass society, and ideology. Soldiers become political beings and citizens, meaningful creatures who fight out of commitment to their national communities and causes.⁴³ Alternatively, they resist or serve without enthusiasm because of the political unpopularity of a conflict, as for some Americans during the Vietnam War. National culture and political ideologies shape the ways in which soldiers act, their willingness to participate in war, and their constructions of particular enemies. Soldiers and armies have a specific 'national character' that determines how and how well they fight. Rather than bureaucratic automatons, in this frame soldiers who behave savagely are filled with race hate. In Omer Bartov's *Hitler's Army*, German soldiers were progressively 'Nazified' by propaganda and wartime experience, becoming 'devoted believers in a murderous ideology'.⁴⁴

A liberal brand of Western triumphalism also informs studies of soldiers and war, best represented by Hanson.⁴⁵ He explains the superiority of Western militaries by reference to values derived from free societies and their expression in a decisive, bloody and powerful way of war. Hanson's Orientalism is naked: 'Western civilization has given mankind the only economic system that works, a rationalist tradition that alone allows us material and technological progress, the sole political structure that ensures the freedom of the individual, a system of ethics and a religion that brings out the best in humankind – and the most lethal practice of arms conceivable.'⁴⁶ For Hanson, the West persists through the centuries, indeed millennia, as some kind of distinct cultural essence based on liberty. Soldiers from free societies fight in particular ways. While Hanson reminds us, among other things, of their capacity for extreme, righteous violence, other scholars seek to identify the military advantages of initiative and individuality, asking whether 'freedom produces better fighters'?⁴⁷ Nowhere in this frame is there room for the legions of colonial soldiers who fought for the West in Western-style militaries but whose condition could hardly be characterized as one of liberty.

As can be seen, the terms of the debate are profoundly informed by conceptions of modernity and Western exceptionalism. In fact, it would seem nearly impossible to think about soldiers and society in the West outside of such categories. While these approaches are by no means entirely or even mostly misguided, there is more at stake than they allow. Thinking about Western soldiers only in Western terms turns out to be limiting. Critiquing this kind of Eurocentrism requires more than telling the story of the non-West, however. Elementary categories and assumptions must be revisited, including the character of the regular military institution, the sources of group solidarity and fighting spirit, and the relations between army, society and politics, in the West as well as elsewhere. Here is the expansive agenda of the postcolonial study of armed forces.

Integral to the rise of the state in Europe were new forms of military organization, addressed in the debate over the 'military revolution'.[48] The regularly organized national armed forces of the sovereign and territorial state became a central construct in the Western political–military imagination. The often implicit but widespread identification of the military institution with the West and its nation-state rivalries works to obscure political–military interconnections constitutive of modern world politics. The regular military is conceived as a product of Western culture, politics and society. At base here is the army of soldier-citizens who fight for their own political communities in a distinctly Western way of war, a set of ideas effectively packaged together by Hanson but which also operate widely as an implicit set of assumptions in scholarly and political life.

Making the military essentially European or Western requires two moves, which can be made in different ways. The first involves the construction of a specifically Western heritage for drilled and disciplined infantry armies which engage in decisive battle. This is usually accomplished via the Renaissance recovery of Greek and Roman military ideas that accompanied the return of infantry formations to battlefield dominance in early modern Europe. But it can also be done in a Weberian and Foucaultian idiom through assumptions about the Western character of modern discipline in general. The second move is to establish an organic connection between the will to combat of soldiers and their polity and culture. Hanson, for example, links Western soldiers' desire for decisive battle with 'freedom' in political arrangements; it is their polity they are fighting for. A more general instance of this move emphasizes the role of nationalism and political ideology in the motivation of soldiers. Putting these moves together produces the state as a community of fate defended by its own soldier-citizens, who fight in a distinct Western style, one powerful enough to achieve Western world dominance. This vision of the disciplined regular military simultaneously establishes a notion of the West as dominant in world terms, but also as consisting of separate nations or political communities, Eurocentrism *and* a system of units. Imagining the military in a particular kind of way helps sustain the core construct of IR and the social sciences: the modern and national Western state.

A place to begin critique is with the association in Hanson's work and that of others between the regular military with the 'Western way of war'. This is the idea that Westerners (and their putative Greek and Roman forebears) invented military discipline and that this way of war is in some way inherently related to 'freedom' in political arrangements and a distinct Western cultural system.[49] In fact, the elementary secrets of drill and organized warfare were discovered and developed without European assistance in many different contexts.

Disciplined Indian infantry opposed Alexander the Great's incursions into the Punjab in the fourth century BC, and drill and organized warfare are found in ancient China and Mesopotamia as well. The Europeans did not introduce firearms drill to the Indian subcontinent in the eighteenth century, as armies there were already using it, as were the Japanese in the sixteenth century. 'As African and Asian archers had released arrows on command for thousands of years, the non-Western world did not have to wait to be told that firearms could be used in the same manner.'[50] These histories caution against Eurocentric understandings of how and why regular military discipline works. That broadly comparable forms of drill and discipline were developed in disconnected places is testimony to the powers of these techniques in generating organized violence in human societies generally.

Nonetheless, it was the specifically European form of the military institution that was exported around the world with the rise of Western power. Early modern Europe saw the return of drilled infantry formations, along with the development of effective musketry, cannon and new forms of fortification. It was in this context that Greek and Roman drill and tactical manuals were recovered, adapted and distributed as they contained well-worn techniques for the discipline and control of infantry formations.[51] Military professionals across Europe learned from contemporary manuals inspired by Vegetius and Aelian, and shared and emulated each other's techniques and innovations, even as they tailored them to local conditions. With colonial expansion, the European form of the regular military institution was carried abroad and its disciplinary techniques used to raise colonial armies in the extra-European world. Modified for a different era and its tactical and political challenges, these processes continued after decolonization with the 'advice and support' of Third World militaries by the superpowers and other metropolitan states. Today, Western soldiers continue to train Iraqis, Afghanis and others in the context of 'nation building' and counter-insurgency. Despite all the transformations in military technology, and the differences in political and social context, nearly everywhere soldiers form in files and ranks, and they drill and parade in ways easily recognizable to a Roman centurion but which also would not seem too foreign to the commander of a Zulu impi. In significant ways, the regular military is a cosmopolitan institution, at home anywhere in the world.

Denoting the regular military as essentially 'Western' can occlude the fact that the institution *was* successfully exported to non-Western places, and that serviceable versions of it were invented outside the West. Whatever its origins, the institution is effective among non-Westerners. Moreover, the notion that early modern Europe and ancient Greece and Rome comprise some kind of common historical subject known as the West is itself tendentious. 'Without continuity between classical Greece and the modern West, Hanson's argument loses much of its force.'[52] A diffuse cultural legacy and a few drill manuals aside, European soldiers were as disconnected from the Greek phalanxes and Roman legions as were the Mesopotamians, Chinese and Indians.[53] The regular military is best thought of as *transnational* in scope and character, and it can and has worked effectively pretty much anywhere, with any given population. This transnational adaptability of military discipline across time and space was already evident in early modern Europe, not least in borrowing ideas from ancient times. European states and other polities employed foreign mercenaries and officers, and responded in similar ways to the technological and organizational challenges of the time. Even as nation-states developed and national militaries created their own distinctive cultures and ways of doing things, the transnational circulation of texts and techniques continued. Soldiers of different armies continued to share a great deal in common.

In thinking of the regular military in Western terms, scholars tend to account for it with reference to putatively Western phenomena, such as the modern nation-state, Western political ideologies, or Western dispositions towards rational institutions. They overlook the possibility that the secrets to this institution's effectiveness may be revealed in its global character, in the fact that it can be exported and adapted to diverse places, rather than in its local Western embodiments, however dominant historically. In this context, it is notable that with the exception of the Japanese, and occasional appearances by the Chinese, the non-Western world rarely appears in the combat motivation literature even broadly conceived. 'Current historiography still concentrates on European armies during the two World Wars – above all the British Expeditionary Force between 1914 and 1918 and the *Wehrmacht* between 1939 and 1945.'[54] The literature suffers from a stunning Eurocentrism by any measure.

A path out of this Eurocentrism is to focus on the historical development and worldwide character of the regular military institution, conceived not as a product of Western culture but as a distinct ensemble of disciplinary technologies and generic ritual practices. These include drill as a general mechanism for training and discipline, officer/other rank hierarchies and obedience to orders, more or less sharp institutional boundaries with civilian society (e.g. uniforms, living arrangements), and regularized subunits combined to form higher formations. This institution lies behind the degree of commonality in soldiering across cultural and historical boundaries. A similar, or at least comparable, organizational context shapes the human potential for soldiering in similar ways in diverse times and places. Such an approach allows for variation in military effectiveness as well as different cultural constructions of soldiering, while not denying the common patterns evident in histories of organized warfare. Instead of distinguishing between European and other kinds of soldiers, or between a Western military and others, humans everywhere are conceived as sharing potentialities that may be actualized in comparable ways by regular military forms of organization.

Focusing on the regular military as an ensemble of disciplinary technologies and generic ritual practices adaptable to different times and places helps shift the combat motivation debate away from Eurocentric and Orientalist constructs of human beings. People are instead conceived as having common capacities and potentialities that are shaped and conditioned by organizational, social and historical contexts.[55] These capacities can be actualized by the regular military, *but only in localized ways*, determined by the specific relations between military and society in any given time and place. What is provisionally universal is that military and society are in relations of mutual constitution, *not* the outcomes and consequences of these relations, which are historically specific. The capacity for combat is a human potential, but it is only realized within specific contexts and circumstances, which shape it in definite ways. That the regular military is an effective generator of discipline does not necessitate seeing the humans subject to its embrace as everywhere the same, as sharing some essential nature, *nor* as necessarily radically differentiated by culture. Explanation can remain alive to both similarity and difference among soldiers without denying either.

The regular military is exported and adapted to diverse social and cultural contexts by professional practitioners seeking to produce a common type of character, the regular soldier, who nonetheless always remains marked by local contexts and who may perform a variety of different military occupations at varying levels of effectiveness. While the focus here has been on combat soldiers, the adaptability of military discipline is equally evident in the widespread use of its basic techniques in many areas of modern society around the world, not least police, prisons and schools, all of which exhibit similarity and difference across cultural boundaries, while transforming localities in myriad ways. As with other forms of bureaucratic organization exported with European imperialism and modified for new contexts, such as the capitalist enterprise and its practices of labour discipline, outcomes were multifaceted.[56]

If the regular military is an ensemble of culturally adaptable practices that more or less readily produces soldiers and will to combat out of diverse contexts, just how and why does it work in different locales and circumstances? To address this issue mainly in Western contexts leaves analysis prey to Eurocentric presuppositions, to assuming that the answers have to do with modernity conceived in Western terms, or with nation-states as distinct political and military communities. For example, a principal assumption in the combat motivation literature is that casualties pose a problem for the fighting spirit of soldiers; too many casualties and either morale breaks down, or some extraordinary ideological or racist belief must be at work to explain why soldiers would continue to fight when death was the only likely outcome. However, if one takes the notion of ritual in the military seriously, and incorporates the findings of that discipline historically most concerned with non-Europeans – anthropology – alternative explanations become possible. One is that casualties are the very *fuel* of fighting spirit, through logics of group sentiment, sacrifice and blood debt. Death releases the life energy of the deceased, *mana*, which circulates among those remaining, binding them together. Ritual invokes and directs this energy, as when a regiment celebrates past victories and mourns its dead as a way of building solidarity in the present. In battle, and on campaign, these dynamics are more immediate and chaotic but their effects can be similar. Each drop of blood can regenerate the forces binding together the remaining soldiers, calling forth energies for reprisal. A unit is never more alive *as a unit* than when it has been bloodied. Death's revivification of social bonds occurs on *both* sides of battle, giving battlefield violence a self-generating character. Two groups of soldierly beings locked together in violent embrace, each wound inflicted generating solidarity and a blood debt that can only be expiated by reprisal, in a recurring cycle that, ideally speaking, can continue to the point of mutual annihilation.[57]

In Eurocentric frames, the suggestion that sacrificial rituals form the heart of combat motivation would hardly get an airing, much less adequate investigation. Eurocentric assumptions work to misconceive Western soldiers, armies and societies just as they do in the case of non-European soldiers. All are bounded and territorialized along national or ethnic lines. But in fact what is notable about the military institution is its transnational character, both in the sense that the transnational circulation of soldiers, texts and techniques was central to the rise and development of this institution, and in the sense that the military can be found anywhere, with soldiers usually having more in common with one another than with their national or ethnic civilian counterparts. Broadly speaking, this institution is remarkable for its effectiveness in a variety of different social and cultural contexts. In saying this, the point is not to deny that there are national armies, or that the nation-state can be a particularly powerful site for the constitution of military power in all its dimensions. Rather, it is to suggest that from the point of view of understanding the military and why and how soldiers come to fight, general answers are not necessarily to be found in national or modern terms. Once the matter is put in this kind of a way, colony and metropole become more directly comparable. The relations between the transnational modalities of military organization and local cultures, so evident in colonial sites like India, are found also in Europe. Local identities provided, and continue to provide, 'traditional' cultural resources for military recruitment, in and out of the West.

Nation-state ontologies attempt to fix relations between state, society and territory, creating a set of putatively isomorphic entities (e.g. Germany, India). But imperialism is about variation in relations between rule, society and territory (e.g. British India, French Indochina). A nation-state ontology misconceives processes of transnational social change, such as those occasioned by imperialism, the expansion of capitalism and the spread of bureaucratic institutions like the regular military, reading them as episodes in the history of territorial societies, rather than centring the transnational relations at work. Such processes were not confined to the world outside Europe. Capitalism, rational bureaucracies and their disciplinary technologies have worked to remake local spaces and populations *everywhere*. These processes are inherently transnational, occurring in interconnected ways across territories and populations. The mutually constitutive play between local cultures and rationalizing institutions like the military or the capitalist enterprise is not particular to the colonies, but is rather one of the basic experiences of modern world history. As always with the postcolonial, the journey out to the periphery helps understand better both the metropole and human social relations in general.

Conclusion: re-envisioning war

Much of history is narrated as the story of clashing nation-states. In this story, war and national identity become closely linked for scholars as well as more popularly.

Benedict Anderson, for example, finds in the 'limited imaginings' of nationalism the reasons 'for so many millions of people ... willingly to die'.[58] There is more than a little here of the primordialism and reductionism Anderson so effectively critiques elsewhere. Such imaginings seem so natural because wars, and representations of sacrifice in war, are engines of reification.[59] They help instantiate an image of the world as composed of nation-states, a geography of war and identity. In circular fashion, war then can be interpreted as a confrontation between reified nations or ethnic groups, rather than a form of social interaction through which identities and polities are made and remade. War becomes a product of political and cultural *difference*, rather than the result of a shared human potential for collective violence, a potential activated by (among other possibilities) a transnational institution, the regular military.

By contrast, if we learn to see war anew, not as a *product* of other social relations and processes, whether economic, cultural or political, but as itself a *generator* of those relations and processes, war appears as a general form of human interaction, a sphere of life with its own dynamics. This is a very different standpoint than a world image of pre-existing territorial polities which have clashes of interest and difference that may issue in war. War becomes a common human property, not that of warlike peoples or states, or merely an occasional interruption in the peacetime processes of social development and political intercourse. A panoply of Eurocentric assumptions about war and armed forces have to be overcome to arrive at this new standpoint, and this chapter has sought to clear some of this brush and open the route to a postcolonial war studies.

Notes

1 This chapter draws in places on Tarak Barkawi and Shane Brighton, 'Powers of War: Fighting, Knowledge and Critique', *International Political Sociology*, Vol. 5, #2 (June 2011), 126–143 and on Tarak Barkawi, 'From War to Security: Security Studies, the Wider Agenda, and the Fate of the Study of War', *Millennium*, Vol. 39, #3 (May 2011), 701–716.
2 Stanley Hoffman, 'An American Social Science: International Relations', *Daedalus*, 106: 3 (1977), 41–60.
3 Tarak Barkawi and Mark Laffey, 'The Postcolonial Moment in Security Studies', *Review of International Studies*, 32: 4 (2006), 329–52.
4 See e.g. Dipesh Chakrabarty, *Provincializing Europe* (Princeton: Princeton University Press 2000); cf. Ranajit Guha, *Elementary Aspects of Peasant Insurgency in Colonial India* (Durham: Duke University Press 1999).
5 Stephen Walt, 'The Renaissance of Security Studies', *International Studies Quarterly*, 35: 2 (1991), 212.
6 See Barry Buzan and Lene Hansen, *The Evolution of International Security Studies* (Cambridge: Cambridge University Press 2009).
7 See e.g. Michael Howard, *The Franco-Prussian War* (New York: Macmillan 1962); Vivienne Jabri, *Discourses on Violence* (Manchester: Manchester University Press 1996); Susan Jeffords, *The Remasculinization of America* (Bloomington: Indiana University Press 1989); Michael Mann, *States, War and Capitalism* (Oxford: Blackwell 1988); Martin Shaw, *Dialectics of War* (London: Pluto 1988).
8 Mann, *States, War and Capitalism*, 147.

104 *Performance*

9. John Keane, *Reflections on Violence* (London: Verso 1996), 14ff; cf. J.G.A. Pocock, *Barbarism and Religion* (Cambridge: Cambridge University Press 2005).
10. Istvan Hont, *Jealousy of Trade* (Cambridge: Harvard University Press 2005).
11. Arden Bucholz, *Hans Delbrück and the German Military Establishment* (Iowa City: University of Iowa Press 1985), ch. 2; Doyne Dawson, 'The Return of Military History?', *History and Theory*, 47 (December 2008).
12. Walt, 'The Renaissance of Security Studies', 212.
13. Carl von Clausewitz, *On War* (Princeton: Princeton University Press 1976), 87.
14. Clausewitz, *On War*, 89.
15. See e.g. Hans Delbrück, *History of the Art of War*, 4 vols (Lincoln: University of Nebraska Press 1990); Michael Howard, *Captain Professor* (London: Continuum 2006).
16. Katherine Herbig, 'Chance and Uncertainty in *On War*', in Michael Handel (ed.), *Clausewitz and Modern Strategy* (London: Frank Cass 1989).
17. Hew Strachan, *Clausewitz's On War* (New York: Grove 2007).
18. Walt, 'The Renaissance of Security Studies', 219.
19. Clausewitz, *On War*, 97.
20. 'But in war more than in any other subject we must begin by looking at the nature of the whole', Clausewitz, *On War*, 75. Cf. Eric Wolf, *Europe and the People Without History* (Berkeley: University of California Press 1997), 3.
21. Clausewitz, quoted in Bucholz, *Delbrück*, 25.
22. Shaw, *Dialectics of War*, 11.
23. Cf. Ernest Mandel, *The Meaning of the Second World War* (London: Verso 1986).
24. The CoW data and explanations of its categories and coding are available on: http://www.correlatesofwar.org/.
25. See Christopher Bayly and Tim Harper, *Forgotten Armies: The Fall of British Asia, 1941–1945* (London: Allen Lane 2004) and *Forgotten Wars: The End of Britain's Asian Empire* (London: Penguin 2008).
26. See Tarak Barkawi, 'War Inside the Free World: the Democratic Peace and the Cold War in the Third World', in Tarak Barkawi and Mark Laffey (eds), *Democracy, Liberalism and War: Rethinking the Democratic Peace Debates* (Boulder, CO: Lynne Rienner 2001), 107–28.
27. Neta Crawford, *Argument and Change in World Politics: Ethics, Decolonization and Humanitarian Intervention* (Cambridge: Cambridge University Press 2002); cf. Bayly and Harper, *Forgotten Armies*, 167–90.
28. Indivar Kamtekar, 'A Different War Dance: State and Class in India 1939–1945', *Past and Present*, 176: 1 (August 2002), 187–221.
29. See e.g. Randolf G.S. Cooper, *The Anglo-Maratha Campaigns and the Contest for India: The Struggle for Control of the South Asian Military Economy* (Cambridge: Cambridge University Press 2005); Dirk Kolff, *Naukar, Rajput, and Sepoy: The Ethnohistory of the Military Labour Market in Hindustan, 1450–1850* (Cambridge: Cambridge University Press 1990); Kaushik Roy, 'Military Synthesis in South Asia: Armies, Warfare, and Indian Society, c.1740–1849', *The Journal of Military History*, 69 (July 2005), 651–90.
30. Fred Anderson, *The Crucible of War* (New York: Vintage Books 2001).
31. See e.g. Jeremy Black, *Rethinking Military History* (London: Routledge 2004) and *War and the World: Military Power and the Fate of Continents 1450–2000* (New Haven: Yale University Press 1998).
32. Mao Tse-tung, *On Guerrilla Warfare* (Urbana: University of Illinois Press 2000).
33. See e.g. Tom Engelhardt, *The End of Victory Culture* (Amherst: University of Massachusetts Press 1998).
34. Paul Kramer, *The Blood of Government* (Chapel Hill: University of North Carolina Press 2006); Mary Renda, *Taking Haiti* (Chapel Hill: University of North Carolina Press 2001).
35. Matthew Clavin, *Toussaint Louverture and the American Civil War* (Philadelphia: University of Pennsylvania Press 2010); Rebecca Karl, *Staging the World* (Durham: Duke University Press 2002).

36 Peter Linebaugh and Marcus Rediker, *The Many-Headed Hydra* (London: Verso 2000).
37 Claire Snyder, *Citizen Soldiers and Manly Warriors* (Lanham, MD: Rowman & Littlefield 1999).
38 John Keegan, 'Introduction', in Victor Davis Hanson, *The Western Way of War* (New York: Oxford University Press 1989), xiii.
39 John Glubb, 'The Conflict Between Tradition and Modernism in the Role of Muslim Armies', in Carl Leiden (ed.), *The Conflict of Traditionalism and Modernism in the Muslim Middle East* (Austin: University of Texas Press 1966), 15. Better known as Glubb Pasha and commander of the Arab Legion 1939–1956, he goes on to point out that the new sovereign Arab armies were adopting the officer/other rank system over their own more 'democratic' Islamic traditions because it was seen as 'Western and therefore "modern"'.
40 See Heather Streets, *Martial Races* (Manchester: Manchester University Press 2004).
41 Edward Shils and Morris Janowitz, 'Cohesion and Disintegration in the Wehrmacht in World War II', *Public Opinion Quarterly*, 12: 2 (1948), 280–315.
42 Christopher Browning, *Ordinary Men* (New York: HarperCollins 1992).
43 See e.g. Barry Posen, 'Nationalism, the Mass Army, and Military Power', *International Security*, 18: 2 (1993), 80–124.
44 Omer Bartov, *Hitler's Army* (Oxford: Oxford University Press 1992), viii.
45 Hanson, *V. The Western Way of War*; *Carnage and Culture* (New York: Anchor Books 2002).
46 Hanson, *Carnage and Culture*, 455.
47 Dan Reiter and Allan C. Stam, *Democracies at War* (Princeton: Princeton University Press 2002), 59.
48 Clifford Rogers, *The Military Revolution Debate* (Boulder, CO: Westview 1995).
49 See Hanson, *The Western Way of War*; *Carnage and Culture*.
50 Randolf G.S. Cooper, 'Culture, Combat and Colonialism', *The International History Review*, 27: 3 (2005), 536–8; Geoffrey Parker, *The Military Revolution* (Cambridge: Cambridge University Press 1988), 140.
51 See e.g. William McNeil, *The Pursuit of Power* (Chicago: Chicago University Press 1982), 125–39; Parker, *The Military Revolution*, 18–20.
52 Stephen Morillo with Michael F. Pavkovic, *What is Military History?* (Cambridge: Polity 2006), 85.
53 As Michael Mallet comments: '[A fifteenth century captain] may have been gratified to learn from one of the humanists in his entourage that his tactics resembled those of Caesar in Gaul, but it is unlikely that he consciously intended it to be so. It was not a study of the Roman republican army which produced a revived interest in infantry but the practical necessities of fifteenth-century warfare.' Quoted in John Keegan, *The Face of Battle* (London: Penguin 1978), 62.
54 Alexander Watson, 'Culture and Combat', *Historical Journal*, 51: 2 (2008), 546.
55 Clifford Geertz, *The Interpretation of Cultures* (New York: Fontana Press 1993), ch. 2.
56 See e.g. Khaled Fahmy, *All the Pasha's Men* (Cairo: The American University in Cairo Press 2002); David Ralston, *Importing the European Army* (Chicago: University of Chicago Press 1990).
57 Cf. Emile Durkheim, *The Elementary Forms of the Religious Life* (New York: Free Press 1965); Rene Girard, *Violence and the Sacred* (Baltimore: Johns Hopkins University Press 1977).
58 Benedict Anderson, *Imagined Communities* (London: Verso 1983), 16.
59 Elaine Scarry, *The Body in Pain* (Oxford: Oxford University Press 1985); Jay Winter, *Sites of Memory, Sites of Mourning* (Cambridge: Cambridge University Press 1995).

6 Deferring difference

A postcolonial critique of the 'race problem' in moral thought

Siba N'Zatioula Grovogui

The ideas of justice and freedom and the categories of history, values and interests through which they are articulated by moral theorists, including cosmopolitans, are equally central to postcolonial thought and criticism. This convergence would suggest the possibility of dialogue between moral theorists and postcolonialists. In a way there is one, but it is one in which postcolonialists visit disciplinary canons for the purpose of re-examining their faithfulness to the formative events of modernity as well as the impact of Western political and constitutional orders on modern trajectories and the positions of today's subjects in the international order. Against this venture, Western liberal and progressive intellectuals have positioned themselves as proprietors and guardians of supposedly universal moral precepts. In this process, as it appears below, many have set their understandings of canons and the past against postcolonial readings of same. Thus, many disciplinary conventions assume falsely a convergence between, on the one hand, canonical prescriptions (mistaken here for tradition) and, on the other, liberal constitutional practices and/or cosmopolitan aspirations. To illustrate this point, I will focus on the manners in which liberal cosmopolitans have appropriated the theories of history, justice and science promulgated by G. W. F. Hegel, Immanuel Kant and others to reposition Europe and the West as legislator and adjudicator of universal values and, therefore, the ultimate authority in world affairs. Sadly, this repositioning depends on discourses and metaphors that still depend on race, metaphors of race, and the dissimulation of the humanity or subjectivity of the formerly colonized.

To illustrate my point I wish to revisit views on recognition, individual freedom, and justice expressed by post-war figures whose overall accomplishments deserve acclaim for their theoretical, philosophical and legal insights. The arguments evolve around views expressed by Chris Brown on the nature and importance of recognition;[1] Hannah Arendt on the status of constitutional principles in public and private lives; and Raphael Lemkin on the nature and forms of genocidal politics and conjointly their prevention and retribution when they occur. The related views are significant in a number of ways. First, they extol the virtues of liberal constitutionalism as expressions of higher forms of reason, morals and law. Second, their arguments depend upon an endorsement of post-Enlightenment philosophical claims and colonial-era anthropological predicates that bear on the positions of postcolonial entities in today's international order. Finally, at least in the cited references, these authors explicitly deploy race and racial categories as a basis for justifying their own moral claims.

The questions raised in this context are also significant on a number of grounds. The first is that the authors and works cited are not isolated. That is, they are not alone in assuming the sufficiency of the languages of post-Enlightenment constitutional arrangements and of the concepts and ideas advanced by philosophers and theorists to defend them. Second, their ideas are founded upon those of historical figures whose views are taken up in theories of international relations by scholars with scant regard to the temporal, spatial and relational dimensions of the politics of their times. Third, the views of the above authors perform the sort of epistemic violence that occurs in moral discourses through unjustified and ill-founded attributions to others and about them for which no one dares bear responsibility in the supposed neutral setting of the academy. As Gayatri Spivak has suggested, a postcolonial criticism should not take for granted that the perspectives taken from disciplinary conventions necessarily contain valid and justified truths, values and institutions.[2] In Spivak's words,

> the mainstream has never run clean, perhaps never can. Part of mainstream education involves learning to ignore this absolutely, with a sanctioned ignorance ...Writing in the metropolis or in the former colony, many of us are trying to carve out positive negotiations with the epistemic graphing of imperialism. ...The challenge of deconstruction is not to excuse but to suspend accusation to examine with painstaking care if the protocols of the text contain a moment that can produce something that will generate a new and useful reading.[3]

She also draws attention to two factors that must be central to any engagement of canonical texts. The first pertains to disciplinary common sense and regimes of truth that are founded upon questionable assumptions and scenarios in which subjects occupy positions in conjunction with their faculties, endowments and capacities.[4] Secondly, the underlying regimes are perpetuated through 'sanctioned ignorance' by 'self-styled academic practitioners'[5] who take up the findings, approaches and thought experiments of historical precursors without any regard to the contingencies of time, space and relations of the latter to the objects of their analyses.[6]

By way of precision, I do not object to any particular method, whether empirical, positivist, or else involved in the analyses under contention. Nor do I want to dispense with the ideas of reason, science and technology as essential to the quest for truth. My primary concern is the reproduction of systems of values, norms and institutions that are intended to preserve vested interests under the guise of truth; what Spivak calls 'axiomatics of imperialism'.[7] Yet, I am concerned with the status of race in their views as well as in the intellectual traditions that inspire them, particularly the underlying received ideas and assumptions about sovereignty, constitutionalism and political subjectivity on the one hand and, on the other, the international system, its political economy and mechanisms and processes of production, distribution and consumption of goods, including ideas. Indeed, much of moral thought today reflexively places faith in regimes of truths advanced by historical figures who should have been subject to self-doubt but were not. It is a truism today that the suppositions and pronouncements of the likes of Thomas Hobbes, Baron de Montesquieu, David Hume, Jean-Jacques Rousseau, Immanuel Kant and G. W. F. Hegel about other peoples, cultures, institutions, practices and dispositions were in fact baseless. Many of them did not observe what they described; when they did, they were ill-equipped to comprehend what they observed; and when they did comprehend they were too ill-disposed toward conquered and dispossessed people or too bound up with the requirements of life in their own societies to question the presumed superiority of Christian and rational Europe – later the West. It is the position of this essay that the attempt to barricade the 'empirical' or 'anthropological' findings of these thinkers from their inquiry into the noumenon of *Man* is impossible. According to Jacques Derrida, even in Kant – the most categorical and systematic of thinkers – 'empirical culturalism' bleeds into the moral discourse.[8] Kant cannot help but restore anthropology's authority as even his most metaphysical depiction of rational man retains its empirical origins in a distinction between the 'raw man' of Tierra del Fuego and the higher 'rational man' of Europe.[9] The mainstream has always been muddy.

I also understand the diversity of disciplinary practices and will admit that my observations do not correspond exactly to every dimension or tenet of the different approaches implicated in my criticisms. Yet, I mean to implicate all perspectives that assumed a uniform West with a unique talent for science, technology and reason and therefore exceptionally endowed with the capacity for redemption, regeneration and progress. These and related propositions and suppositions are advanced without due regard to the historicity of the West, its role in the modern human drama, and the existence elsewhere of valid moral, intellectual and institutional resources bearing on peace, security, justice and other key disciplinary concerns. The appropriate postcolonial response[10] is not merely to offer a menu of events and practices that disprove disciplinary assumptions about the 'non-West' or 'the Rest'. Nor is it merely to contest the conceptions of reason, rationality and humanism proposed by various theories as foundations for thinking or making sense of the international order. It is to debunk their modes of representation and signification outside by revisiting the prevailing narratives of history, literature and philosophy among others. This exercise must be complemented by the expansion of disciplinary archives to include moral thought suppressed or lost in the wake of conquest, imperialism and colonialism. The ultimate aim would be to open the discipline of international relations up to new imaginaries that reside in so-called local memories, arts and forms of knowledge without being wedded to nativism or native essentialism. The latter two tasks are beyond the purview of this essay.[11]

In the following, I wish to combine productive engagements with disciplinary common sense and regimes of truth with wariness of disciplinary practices and the philosophical and political instrumentalism that underpin them: for instance, Immanuel Kant's pre-emptive foreclosure of the aboriginal as subject; G. W. F. Hegel's racialized dialectics and rationality; and Karl Marx's treatment of labour as central to understanding difference and hierarchy, to the exclusion of race and colonization. This essay is therefore an exercise in deconstruction of liberal regimes of truth, their modes of production, and the discrete mechanisms of their enactment as disciplinary common sense. Consistently, it pays attention to the constitution of disciplinary common sense on justice, freedom and international morality. It does so by examining the uses of history, hermeneutics and ethnography, which enable racialized understanding of both moral theory and the postcolonial condition.

The most important moral question of the day

Academic culture is theoretically predicated upon freedom of conscience and uninhibited practices of science. It is assumed that, without the above, the quest for truth and the orderly production of knowledge would be impossible. Perhaps! Yet, one need not be attentive to Michel Foucault to observe that the context for the related practices is enmeshed in expressions of power and ideology in the interest of a normative order. From this perspective, it is a feature of postcolonialism that it pays attention to the manners in which discipline inhibits certain lines of inquiry and promotes others through practices of intimidation, self-censorship and instrumentalism. The intimidation often originates from self-appointed guardians of disciplinary boundaries and practices in the guise of a commitment to the preservation of science and scientific norms and the coherence of practices by a scientific community united by tradition, value and interest.[12] To this end, the discipline (in the sense of intimidation) depends upon the tying together of concepts and ideas in defence of parochial values, interests and institutions on the grounds of their legitimacy and immutability as demonstrated by 'canonical' texts and 'universal' maxims of politics, morality and ethics.[13] The above are predicated upon institutions that guarantee preferred outcomes: social, political, economic and/or otherwise.

The above dispositions are more readily observable in analytic philosophy, which focuses on clarifying, by analysis, the meaning of statements and concepts. Throughout the twentieth century, analytic philosophers inspired International Relations scholars to focus on the constituents of the ideas and concepts inherited from supposed canonical figures and thereby commit their inquiries to clarifying the language and arguments of their chosen predecessors. The result is that the discipline is now replete with arguments and counter-arguments about the logic of arguments, the rationality and/or pragmatism of given ideas, and the ethics of positions that are often more or less internally coherent. Yet, although many claim to be so, few IR theorists who borrow from the methods of analytic philosophy are sufficiently mindful of the temporal, spatial and relational contingencies of politics both at the time of inception of their preferred texts, and now. Instead, today analysts are obsessed with the need to eliminate 'confusions' of thought in order to resolve legitimate and practical philosophical problems in the interest of a common language in our reflections on the past and our own common experiences. This tendency is more pronounced in moral philosophy and normative thought where deliberations on rights, morality and science are intricately linked to questions of standing (or subjectivity), entitlements (rights) and justice (truth).

In the following section, I hope to accomplish two things. The first is to show the dependence of post-war normative IR theory on propositions, deductions and affirmations made by G. W. F. Hegel and Immanuel Kant among others. The second point is to show that, contrary to its image of itself, the discipline is not open enough to allow all practitioners equal input in the analysis of the texts advanced as the basis for inquiry and argumentation. In this regard, disciplinary debates depend on the contours and conditions of disciplinary practices, including the intolerance and authoritarian impulses of self-appointed guardians of the discipline and its practices. From a postcolonial perspective (and not only from such a perspective), abstracting the ideas of the above authors from the space and time of their origin, as well as from the contemporary moment of hegemonic subjugation, on the grounds that such ideas are 'universal', enables opportunities for epistemic violence and (re)colonizing discourses.[14]

My illustration begins with an incident at the 2007 annual meeting of the International Studies Association, at a panel on the relevancy of the views of G. W. F. Hegel on race. One of the questions that arose was whether the slave revolt in Haiti had any bearing on Hegel's master–slave dialectic, and if so what that would say about some of the German philosopher's conclusions on race in *The Philosophy of History*. The chapter was presented by Naeem Inayatullah and David Blaney under the title 'Shed No Tears: Wealth, Race, and Death in Hegel's Necro-Philosophy'.[15] One of the participants was Professor Chris Brown, who retorted at some point that Hegel could not be said to be racist because, I am paraphrasing here, 'he took the courageous position on the most important moral question of his day: the Jewish Question.' Of course, Brown was technically right that, in *The Philosophy of Right*, Hegel advocated a constitutional (or legal) resolution to the marginalization of Jews for an orderly regulation of civil society.[16] However, the comment brought to mind two concerns. The first was that the comment sought to reject a legitimate reading of one of Hegel's essays by referring to the central arguments but to an equally important but peripheral issue discussed in another essay in a different context. My second concern was the idea that one form of exclusion and violence born of a particular form of difference morally outweighed another form of exclusion and violence born of difference, even if it may be established that the relevant forms of difference are historically rooted in different forms of subjectivity.

For a host of historical reasons, I share Chris Brown's view that the Jewish Question was significant in nineteenth-century Germany. Jews faced more than subtle hostility; and violence against this community survived even the Renaissance, Reformation and nearly all modern European political settlements. This is to say that constitutionalism under liberalism and its subsequent formulations of political tolerance, property rights and personal security did not prevent pogroms and other acts of violence against Jews leading up to the Holocaust. Brown is therefore correct that Hegel gave expression to an emergent progressive view on the necessity of granting civil rights to Jews at a time when conservative and religious groups advocated excluding Jews from formal constitutional rights. The reason given by many was that Jews were members of a 'foreign' religion and a 'foreign' nation. Hegel noted that, 'although it may well have been contrary to formal right to grant even civil rights to the Jews, on the grounds that the latter should be regarded not just as a particular religious group but also as members of a foreign nation, the outcry which this viewpoint and others produced overlooked the fact that the Jews are primarily human beings.'[17] Hegel acknowledged that the question of civil rights for Jews was not neutral or abstract and that 'the granting of civil rights gives those who receive them a self-awareness as recognized legal persons in which society, and it is from this root, infinite and free from all other influences, that the desired assimilation in terms of attitude and disposition arises.'[18] Finally, if they had not been granted civil rights, according to Hegel, 'the Jews would have remained in that isolation with which they have been reproached, and this would rightly have brought blame and reproach upon the state which excluded them; for the state would thereby have failed to recognize its own principle as an objective institution with a power of its own.'[19] In sum, 'While the demand for the exclusion of the Jews claimed to be based on the highest right, it has proved in practice to be the height of folly, whereas the way in which governments have acted has proved wise and honourable.'[20]

The above is not an unambiguous endorsement of formal rights for all. But it sufficed to put a dent in the view that foreigners within society were undeserving of protection. Hegel's defence of the rights of Jews also rested on his articulation of the realities of the state and nation (particular kinds of state and nation) as well as private property. These were all bound in Hegel's views of Christianity, reason, rationality, and a historical conscience of the connections between Christianity and Judaism that could be called upon to shame the state and nation. Anything less than recognition would be a moral blemish upon the nation. For instance, Hegel argued that Jews should not have to lose property 'merely because of an external consideration at variance with right in its strict sense – that is, in order to terminate the disputes and confusions with which old claims would threaten the security of property, etc.'[21] The reality of property, Hegel assumes, is based on the will of the owner to possess something, of the will's need to express itself in order to possess something, which is revealed by the remembrance and honour which gives property its validity as a living and self-sufficient end.[22] There are already two conditions attached to this right to property. One is prescription, by which the nation may render someone ownerless and contingently turn the thing into public monument or universal property. The other condition is disuse, or when 'Mere *land*, consecrated as a place of burial or even dedicated in its own right ... embodies an empty arid absent arbitrary will.'[23] Hegel is not only convinced of the existence of non-will relationships to land, he does not believe that individuals who maintain such relationships to land could be injured by its taking. In fact, he conceives of circumstances when the claim to property cannot be guaranteed or respected.[24] Therefore the recognition of assimilation of the Jews into the political order of property relations is also an exclusion of those varied peoples for whom wilful determination of ownership could be discounted on the basis of cultural differences such as collective ownership or hostility towards the notion of owning the earth rather than inhabiting it. In this way generosity to the Jews is part and parcel of the Western project of enclosure and expropriation that underwrote colonial acquisition of land and of persons as slaves.

In the above, Hegel was engaged in the completion of an historical effort within Europe to protect Jews as a minority, and Jewish rights as minority rights. Still, Jews were not the only entities subjected to violence. Hegel was writing under the shadow of abolitionism and the quest to end slavery, which it was known even in Hegel's time cost millions of lives and wrought untold devastation on an entire continent and its populations. To evaluate Hegel's views of non-Christian Germans (or Europeans), one must place the text debated by Inayatullah and Blaney in the context of Europe and its others. In this sense, *The Philosophy of Right* was about an internal other whose faith was intricately linked to the survival of civil society as a central dimension of constitutionalism (and liberalism). *The Philosophy of History* was a different justificatory text, one about the legitimacy and rightfulness of European ascendency and treatment of another 'other' both in theological, spatial and affective terms: Muslims (Arabs), Africans, Asians and the native populations of the New World. The violence against these other others did not proceed along the same grammar as that done to Jews.

It is not surprising, given the political and legal movements that followed the Enlightenment, that liberal theologians, politicians and intellectuals would take up the defence of the Jews. This defence was easily couched in biblical and constitutional terms that were concurrently negated through affective dispositions born of historical recollection of the Crusades (in the case of Muslims), anthropological self-justifications (in relation to Africa and the New World) and political vindication (towards Ottomans, Chinese and others). The differences in language and approach to these other others were not merely political in nature. They were also philosophical and scientific, beginning with seventeenth-century natural law theory and culminating in nineteenth-century natural history. Consistently, Hegel was preceded by generations of English, Scottish, French, Italian and German scholars whose visions of humanity and human faculties and entitlements (rights) were founded on simple but dangerous ideas of providential desert, according to which the elect or chosen assumed privileges and immunities, while the damned or fallen were assigned obligations and duties to comply with their assigned stations in life, under the pain of dispossession, isolation and/or death. Likewise, Hegel has been followed by generations of liberal constitutionalists whose visions of the constitutional order – and therefore of the state, society, law – accommodate some subjects through inclusion and assimilation while casting others to the status of permanent outsiders. In any case, the relevant arguments hint at or contain distinct forms of violence for each category of subject.

Deferring difference 113

The grammar of antipathy that formed the background to violence was moulded in affective dispositions that are no longer available for examination. For instance, the grammar of antipathy towards Muslims –referenced over the centuries as Mahometans, Saracens, Turks, etc. – can be traced back to the Crusades and subsequent narratives on the origins and significations of conflict between Muslims and the other two Abrahamic religions: Christians and Jews. For their part, the native populations of the New World and Africans were subjected to violence under different theological views and corresponding philosophical conceptions of the human and life. Each grammar of antipathy provided the symbolic structures for consideration of violence, or the context within which the form and appropriateness of violence was considered: war, expropriation, expulsion, pogroms, transfer to reservations and the like. We know today that violence was difficult to contain and that over time the constitutionally assimilated and the socially integrated European minorities (for instance Jews) did not fare any better than those populations that were excluded (Muslims for instance) in the Western quest for national sovereignty through communal will. However, the grammar and tactics of liquidation remain different and worthy of disaggregation.

Hegel's plea for the inclusion of Jews into the German social compact remains significant in legal, political and moral terms. But why deny Hegel's other inclinations and the fact that he could have maintained contradictory and conflicting stances towards different entities? I am not sure of Brown's motivation in countering discussions of Hegel's views of history with argumentations from the unrelated subject of Hegel's political pragmatism on the Jewish question. Lest I be misunderstood, Brown's own personal morality is not at stake. He has otherwise been at the forefront of calls for mutual respect in international relations, based on a rebuke of what he terms 'The Modern Requirement', which recalls the injustice done to the native populations of the New World by the Spanish conquistadors and later colonial powers.[25] Brown has also advocated the observance of public morality in international relations, and a corresponding ethic of coexistence among states and respect for individual human rights.[26]

The stake is the reading of the Black World that occurs when theorists imagine, as do analytic philosophers, that the terms, concepts and justifications of philosophy and modern constitutional orders are sufficient unto themselves as terms of contemporary politics.[27] It is not merely that there are faults with the conceptions of truth, justice and rights advanced by Kant and Hegel for instance. Nor is it that given extrapolations from their ideas may or may not be adequate. The problem is that some historical figures more than others espoused views of subjectivity and therefore of certain subjects that are morally dubious. Such are Hegel's views of race, the customs of non-Europeans, and providence in *The Philosophy of History*. The related ideas are at times erroneous and/or offensive in their determinations. For instance, Hegel held in *The Philosophy of History* that the inferiority of the Native Americans 'in all respects, even in regard to size, is very manifest', and that the indigenous populations of the New World are 'still abiding in their natural condition of rudeness and barbarism'. He also held that the Negro

114 *Performance*

'exhibits the natural man in his completely wild and untamed state'.[28] In these and other instances, Hegel presented so-called barbaric people as the antithesis of Europeans, whose 'negative existence' laid the foundation for the clash of cultures that would complete a plan chartered by Providence itself.

From a postcolonial perspective, no amount of clarification and/or elucidation of modern political debates and of the terms of constitutional settlements or the language of such settlements would elide this simple fact. Indeed, the desire and tendency to extricate race, racial sentiments and racism from modern European and Western thought only leads to confusion about the end of associated projects. Postcolonial concern grows exponentially when obfuscation is conjoined with a project to negate the subordination of others in both philosophical texts and politics; to substitute affect for truth in total disregard of otherwise applicable norms of inquiry; and to cleanse canonical memory of unpleasant facts emanating from Western institutions and political traditions.

The most important constitutional question

Brown is not alone in assuming the moral rectitude, sufficiency and universality of liberalism and Western constitutional orders. Hannah Arendt, perhaps the best critic of totalitarianism, also assumed that the objective of modern constitutionalism had been to advance freedom, liberty and the rights of Man as individual and universal being. She included Blacks among the subjects of the rights in the US constitution although their status, standing and position in the body politic had been largely uncertain: whether as slaves or 'freemen' before, during and long after Reconstruction. Consistently, Arendt sided with US conservatives in Little Rock, Arkansas during an incident in 1957 in which nine Black children were barred by a white mob from entering a previously white school. This happened following the US Supreme Court's 1954 *Brown* v. *Board of Education* ruling allowing school integration, when President Dwight D. Eisenhower sent Federal troops to enforce the integration of Central High School in Little Rock.

In an article in the magazine *Dissent* written for this occasion, Arendt expressed qualms about the intervention of the Federal government in what was to her the private province of states and the individuals involved.[29] To be sure, Arendt's article appeared two years after the initial event and she was careful to express misgivings about her own intervention. These are her words:

> Like most people of European origin I have difficulty in understanding, let alone sharing, the common prejudices of Americans in this area ... I should like to make it clear that as a Jew I take my sympathy for the cause of the Negroes as for all oppressed or underprivileged peoples for granted and should appreciate it if the reader did likewise.

So, it is not that Arendt supported segregation. She was seeking a higher constitutional principle upon which to ground private relations, in contrast to the assumption of duties in the public sphere. Arendt brought many influences to bear on this quest, including ones from the phenomenological and existential traditions espoused by Edmund Husserl, Karl Jaspers and Martin Heidegger. Likewise, her liberalism was textured by a political philosophy steeped in a civic republicanism that was broadly Kantian in outlook. It should not be surprising therefore that she envisaged politics along the lines of categorical imperatives derived from well-established political maxims and institutions to support them. Consistently, Arendt's politics drew upon the public performance of freedom of the Greek 'polis', American townships, the Paris Commune, the civil rights movements of the 1960s and the Hungarian uprising of 1956. Above all, she built her conceptions of freedom on the founding principles of the founding revolution of the US republic.[30]

It should not be surprising that Arendt would maintain that, in the context of the Little Rock incident, it was more important to support the basic constitutional right of freedom of association, which could not survive government interference, than articulate a federal responsibility due to citizens who had been previously excluded from the constitutional compact. To her, the most important constitutional question was whether citizens or persons could freely decide to enter into associations of their own liking without government interference mandating the inclusion of everyone, regardless of the ends of such associations. Arendt thus contrasted the public/political realm of constitutional equality, where discrimination should not be allowed, with the private realm of the social, where choices and preferences (even ones based on discrimination) must be allowed. She correctly asserted that a central principle of private association was to discriminate and/or to discern on subjective grounds – grounds that others might find objectionable. Once again, it was a valid argument suited for a context other than the one for which it had been penned.

Distinguishing between the political and the social had been central to many of Arendt's arguments on the relationships between state and civil society, individuals within civil society, and capital labour relations. In these instances and others, she was mindful of the desire of groups to subordinate the public realm of human freedom to their own needs or social requirements. She displayed the same reservation in her Little Rock essay about the sorts of events that she imagined had led to the rise of authoritarianism elsewhere. It is hard to object to an abstract principle or a moral category when it is associated with justice, individual rights, and duty and/or virtue for the preservation of a republican form of government. However, as with Brown, Arendt sought logical consistency without regard to particularity, and devoid of any historical analysis of the sort of ethical concerns that informed the ruling in *Brown* v. *Board of Education*. Put differently, Arendt interpreted constitutional logic through abstract philosophical principles that are now excised from social dynamics that are themselves anti-republican and worse. Therefore, she sought to resolve a problem that is internal to the constitution by its very externality to it by defending the internal logic of the said constitution without due regard to the condition of possibility of racial discrimination in both post- and antebellum America, and the *Brown* ruling itself.

From a strictly Kantian perspective, the above is understandable. But this understanding has an edge. Arendt's work deals with the nature of power; more concretely, political authority, political subjects and totalitarianism. She associated the rise of the latter, or at least its conditions of possibility, with anti-Semitism and imperialism, among other things. This means that she was keenly aware of the circulation of the categories of race in political thought, but also of the implication of this fact for politics. Ironically, she omitted to note the connections between liberalism and race; omitted to note that Western entities were primary purveyors of racial and racist ideologies, from the 'discovery' of the New World to the institution of chattel slavery, empire and colonies. Arendt also omitted to note and to elaborate on the manners in which race was inscribed in the new conceptions of freedom, and in the constitutional form which was meant to give expression to these conceptions. As a consequence, the resulting analysis of freedom is envisaged strictly from the perspective of the historical freemen: the original subjects of the American Revolution – white men augmented by white women and generations of white immigrants. The related construction of citizen – and of the human – was founded on a historical anthropology of race without which the plantation economy and its regimes of entitlements and immunities would have been impossible. Without those omissions, Arendt could have complemented her forceful defence of the historical novelty and innovations of the American Revolution[31] with an indication that the manner in which race shaped the nature and contours of citizenship also had no parallels in ancient Greece or Rome.

Arendt's omissions were not without effects. They led her to mistaken assumptions on a number of issues related to the distinction of the political from the social and their operation during and after the American Revolution. She was mistaken for instance that the post-revolutionary constitutional order would open itself up to universal freedom without other kinds of revolutions – equally modern and equally profound. She was unable to perceive the significance of the related events because of a distinction to which she was committed between practices of freedom and social disturbances. This distinction was the basis of her analysis of the Little Rock incident: a view of the subjects based on Enlightenment-era bourgeois assumptions on the composition and operations of human faculties as well as the depoliticization of the history of racial subject formation. These assumptions had racial and racist connotations underscored by the American constitutional compromise that reduced Blacks to three-fifths human, and which were affirmed by juridical events up until the *Brown* ruling and the corroborating political events of the Civil Rights era in the 1960s. Thus, while it may be correct to say that 'Freedom in the Republic is not identical with "liberation" (with negative freedom)', it is erroneous to reduce the Civil Rights Movement to a social problem or a problem of 'civil rights'. That movement too was a practice of freedom aiming to redefine freedom itself within new moral, political and institutional political boundaries. In short, the Civil Rights Movement was no social disturbance because, contrary to Arendt's view, the American Republic was initially committed to the cause of freedom for the particular groups that initiated the Mayflower Compact and established colonies at the expense of the native populations and on the labour of Blacks and others. That compact had to be denounced, the constitution amended multiple times, and the institutions of the Republic 'revolutionized' anew to give birth to today's American Republic. This draws attention to the politics inherent in Arendt's decision upon where the 'political' ends and the 'social' begins. Hence the designation of the social or the private is itself political, much in the way that Kant's determination of the metaphysics of Man always necessitated an anthropological knowledge of Man. Philosophers cannot jump over their own historical and empirical shadow. To do so merely immunizes thought against necessary ethical debates; it does not undo the founding violence of its pre-theoretical commitments.

The analytical method and discursive strategy used by Arendt in this context is commonplace in liberalism after colonialism. It consists of defending the constitutional order enacted by conquerors after disposition as a matter of moral imperatives, including the protection of property (without reference to origin) and individual freedoms (without reference to the appropriation of the commons as condition of the constitution of the private). Several liberals have accomplished the same feat, most notably Isaiah Berlin, in his famed distinction between negative freedom which is intended to keep government at bay and away by those seeking immunities in order to protect their entitlements and privileges against the expropriated seeking redress through government intervention or revolution.[32] In most of these instances, the neutral distinction between the social and the political often has a racial undercurrent: those whose problems are relegated to the status of the social are invariably racial minorities or inhabitants of the postcolonies.[33]

The most abhorrent evil imaginable

Kant stipulated in *The Metaphysical Elements of Justice* that, as legal principle, 'Judicial punishment can never be used merely as a means to promote some other good for the criminal himself or for civil society, but instead it must in all cases be imposed on him only on the ground that he has committed a crime.' He was talking of course of retributive justice which, according to him, should aim to punish specific individuals for particular acts and also aspire to set standards of conduct for others.[34] It should not be surprising therefore that this Kantian principle, combined with a Cartesian commitment to truth, should guide judgment on the most hideous crime of war committed during the Second World War: the Holocaust.

There are many certainties about the Holocaust. The fact that it was a crime that targeted Jews, as both a religious and ethnic entity, is among them. Another certainty is that Jews had been demonized for a host of baseless reasons, but the immediate condition of the crime of near-extermination against them was their ethnicization and racialization. This was possible through a combination of factors ranging from theology (during the Middle Ages), science (particularly nineteenth-century natural history) and ideology (under colonialism and later Nazism).

118 *Performance*

This much is established by Raphael Lemkin, the Polish lawyer of Jewish descent who coined the term genocide.[35] The conventional wisdom today is that, while the Holocaust was the outcome of sustained and purposeful policy based on a distinct ideology, it nonetheless defies analysis and comprehension.[36] As a lawyer, however, Lemkin sought to give the Holocaust a designation that identifies the act of genocide: the physical destruction of collectivity through direct and/or indirect means so long as the means interfered with the biological and social reproduction, or led to the extermination, of the group against whom they are directed.[37]

Lemkin's work in this regard complies with the available norms of empirical studies: thorough, systematic, falsifiable and, more importantly, compelling. He was determined to demystify the act of genocide but also to guard against its banalization through linguistic obfuscation and empirical omissions. Lemkin achieves these goals without diminishing, tarnishing or pre-empting the experiences, memories and future narratives of survivors. To Lemkin, genocide is a legal offence, which we now associate with war crimes. In this regard, it was important to Lemkin to determine the characteristics of the legal fact of genocide, such that they could be easily established and verified by courts and other institutions when suspicion arose. The post-Nuremberg Geneva Conventions seem to have done just that by distinguishing acts of war from war crimes and the crime of genocide.

It is to Lemkin's credit too that he did not understand the act of genocide as merely a legal fact. He was keenly aware of its anthropological and ethical dimensions. This is to say that genocide was a specific crime of war that targeted an entity on account of racial or ethnic identification: to my recollection, Armenians, Herero, Jews and perhaps Tutsis in the twentieth century. The ethical dimension of genocide is more complex for postcolonial readers. It includes a number of questions: the first is who should be included under the category of the human for the purpose of defining such crimes against humanity as genocide. Should it include Native Americans, Aborigines, the victims of the St Bartholomew massacres in France, the Irish victims of British policies, sexual minorities, Communists and the disabled (the latter also targeted by the Nazis)? The question exceeds the limits of Kantian retributive justice because the purpose of edification is not merely to punish, to exact revenge, or to ask for reparation. Another question is who speaks for humanity, or what juridical or political entities define genocide and what should be included under the designation? Put differently, who is the resident repository and guardian of the memory, morality and laws of the collective? The questions above have moral and political implications beyond the definition of crime and the judicial determination of punishment. I raise them merely to provoke thought at this moment, but I will return to the question later in relation to the facts of colonialism.

The authoritative anthropology of genocide on the other hand has been murkier around the question of race – an irony in itself. I said 'authoritative' to demarcate the ethnography underlying this particular form of knowledge from the prevailing academic findings then and now. The irony is that the form of racism implicated

Deferring difference 119

in the authoritative discourse proceeds from near accurate understanding of the racism of the crime of genocide itself: that it is an assault on groups mostly on account of their origin. As intimated above, the same attention to the empirical applies to the execution of the crime itself. This attention to the empirical gives way to racial demonization owing to historical grudges and their affective manifestations in theological and ideological imaginaries. This occurs when the disposition to genocide is determined to be a regressive or alien act, one conceivable only in different times (distant past) and spaces: the Barbary Coast for instance. In effect, the entities that conceived, planned and executed the Holocaust were indexed as historically and spatially distant communities and therefore European culture was exonerated. The end of this indexing is of course to reproduce and reintroduce racial categories into moral thought in order to re-establish the image of Europe as producers of universal values as well as endorse the view of the West as the legitimate adjudicator of values, norms and institutions.

Lemkin begins his sociology of the Holocaust with incontestable remarks. The first phase of genocide, he held, was the destruction of the 'national pattern of the oppressed group', followed by 'the imposition of the national pattern of the oppressor upon the oppressed'. Examining German actions, Lemkin also noted that occupation and the transformation of the political landscape of colonized entities were essential components of genocide. Further, genocide is not possible without the collaboration of the intelligentsia of the genocidal power and the concurrent 'silencing' of the cultural elite that provides leadership for the targeted communities, which may also organize resistance if left alone. Further, the degrading of the arts, literature and scientific endeavour of the population to be destroyed is a prerequisite to genocidal propaganda. In addition, the destruction of the foundations of the economic existence of a national group is a necessary if not a sufficient condition of preparation for genocide. Finally, a genocidal policy must necessarily denigrate or disrupt the communal (national) or religious identity of the oppressed group in preparation for genocide.

A lawyer desiring precision, Lemkin was attuned to the fact of the plurality of actions and policies of genocide. In his analysis of the facts, however, he regrouped the related actions and policies into two categories: the crimes of Barbary and crimes of Vandalism. These categories effectively placed Africans (the Blacks) and Germanic tribes at a crime scene which, at least in the case of Africans, the majority had not seen. They were likewise indicted for actions that they could not imagine or execute. Barbary, it must be recalled, entered European expressions in the sixteenth century with the 'Barbary Coast' as a reference to what is today's Maghreb, or the middle and western coastal regions of North Africa – what is now Morocco, Algeria, Tunisia and Libya. Ironically, the term used to derive Arab Muslims eventually referred to the majority Berber populations which had occupied the region long before Arabs, and who were not implicated in the Crusades during which North African Muslims are said to have acted, forgive me, barbarically.

I do not attribute racist motives to Lemkin. I actually think the opposite. My concern is the power of language in mobilizing images and restoring a particular common sense to memory – and to remould affect. It is in this sense that Lemkin contributed to marking genocide metaphorically as the fall of Europe and a turning away from its destiny. In so doing, Europe fell into a temporal abyss inhabited by vandals and barbarians. He thus subscribed to the idea that, in committing genocide, Europe had become its (opposite) other: the Moor, Berber, Arab and other Muslim of the so-called Coast of Barbary. It did not matter that in other equally charged racist discourses the same populations of the northernmost coast of Africa were said to possess inferior, even inhuman, theology, science and ideology, Lemkin's own prerequisites for genocide. Nor did it matter that these populations were never found at the scene of the crime. Europe and European rationalism and bureaucratic technologies could be exonerated if those responsible for the Holocaust could be said to experience the biblical fall.

The reproduction of racism and racial ideologies had its own consequences. One was to obscure very significant points made by Lemkin himself. One is that genocide is as likely within the nation-state (read Germany) as under occupation (German occupation of Poland). What is left unsaid by Lemkin is the likelihood of genocidal policies during European conquest and settlement or colonization as well as colonialism during the era of imperialism. Having subscribed to the distinction of Europe (and of Judaeo-Christianity) as a separate sphere of morality, Lemkin could not envisage Jean-Paul Sartre's view that 'the relationship between the colonized and the colonizer is potentially genocidal if not by intent at least in practice given discrepancies in power and the means of violence, on the one hand, and, on the other, the proclivity of the former to fight occupation against the determination of the latter to maintain control.' Sartre's point may be hyperbolic but it is supported by events from the New World, during European conquest and settlement; Africa during the slave trade and colonialism (for instance in what is now Namibia); and elsewhere, including in the Pacific and Indian Ocean island territories.

Conclusion

The above suggests that race is differently different from other forms of difference in post-Enlightenment moral thought. It also suggests that the universality of moral categories has been predicated on the erasure of the racialization of difference under modern Western constitutional arrangements. This difference of race manifests itself in multiple ways in moral thought, of which I have explored three. In the first instance, the omission of race or the exoneration of the racism of original texts is the condition of the universalism of the contained ideas. This is the path taken by Chris Brown in his defence of Hegel. Whatever the motivation, the attitude is unnecessarily defensive and does not do justice to the ability of the postcolonial interlocutors of liberals and other cosmopolitans to discern. In the second instance, the denunciation of racism in one context only foregrounds the most pernicious kind of racism, one so embedded in the psyche and so far removed from constitutional and moral concerns that it is no longer visible as racism. This is why Lemkin seems to be oblivious to the affective power Barbary holds as a metaphor for genocide. In the last instance, liberal theorists often obscure the signification of race by deploying morally irrefutable categorical signifiers, including respect for individual rights as a necessary condition of freedom and justice, while obscuring the non-neutral implementation of the said categories in the constitutional order and related economies of rights, privileges, entitlements, immunities – that denote racial subordination or oppression. Hannah Arendt's so-called Little Rock essay did just that.

Although it may seem like a paradox, liberalism and cosmopolitanism are not immune from the double urge to simultaneously suppress and instrumentalize race, attesting to the epistemological instrumentality of race in the conception and implementation of modern thought and institutions. I hasten to add that it would be an injustice nonetheless to assume that the related philosophical arguments and institutional practices are indistinguishable from those of other ideologies, approaches and the resulting practices. The interest in focusing on a single lineage was to highlight the manners in which philosophical and theoretical precepts become common sense in the creation of normative regimes that are at their core technologies of power, legitimation and affect, or sympathy and antipathy. Once constituted, these technologies are deployed toward the institution of commonplaces, or common understandings and practices, and their moral landscapes and their spaces of deliberation – for the determination of crimes, guilt and judgment – and the spaces of deliverance – where the application or suspension of the law, morality and ethics is decided. These moral landscapes may also harbour spaces of suspicion, or mythical zones of pathology as determined by speculations based on banalized theology, anthropology, literature and the like about the nature and dispositions of other people. This is how Barbary and Vandalia came to prominence as an explanation for the crimes of Europe.

Postcolonialists should therefore pay attention to the constitution of knowledge and archives. Indeed, it matters how historical narratives and archives are constituted, particularly where truth, justice and rights are concerned. This is not to say that postcolonial archives stand outside of history and that Cartesian notions of truth, Kantian views of justice, or Hegel's perspective on rights do not hold standing with the constitution of such archives. The obverse is equally true: the Black world was never outside of history and such an acknowledgment must compel theorists to move past their own canonical extrapolations. The way forward requires analyses of disciplinary practices. The tendencies decried in this space are of three sorts. The first is the tendency to conceal the mechanisms of subordination and social relations that operate through time and space through scientific method or irrelevant philosophical themes. The second involves the suspension and/or disregard in the study of the Black world of empirical and normative events that may put into question received disciplinary wisdom on sovereignty, subjectivity, modern identities and their base claims regarding justice and freedom. My third concern pertains to disciplinary views of society, morality, freedom and justice. These are ethnographic, philosophical, ethical and legal questions at their core; but they also pertain to our understandings of the social, the philosophical, the ethical and the legal.

Notes

1. Chris Brown, 'Hegel and International Ethics', *Ethics and International Affairs*, 5: 1 (1991).
2. Gayatri Chakravorty Spivak, *A Critique of Postcolonial Reason: Toward a History of the Vanishing Present* (Cambridge: Harvard University Press 1999).
3. Spivak, 3, 65, 98.
4. Spivak, 32.
5. Spivak, x (preface).
6. Spivak, 98.
7. Spivak, 34.
8. Spivak, 32.
9. Jacques Derrida, *Margins of Philosophy*, (Chicago: University of Chicago Press, 1985), 121–2.
10. As used here, postcolonialism stands in for a multiplicity of perspectives, traditions and approaches to questions of identity, culture and power. Indeed, postcolonialism has multiple points of origination in Africa, Asia, Australia, Latin America and the New World (see, for instance, Paul Gilroy, *Postcolonial Melancholia* (New York: Columbia University Press 2005); Albert Memmi, *The Colonizer and the Colonized* (New York: Penguin 1965); Ranajit Guha, *Subaltern Studies: Writings on South Asian History and Society* (Oxford: Oxford University Press 1996); Gayatri Chakravorty-Spivak, *A Critique of Postcolonial Reason: Toward a History of the Vanishing Present* (Cambridge, Mass.: Harvard University Press 1999); Walter Mignolo, *Local Histories/Global Designs: Coloniality, Subaltern Knowledges, and Border Thinking* (Princeton: Princeton University Press 2000); Homi Bhabha, *Nation and* Narration (New York: Routledge 1994); and Edward Said, *Orientalism* (New York: Vintage 1979)). These regions were subjected across time to different forms of governance and political traditions that account for the diversity of approaches to society, science and knowledge. Colonial histories also explain the overture of postcolonialism to a variety of theories, including liberalism, Marxism, postmodernism and feminism and their applications to history, philosophy, sociology, psychology and political science. This diversity has led to confusions compounded by the academic confinement of postcolonial studies to ethnic, cultural and regional studies programmes or departments. Yet, postcolonialism does not limit itself to a single region or discipline. Finally, I wish to stress the precarious relationship between 'freedom' and politics in the postcolonial context.
11. Siba N. Grovogui, 'Counterpoints and the Imaginaries Behind Them', *International Political Sociology*, 3: 3 (2009).
12. See Steve Smith, 'The United States and the Discipline of International Relations: Hegemonic Country, Hegemonic Discipline', *International Studies Review*, 4: 2 (Summer 2002).
13. R. B. J. Walker and Richard K. Ashley, 'Speaking the Language of Exile: Dissident Thought in International Relations', *International Studies Quarterly*, 34 (1990).
14. Siba N. Grovogui, 'Regimes of Sovereignty: International Morality and the African Condition', *European Journal of International Relations*, 8: 16 (2002).
15. Naeem Inayatullah and David Blaney, 'Shed No Tears: Wealth, Race, and Death in Hegel's Necro-Philosophy'. Panel on Hegel and International Relations, 48th annual meeting of the International Studies Association, Chicago, 28 February–3 March 2007.
16. G. W. F. Hegel, *Elements of the Philosophy of Right*, Allen W. Wood (ed.) (Cambridge: Cambridge University Press 1991), 295–6.
17. Ibid.
18. Ibid.

19 Ibid.
20 Ibid.
21 Ibid., 94.
22 Ibid.
23 Ibid.
24 Ibid.
25 See, for instance, Chris Brown, 'Cultural Diversity and International Political Theory: From the Requirement to "Mutual Respect"?', *Review of International Studies,* 26: 2 (April 2000), 199–213 (Cambridge University Press, available at: http://www.jstor.org/stable/20097670).
26 Ibid.
27 Siba N'Zatioula Grovogui, 'Mind, Body, and Gut!: Elements of a Postcolonial Human Rights Discourse', in Branwen Gruffydd Jones (ed.), *Decolonizing International Relations* (Lanham, MD: Rowman & Littlefield 2006).
28 G. W. F. Hegel, 'Geographical Basis of History, Part I', *Philosophy Of History,* trans. by J. M. A. Sibree (Kitchener, Ontario: Batoche Books 1857), *passim.*
29 Hannah Arendt, 'Reflections on Little Rock', *Dissent* (Winter 1959), 47–58.
30 Hannah Arendt, *On Revolution* (New York: Faber and Faber 1965), 24–25.
31 Hannah Arendt, *On Revolution* (New York 1965), 24–25.
32 Isaiah Berlin, 1969, 'Two Concepts of Liberty', in Isaiah Berlin, *Four Essays on Liberty* (London: Oxford University Press, New ed. 2002).
33 See, for instance, Robert H. Jackson, *Quasi-states: sovereignty, international relations and the Third World* (Cambridge: Cambridge University Press 1994), 26–9.
34 See, for instance, Stuart Hopkins, 'Kant and the Morality of Anger', available at: http://www.philosophypathways.com/essays/hopkins2.html
35 See, for instance, The United States Holocaust Museum, *The Holocaust Encyclopedia,* available at: http://www.ushmm.org/wlc/en/article.php?ModuleId=10007050
36 See, for instance, Dominick LaCapra, *Representing the Holocaust: History, Theory, Trauma* (Cornell University Press 1996).
37 Most references regarding genocide are drawn on Raphael Lemkin, *Axis Rule In Occupied Europe: Laws Of Occupation, Analysis Of Government, Proposal for Redress* (Clark, NJ: The Lawbook Exchange Ltd 2005).

7 IR and the postcolonial novel
Nation and subjectivity in India

Sankaran Krishna[1]

The postcolonial condition produces selves that are not satisfied and sovereign, but split and rest uneasily with themselves and their milieu. The postcolonial nation is a serrated – not smooth – space, led and represented by middle classes but not inclusive of vast members of society who are strangers to what one might call, following Spivak, the 'culture of imperialism'.[2] It is a middle class that resides *amongst* but rarely *with* one's countrymen. The different classes of people that comprise the postcolonial nation are arrayed by this middle class in terms of their familiarity with, and comfort within, the cultures of imperialism. Their distance from or proximity to this culture becomes a metric by which people are classified as sophisticated, desirable and cosmopolitan versus provincial, unsophisticated and anachronistic. I argue that the locus of enunciation of the postcolonial novelist is one that hierarchizes various national and international characters as subaltern, provincial or cosmopolitan depending on their knowledge of and ease within a culture of imperialism.

The life-world of such a postcolonial middle class hinges upon a continuous negotiation between inside and outside, home and world, East and West, nation and international, provincial and cosmopolitan. In other words, the postcolonial locus of enunciation as outlined above might be said to produce a certain 'distribution of the sensible', which is, of course, precisely how the French social theorist Jacques Rancière defines politics.[3] This class's yearning for an impossible elsewhere authorizes certain plot-lines, delineations of character, narrative structures, and dialogue or interaction between characters that may be read as an aesthetic practice which is also profoundly political. Such negotiations would perhaps be most evident in the understandings of selfhood and the nation as they appear in this literary form.

This chapter analyses these negotiations in three novels by Indian authors Amitav Ghosh, Arundhati Roy and Kiran Desai. How does familiarity with the culture of imperialism help distinguish class, region, nation, cosmopolitanism and other attributes of the characters in their novels? How is 'India' continuously worlded through the characters, the interactions between them, the dialogue, and pivotal moments in these novels? To what extent do these novels exemplify postcoloniality as a locus of enunciation constantly animated by an impossible desire for decolonization, to escape the alienation from oneself and from many of one's fellow citizens, and relations with the West marked by a deep and profound ambivalence? How does such prose, to the extent that it is honest about its class origins and hews closely to that which it knows intimately, also serve to fracture and render impossible the nation project itself? How do we as readers empathize with the depictions of those outside the culture of imperialism – namely the subaltern classes or individuals?

In a tangential way, my chapter engages with the discipline of international relations. Notwithstanding a vast literature – both in the humanities and social sciences – that shows the coevality of the nation and the novel, and technological, cultural and historical forces that impelled both their formations, IR discourse[4] tends to regard the nation – the constitutive unit of the discipline – as an unremarkable given, something that 'goes without saying because it comes without saying' (to use a phrase from Bourdieu).[5] IR discourse is preoccupied by the study of what nations do to each other; it is not habitually reflective of what the nation is, or the processes by which nations constitute and reproduce themselves, that is, the extent to which their performance produces their being. From a different, postcolonial vantage, instead of viewing performance (that is, international relations) as the actions of an already-constituted being (the nation) upon an already extant world of other nations, one could view both performer and stage as mutually constitutive and coeval. In other words, IR is what nations do, and it is in the doing that the world of nations is produced and reproduced.

Through these novels, I show that the nation is an emotive structure of belonging, a mental landscape as much as it is a demarcated territory on a physical planet. What a nation is, what it represents and evokes, depends a great deal on who is thinking about it, how they regard the near and the faraway, and the ways in which they have been formed as thinking subjects through narratives and other representational practices that have inscribed the world and their place in it. How are the nation and the international imaged in the novels of these writers? How do these images constitute them as cleft subjects? I realize that for much of IR, literature is epiphenomenal or ornamental. And yet, literature may do more than just enhance and enrich our understanding of the multiple layers of meaning congealed in that term we take so much for granted – the nation. It may enable us to stop regarding nations as things or entities that are already known to us – and instead regard them as fractal (in the sense of constantly changing and indeterminate) mindscapes.

Worlding *The Shadow Lines*

Published in 1988, *The Shadow Lines*[6] was Amitav Ghosh's second novel following his brilliant debut in *The Circle of Reason*. Ghosh's writing has always been marked by an acute awareness of the epistemic and physical violence that national boundaries, borders and identities wreak on people. His fiction (and his prose) complicates and questions the redemptive narratives that seek to justify the coercion and mass murder perpetrated by modern states and oppositional insurgent movements. His work is especially notable for its deep insights into the way postcolonial states and middle classes have thoroughly internalized and reproduced notions of realpolitik, or amoral statecraft, in their desire for parity with the West in what one might call the killing arts. For those who view IR discourse as problematic (in that it seems to naturalize violence in the name of a teleological narrative of nation-building) and arbitrary (in the sense that it could be otherwise), Ghosh has always offered a great deal.

The Shadow Lines is narrated in the voice of an introspective and observant boy growing up in the Calcutta of the 1950s and 1960s. We never find out the protagonist's name at any point in the novel and I will refer to him from here on as N (for narrator). N is Bengali and in many ways typical of India's urban middle class of that time. He is the son of a middle manager in a local rubber factory, attends an English-medium school, has a capacious and precocious awareness of world affairs, politics, geography, science and history that may seem remarkable in other contexts but was hardly so in his milieu, and is mildly obsessed with cricket. Importantly, he is somehow convinced that his life in Calcutta is a vernacular or provincial apprenticeship to a later, fuller life that would be international, cosmopolitan and Western in various senses of those terms. N's schooling in Calcutta is followed by college in New Delhi and then a PhD in history from Oxford on a scholarship (an itinerary that, incidentally, is not very different from Ghosh's own in real life).

The milieu of the novel traverses Calcutta, Dacca, Delhi, Oxford and London. Yet given the nature of Bengali/Indian /postcolonial middle classes, it simultaneously involves the entire world. The intellectual and epistemic life-worlds of N, his friends and relatives are thoroughly reworked by ideas, books, magazines, and literatures from everywhere. They avidly read newspaper reports of faraway events, and their lives are intercrossed with arrivals and departures of various friends and relatives who shuttle between India and the world outside. Theirs was a cultural formation in which one moved seamlessly between Rabindranath Tagore and William Shakespeare, Karl Marx and M. N. Roy, Prasanta Mahalanobis and Harold Laski, the movies of Vittorio de Sica and Satyajit Ray. It was a place where legendary soccer players like Pushkas or Pele were household names, spoken of with tactile familiarity and vivid detail – and yet no one had ever actually seen them play, not even via television. Living in Calcutta, this middle class was always plugged in to the intellectual, cultural, political, social and other currents of a world at large. It was also possibly aware that its own obsession with the rest of the world was in many ways one-sided: that same world did not much care for the lives and times of an audience it did not even know it had.

N's larger family was also worlded in a more literal or physical sense. They had lived for generations on both sides of what would become the border between India and East Pakistan/Bangladesh. Various relatives had made their living working in Rangoon, Burma or other outposts of the British Empire, and relatives were renowned for having acquired high distinctions during their education in England. Others were marked out as special because their careers – as diplomats, development experts, academics – took them all over the world, and still others emigrated to places like the United States or Canada. Mid-twentieth-century Calcutta or India was a place thoroughly and explicitly made and networked by global connections, migrations and movements, both intra-Third World and linking colonial and ex-colonial spaces to Western metropolises.

The 'worlding' of the novel's characters and spaces is reflected in its opening lines: 'In 1939, thirteen years before I was born, my father's aunt, Mayadebi, went to England with her husband and her son, Tridib.' Tridib, who is N's uncle-once-removed, but really more like an older cousin, is somewhat distractedly pursuing a PhD in archaeology at Calcutta University. His father is a suave, urbane and cosmopolitan diplomat in the Indian Foreign Service. Tridib himself, though he had spent much of his life in the ancestral home in Calcutta, had eclectic interests and a wide (if also eccentric) knowledge, with the added gloss of actually having lived in England for a year when he was just eight. He is seen (by some of his older relatives at any rate) as a dilettante squandering his talents in 'adda' – or gossip – on street corners and in parks instead of leaving a footprint on his world.

Tridib is one of N's most important windows to the world. His recollections of the London of the German blitzes, air-raid sirens, bomb shelters and blackouts evoked in N's mind a space at once fabulous and real. The minutiae of Tridib's year in London would be recalled with Proustian detail and texture by N in the years that followed, especially during his own time as a student at Oxford. As with many a postcolonial, London and England were spaces imagined, felt, examined, encountered, recollected, experienced and lived in long before one actually reached the place.

Early in *The Shadow Lines*, we encounter a classic instance of how fellow citizens are graded in terms of their approximation to a desired international culture – and I mean grading in a literal sense. The occasion is a visit to N's home by Tridib's dad, the jet-set diplomat on one of his periodic trips to Calcutta. As his car, a grand Studebaker, draws close to N and his family who wait on a sidewalk, the excitement mounts. The Shaheb is wearing, in the searing heat of Calcutta's summer, a pale-green corduroy jacket with a silk cravat. After alighting, he asks solicitously of N's mother if eggs, vegetables and kerosene still remain affordable in nearby Gariahat market. Awed at this interest in the quotidian by one so august, N's mother is completely won over. N's father, who is painfully aware that Shaheb's effortless cosmopolitanism and grace are never to be his, puzzles over his interest in a Bengali housewife's shopping basket. The mystery is solved some years later:

> my father in the course of a business trip to Africa happened to spend a few days with ... the Shaheb ... There at an embassy dinner he overheard the Shaheb conducting precisely the same conversation, merely substituting mutton for eggs, with the wives of two third secretaries successively. Those are the right things to say to a Mrs Third Secretary, he explained to my father on the way home. They're new to the business you see, and it keeps their morale up: they like to know that H.E. himself takes an interest in their little difficulties.

> So you see, my father explained to my mother when he came back from his trip to Africa ... that day ... he had given me parity with a third secretary.
>
> (*The Shadow Lines*: 41)

When N's father achieved unexpected success and a promotion at his firm, Shaheb was momentarily at a loss to locate him on the protocol ladder. He eventually 'resolved the question of precedence by raising him to the rank of First Secretary (Commercial)' (p. 41). The Shaheb's precise metric for evaluating the worth of people in terms of the organization chart of the Indian Foreign Service recurs in less literal forms throughout *The Shadow Lines*, as various characters eye each other's worth in terms of their cosmopolitanism or provinciality.

A central thread running through *The Shadow Lines* is N's unrequited love for his second cousin Ila, who is the granddaughter of the Shaheb and is Tridib's niece. N's desire for Ila showcases the ambivalence, impossible longing, and desiring whiteness[7] that constitute the postcolonial. Ila's father was an economist with the UN and they had lived and travelled all over the world. Ila, who was the same age as N, had gone to a series of international schools, and would return every few years with her family to the ancestral home in Calcutta. She was bathed in an aura that was worldly, cosmopolitan and alluring. Ila brought the world into N's existence, and that world both animated his desire for his cousin and made her irresistible to him.

Ila, of course, consistently failed to live up to N's expectations of her worldliness or share his enthusiasm for the supposedly exotic places she travelled through. In one of their encounters, when both were in their early twenties, N recalls:

> I asked her then if she had any memory of the stratagems we used to employ to get Tridib to tell us about the year he had spent in London, during the war; of how we used to pore over his photographs when we could persuade him to bring them out; of how he used to tell us about the people in them, pointing out Mrs Price with May in her arms, or Alan Trewasen, her brother, with his bad arm hanging limply by his side, and her husband Snipe, who used to treat himself with Yeast-Vite tonic pills for his neuralgia and Bile beans for his blood, Doan's kidney pills for his backaches and Andrews Salt for his liver, Iglodine for his cuts and Mentholatum for his catarrh; Snipe, who had once sent Tridib to the chemists' shop on West End Lane to buy him a glue called Dentesive so that his dentures would not be shaken by the bombs.
>
> Yes, she said nodding, mildly puzzled by my insistence, she did have a faint recollection, but she could not exactly say she remembered.
>
> But how could you forget? I cried. She shrugged and arched her eyebrows in surprise and said: It was a long time ago – the real question is, how do *you* remember?
>
> (pp.19–20; emphasis in original)

For N, remembering worlds that were distant, exotic and yet achingly desired, was effortless. Each of the unremarkable commodities that dotted everyday life in the London of 1939 seemed to him to embody a richer, more plenitudinous and significant world. For Ila, those same worlds were proximate, mundane, lived-in and transited through – nothing more than an indifferent series of milestones on a seemingly endless journey. As N elaborates,

> I (never) succeeded in explaining to her that I could not forget because Tridib had given me worlds to travel in and he had given me eyes to see them with; she who had been traveling around the world since she was a child, could never understand what those hours in Tridib's room had meant to me, a boy who had never been more than a few hundred miles from Calcutta. I used to listen to her talking sometimes with her father and grandfather about the cafes in the Plaza Mayor in Madrid, or the crispness of the air in Cuzco, and I could see that those names which were to me a set of magical talismans because Tridib had pointed them out to me on his tattered old Bartholomew's Atlas, had for her a familiarity no less dull than the Lake had for me and my friends; the same tired intimacy that made us stop on our way back from the park in the evening and unbutton our shorts and aim our piss through the rusty wrought-iron railings.
>
> (p.20)

Ghosh articulates the postcolonial desire for other spaces with acuity:

> He (Tridib) said to me once that one could never know anything except through desire, real desire, which was not the same thing as greed or lust; a pure, painful and primitive desire, a longing for everything that was not in oneself, a torment of the flesh, that carried one beyond the limits of one's mind to other times, and other places, and even, if one was lucky, to a place where there was no border between oneself and one's image in the mirror.
>
> (p.29)

N slowly realizes that Ila was a misfit in the international schools she attended. The yearbook photographs invariably showed the stars of the school – tall, broad-shouldered, handsome, athletic boys with their arms around beautiful girls – at the centre, and Ila herself at the margins: bespectacled, dressed in grey, wearing her hair in braids, and looking studiously at the lens while clutching a book. Her visits to Calcutta were occasions to fashion a fictitious persona desired by handsome school mates as she moved gracefully through the international – a fiction that N was only too glad to co-construct with her. The reality was that race, class, colour, looks, Third World origins and Indian petit bourgeois aspirations constantly left Ila out of the circles of the bold and the beautiful. Her white 'friends' sometimes disdained to be seen with her, and her proficiency in a tongue other than her own left her ambivalent even about the one domain she excelled in – her studies. If N saw in Ila a cosmopolitan life lived in the limelight, about the only time Ila's life actually approximated that fiction was during her visits to Calcutta, and that too only in the eyes of her relatives, especially her cousin N.

The geocultural inequality between the postcolonial nation and the international, between developed and the supposedly still-developing and in-transition, between foreign and local, was transmuted into their relations as young cousins. On one occasion, as Ila's family arrives in Calcutta on one of their visits, the pre-teen N awkwardly clings onto his mother's sari, too shy to step forward and greet Ila.

> Why are you staring at her like that? my mother said. Go and talk to her.
> At that I shrank even further back.
> I don't know what the matter with him is, my mother said, complaining loudly, to everyone. He's been waiting for her for days. He talks about her every night: where's Ila? when is she coming? He won't go to sleep at night until I tell him, she's coming soon, don't worry ...
> Now listen to that, said Queen Victoria [the family's nickname for Ila's domineering mother], looking at me fondly. What a sweet little man. Do you hear that Ila? He asks about you every day.
> Ila smiled and turned her head away with a tiny shrug.
> I knew then, for certain, that she had not asked about me as I had about her.
> At that moment I hated my mother. For the first time in my life she had betrayed me. She had given me away, she had made public, then and forever, the inequality of our needs; she had given Ila the knowledge of her power and had left me defenceless; naked, in the face of that unthinkable, adult truth: that need is not transitive, that one may need without oneself being needed.
> (pp.43–44)

The ache of N's love for Ila would only increase with her indifference. And her indifference to him was not so much willed as it was inescapable.

Ila had her sights elsewhere – to find that person who would somehow move her from the grey edges of those yearbook photographs to their glowing centre. During her BA at the University of London, she falls for Nick – the grandson of the Trewasens – who had been a classmate of hers in middle school. Nick is a lazy layabout, back in London after being fired from his job as an accountant in a bank in Kuwait for embezzling funds. He too is awash in a postcolonial melancholia[8] of his own, and laments the passing of an era in which Britannia ruled the waves to one in which she barely counts for anything at all. Unaware of the enormous privilege that whiteness still bestows upon him, and the undeserved afterglow that still shines on Britons in far outposts such as Kuwait or Singapore or Hong Kong, Nick has a provinciality and incuriousness that is the special privilege of the latter-day dregs of empire. He sardonically observes at a Christmas Eve party in London in the presence of Ila and N:

> Now Grandpa Trewasen had a good time. How wonderful it must have been to go around the world like that: like some great Dickensian show on a stage. There's never been anything like it before and there'll never be anything like it again.

> He turned to me and shrugged, making a rueful face.
> And what do I get? he said. Bloody old Kuwait. That's what comes of being born too late.
>
> (p.108)

N's discovery that Ila is in love, or at any rate physically intimate, with Nick comes with a realization that this is a contest which he, by far the better man, will always lose. Ila's desire for an unattainable whiteness can never be sated by anything N can offer. He is, in fact, all that she is seeking to distance herself from. Horrified by the patriarchy and dual standards of Indian society, Ila cannot find herself at home in Calcutta. Yet, marked as an outsider in the West, she cannot find her feet there either. A disastrous marriage to Nick follows – one in which she can disparage his utter ineptness in a world requiring hustle and enterprise, and he can exact a daily revenge by sleeping with every Third World woman he can lay his hands on in London. For both Ila and Nick, the nation is a hollowed-out space they had sought to fill with hope and redemption through an elsewhere, the international. Nothing there or here can quite match the voracity of their needs – setting them up for the drudgery of lives lived out of place and time.

Ghosh expresses the sanguinary nature of nationalism through the unlikely character of N's grandmother. She had come of age politically during the era of the anti-colonial nationalist movement against the British and had idolized the so-called Bengal terrorists. These youth were mostly from educated middle-class and upper-caste backgrounds and believed an armed uprising against the British was the only legitimate, that is, manly, way of securing independence. Her nationalism had been forged in the crucible of the uncompromising and self-sacrificing idealism of Jugantar and Anushilan, and she had little patience with the woggish pretensions of Shaheb and his granddaughter Ila. She sensed N had a soft corner for Ila and intuited as well the reasons for this – that it must have had something to do with Ila's location in the realm of the international and the cosmopolitan. On one occasion N returned to Calcutta during a break in term at his college in Delhi to find his grandmother on her deathbed, surrounded by IV-tubes, bedpans, oxygen cylinders and the like. As they conversed, N recounted to his grandmother the racism and exclusion that Ila had experienced growing up, and still endured in London. His grandmother spat:

> But she shouldn't *be* there [England] …. Ila has no right to live there … She doesn't belong there. It took those people a long time to build that country: hundreds of years, years and years of war and blood-shed. Everyone who lives there has earned the right to be there with blood: with their brother's blood and their father's blood and their son's blood. They know they're a nation because they've drawn their borders with blood. Hasn't Maya told you how regimental flags hang in all their cathedrals and how all their churches are lined with memorials to men who died in wars, all around the world? War is their religion. That's what it takes to make a country. Once that happens

people forget they were born this or that, Muslim or Hindu, Bengali or Punjabi: they become a family born of the same pool of blood. That is what *you* have to achieve for India, don't you see?

(pp.77–78; emphasis in original).

N realizes dismissing his grandmother's rant will not do: there is too much there that he shares and empathizes with – the mixture of emotions, of love and hate, of self-hate and self-love, the redemptive nature of violence against one's oppressors, and the annealing power of violence upon one's own, in the making of national communities. He knows fully that his grandmother cannot be dismissed as a simple-minded nationalist. She

> was only a modern middle-class woman – though not wholly, for she would not permit herself the self-deceptions that make up the fantasy world of that kind of person. All she wanted was a middle-class life in which, like the middle-classes of the world over, she would thrive believing in the unity of nationhood and territory, of self-respect and national power: that was all she wanted – a modern middle-class life, a small thing that history had denied her in its fullness and for which she could never forgive it.
>
> (p.78) [9]

His grandmother's quest for an unremarkable and just-so way of being, an unalienated and comfortable self, is in many ways the quest of nearly all the characters in *The Shadow Lines*. Each of them tries and fails in their own way to repair the sense of injury that cannot be named because it predates their very entry into this world.

When the postcolonial reaches the international, s/he finds that the remembered and anticipated space of one's mind is vastly more hospitable and interesting than the reality. For N, Tridib's London of 1939 on the eve of war would ever be a far more interesting and alluring place than the one he actually encountered many decades later. As he thought, 'I wanted to know England not as *I* saw her, but in her finest hour – every place chooses its own and to me it did not seem an accident that England had chosen hers in a war' (p.57, emphasis in original). For Nick, home had become a reminder of failure – of his nation and of himself. If Ila felt out of place, he felt out of time. N's grandmother's dying rant was suffused with anger at the distance that still separated her milieu from arrival as a nation, and his various friends and relatives struggled to find the peace that must come with an unalienated sense of being. And so it went for each of them: injured selves oscillating between the home and the world, the national and the international, vainly looking for that moment when they could go through the looking-glass, and finally reunite with the split self staring back at them.

The God of Small Things and the life-world of the elsewhere

As those familiar with Arundhati Roy's *The God of Small Things*[10] know, a crucial turning point in the novel is the arrival into Cochin and Ayemenem of Sophie, the first cousin of the twins Estha and Rahel, and her mother Margaret in December 1969. Margaret is English and the ex-wife of Chacko, the twins' maternal uncle, and has come with Sophie to India from London to get over the grief of a recent tragedy, the death of her second husband, that is, Sophie's stepfather. A few days after their arrival, the three young cousins – Sophie, Estha and Rahel – steal a boat and row into the strong currents of Ayemenem River where it capsizes, drowning Sophie. The twins survive, but they and their single mother Ammu (Chacko's sister) are blamed for the horrific accident. Their lives disintegrate after this event: the twins are separated from each other and from their mother, with Estha being 'returned' to his alcoholic father on a faraway tea plantation in north-eastern India, Ammu dying a few years later of illness and heartbreak, and Rahel (through whose eyes the whole novel unfolds) careening from one unsuccessful career or relationship to another. The pivotal moment in the novel is evocatively described by Roy as 'the kind of time in the life of a family when something happens to nudge its hidden morality from its resting place and make it bubble to the surface and float for a while. In clear view. For everyone to see' (p.35).

The scene I want to focus on is the one where Chacko, Ammu, the twins and the spinster aunt Baby Kochamma are travelling by car from Ayemenem to Cochin airport to receive Sophie and her mother. The previous week had been hard on the feisty twins as everything they did was vetted through 'what will Sophie Mol think?' and found seriously deficient. They were fined every time they slipped back into their mother tongue Malayalam and made to write 'I will always speak in English' a hundred times under Baby Kochamma's strict watch. They practised their English pronunciation and were forced to recite verses of poetry in anticipation of amusing their foreign cousin.

At the airport, Roy lays out an assemblage of ethnicity and provinciality that distinguishes the twins' family and their cosmopolitanism from the Kerala-India that surrounds them.

> When Sophie Mol's plane appeared in the skyblue Bombay-Cochin sky, the crowd pushed against the iron railing to see more of everything.
>
> The Arrivals Lounge was a press of love and eagerness, because the Bombay-Cochin flight was the flight that all the Foreign Returnees came home on.
>
> Their families had come to meet them. From all over Kerala. On long bus journeys. From Ranni, from Kumiti, from Vizhinjam, from Uzhavoor. Some of them had camped at the airport overnight, and had brought their food with them. And tapioca chips and chakka velaichathu for the way back.
>
> They were all there – the deaf ammoomas, the cantankerous, arthritic appoopans, the pining wives, scheming uncles, children with the runs. The fiancées to be reassessed. The teacher's husband still waiting for his Saudi visa. The teacher's husband's sisters waiting for their dowries. The wire-bender's pregnant wife.
>
> 'Mostly sweeper class,' Baby Kochamma said grimly, and looked away …

> 'Don't forget that you are Ambassadors of India,' Baby Kochamma told Rahel and Estha. 'You're going to form their First Impression of your country.'
>
> (*The God of Small Things*: 138)

In Roy's rendition, even as Rahel and family 'English' themselves in anticipation of Sophie's arrival, the proletarian and petit bourgeois Indians returning from abroad were doing their own best to hang on to the aura of foreignness, and viewing their former (and future) selves through alien eyes:

> And there they were, the Foreign Returnees, in wash'n'wear suits and rainbow sunglasses. With an end to grinding poverty in their Aristocrat suitcases. With cement roofs for their thatched houses, and geysers for their parents' bathrooms. With sewage systems and septic tanks. Maxis and high heels. Puff sleeves and lipstick. Mixy-grinders and automatic flashes for their cameras. With keys to count, and cupboards to lock. With a hunger for kappa and meen vevichathu that they hadn't eaten for so long. With love and a lick of shame that their families who had come to meet them were so ... so ... gawkish. Look at the way they dressed! Surely they had more suitable airport wear! Why did Malayalees have such awful teeth?
> And the airport itself! More like the local bus depot! The birdshit on the building! Oh the spitstains...! Oho! Going to the dogs India is.
>
> (p.140)

Commodities stratify the different classes in this scene at the airport. 'They' will return from the Gulf with the bric-a-brac of polyester suits, rainbow sunglasses and mixy-grinders while 'we' return with Oxbridge degrees, propah accents and cultural capital. The Fanon-esque dance of alienation from self continues as Baby Kochamma suddenly begins to speak with an English accent and feigns a familiarity with Shakespeare to endear herself to the befuddled Sophie and distance herself from the 'sweeper class'. The twins refuse to perform their much-rehearsed lines for the benefit of their cousin and her mother. A combination of youthful recalcitrance, a keen sense of exactly where the jugular of pretentious elders lay, and panicked stage fright combine to render them alternately mute and rude. Rahel wraps herself in the dirty curtains of the Cochin airport's lounge and refuses to come out to greet her English relatives by her uncle's ex-marriage. All that is visible of her are her Bata sandals.

Eventually, when Ammu corners the twins and scolds them for their behaviour, and for disobeying her in public, what she has to say is critical for the eccentric locus of enunciation that characterizes the postcolonial.

> 'And the other thing, Rahel,' Ammu said, 'I think it's high time that you learned the difference between CLEAN and DIRTY. Especially in this country.' Ambassador Rahel looked down.
>
> (p.149)

Ammu, Rahel and Estha had never left India. What on earth could the qualifier 'especially in this country' then refer to? 'Especially in this country' directed at a seven-year-old girl is an admonition with an uncanny prolepsis into the future: as long as you are here, you will not drape yourself in dirty curtains in airport lounges. Your 'here-ness' is possibly temporary and, ideally, if all goes well, your future trajectory and travels will include other airports – non-Indian, international airports – with clean curtains and drapes that you will have no reason to wrap yourself in. But here and now, in this postcolonial space, this anteroom of history, this waiting lounge for a launch into the realm of the international, you ought to know how to comport yourself.

Roy completes the irony in this episode by ending it with: 'Ambassador Rahel looked down.' The postcolonial ambassadorial class is clearly not so much a *representative* of India to the world as it is a sign to the world that some Indians' cosmopolitanism and culture are at least an equal to the best to be found in the West.

Lest I give the impression that the postcolonial as the ante-space of the international occurs only in what one might archaically call the 'Third World', Roy's novel depicts all too well the Third World within the first. When Margaret and Chacko first meet, he is the exotic Rhodes Scholar at Oxford from faraway India, and she is a dull-as-ditchwater waitress in a linoleum-floored restaurant in a university town where the likes of her could never afford – financially, culturally or socially – to ever enter the university.

> She had always thought of herself as a somewhat uninteresting, thick-waisted, thick-ankled girl. Not bad looking. Not special. But when she was with Chacko, old limits were pushed back. Horizons expanded.
>
> She had never before met a man who spoke of the world, of what it was, and how it came to be, or what he thought would become of it – in the way in which other men she knew discussed their jobs, their friends or their weekends at the beach. Being with Chacko made Margaret feel as though her soul had escaped from the narrow confines of her island country into the vast, extravagant spaces of his. He made her feel as though the world belonged to them.
>
> (p.245)

Chacko and Margaret become sites for projecting desires for an other, a foreign, and an international. Inevitably, their brief marriage collapses as they realize that reality is far too mundane to bear the weight of such anticipation. The desired realm of the international works in Roy's novel to delineate love between Chacko and Margaret, as well as occasions the reasons for their falling out of it.

Roy's book is a tragedy in the classic sense of the term – the destruction that awaits many of its main characters is foretold and they are dimly aware of their fates and yet act in ways that do not/will not deflect that outcome. When Ammu (the separated single mother from an upper-caste family) and Velutha (the lower-caste carpenter) consummate a love that goes back to their childhood, they violate societal taboos that they surely knew would evoke a violent death for him and complete ostracism for her. They proceed to do so. Roy's prose works exceptionally hard to depict the incredible savagery and barbarism with which Velutha is killed by the police, in cahoots with the local communist party apparatchik. She lovingly and glowingly etches his beautiful and muscled body throughout the novel, making clear that his strength was hewn from everyday tasks like carpentry and fishing. The mixture of gentleness and power with which he makes love to Ammu is as alien to the flaccid physiques of the likes of Chacko or Ammu's ex-husband as one can imagine.

Yet, one cannot help but feel that the excessive attention to the musculature and rugged physical beauty of Velutha is a compensation by Roy for her (and our) inability to get into his mind in the way she is able to do for the other characters of the novel. The insight with which she can describe Ammu's love for Velutha is not matched by anything similar to describe his feelings for her. Despite Roy's strenuous efforts (all the more striking in a novel staggering for the ease and flow of its prose), when he meets his violent denouement, what preoccupies us is the impending destruction of the precarious world that Ammu, Rahel and Estha had survived in until then and now must surely be destroyed. The incredible pathos the novel induces centres less on Velutha's horrible fate and more on the spiralling and slowly drawn out tragedy that engulfs Ammu, Rahel, Estha and their wonderfully cosmopolitan yet precarious Indian middle-class world. Unlike Ghosh, whose cast of characters in *The Shadow Lines* does not include anyone who might be termed 'subaltern', Roy writes Velutha into the novel. It is perhaps less a critique of her prose that we are unable to adequately get into Velutha's mind and therefore be suitably outraged at the circumstances of his murder – and more an indictment of the cleft self and nation that is the postcolonial condition that we are unable to do so.

Reliving the international in north-eastern India

Kiran Desai's *The Inheritance of Loss*[11] is set in the sleepy and bucolic hillstation of Kalimpong in north-eastern India even as that space begins its slide into ethnic insurgency and political turmoil in the 1980s. An interesting menagerie of characters animates the novel, each of them differently out of place and time. There is the ostensible anglophile Jemubhai, a retired judge of the Indian Civil Service (ICS) who had studied in England as a young man and now lived in a sprawling bungalow that is a relic of colonial times. Jemubhai had been resolutely Gujarati and never spoke or interacted with anyone while studying in England, and became staunchly English once he returned to serve in India. Two ageing Bengali sisters – Noni and Lola – lived in a picturesque cottage nearby and tried hard to lead a life straight out of the English version of *Town and Country* magazine. Their neighbours were Father Booty and Uncle Potty – the former a Swiss missionary who had lost the faith and made Kalimpong his home for over thirty years now, and the latter a Colonel Blimp-ish character. The judge's ageing cook had a son, Biju, who worked as an illegal alien in New York City, desperately trying to earn enough to escape up the class ladder back home. The story is mostly told through the eyes of sixteen-year-old Sai, Jemubhai's only granddaughter, whose parents are killed in an accident and who is suddenly and unpleasantly foisted upon him as a ward.

Jemubhai hangs on to his anglophilia although every moment of his actual life in England was torture. His English back then was incomprehensible, and his rural and lower-class origins rendered him a comical outsider. In his misanthropic retirement in Kalimpong, he is often 'grumpy because the heat reminded him of his nationality'. (p.70). Jemubhai constantly lives and relives the insults of his brief stint in England while preparing for exams to enter the ICS. Although his written performance had been stellar, the inadequacies of his class origins caught up with him during the interviews. Asked to recite a poem, he chose Scott's *Lochinvar* but declaimed it in what sounded like Gujarati to the Englishmen evaluating him. They could barely contain their guffaws. Jemubhai eventually squeaks into the ICS and returns home in triumph, but has been hollowed out by the experience.

More than fifty years later, at dinner with his granddaughter Sai and her physics tutor (a young local lad named Gyan), the shame of it all suddenly rises within him like bile. Gyan had just amateurishly recited a poem by Tagore in response to Jemubhai's inquiry as to what, besides physics, interested him. As Gyan finishes his recital, Jemubhai responds with an anger that is as inexplicable as it is excessive. We soon realize that it has nothing to do with Gyan but with the *Lochinvar* episode from his own past, one that still brought a flush of shame to Jemubhai's cheeks. Gyan's clumsy rendition of Tagore's poem brought back all the pain and self-hate of that distant day of his interview to Jemubhai.

> The Judge shook himself. 'Damn fool,' he said aloud, pushed his chair back, stood up, brought his fork and knife down in devastating judgment upon himself and left the table. His strength, that mental steel, was weakening. His memory seemed triggered by the tiniest thing – Gyan's unease, his reciting that absurd poem ... Soon all the judge had worked so hard to separate would soften and envelop him in his nightmare, and the barrier between this life and eternity would, in the end, no doubt, be just another such failing construct.
> (p.112)

The blurring of identities in Jemubhai's mind is reflected in the uncertainty of the pronouns in the above quote. Who is the 'damn fool'? Is it the Jemubhai of now, or is it the young Jemubhai aspiring to the Civil Service, or is it Gyan? More improbably, is the 'damn fool' a reference to one of his supercilious white interviewers? Who was the 'he' that recited the absurd poem: Jemubhai or Gyan? Time past and time present are mixed inextricably, and the shame of remembered humiliations comes to suffuse Jemubhai's contemporary encounters. He is living in and trying to settle scores on past battles long after most of his antagonists have left this world. As often with a postcolonial, he is preoccupied in twin senses of the term: he is both out of place and time, living anywhere but in the present; and

138 *Performance*

preoccupied in the sense that his mind is already filled and occupied with obsessions of past encounters, humiliations and episodes.

Five decades after Jemubhai's return to India, after a stay of perhaps no more than a year or two in England, it seemed as if the quantitative disparity between the lengths of stay in the two countries was utterly irrelevant. For Jemubhai's mental and physical life-world seemed one constant, ever-losing and ever-obsessive battle to set right the insults, isolation and utter misery of those months in England. His treatment of his hapless young wife (fixed for him by an arranged marriage) is beyond cruel. The humiliations of the outside world get refracted into the domestic space of the nuclear family, and Jemubhai's wife comes to bear the burden of events unbeknownst to her. Every act of ineptness on her part (in the role of an ICS officer's wife) was a reminder to Jemubhai of his own searing experience in England – and his lashing out at her is little more than displaced self-flagellation for his own prior inadequacies.

As the peace and beauty of Kalimpong, so evocative of the English countryside to its ensemble of characters (most of whom had never been to England), begins to unravel with the ethnic insurgency, Noni and Lola's cottage and its gardens come to be occupied by the militants. They set up camp, shit on the lawns, bathe in the fountains and string their underwear up to dry on the trellises of their lovely gardens. As the ageing sisters watch their world crumble, and the walls that separated them from 'India' fall before their eyes, they begin to realize the artifice of their lives.

> Noni returned to sit on the dragon cushions on the sofa. Oh, they had been wrong. The real place had evaded them. The two of them had been fools feeling they were doing something exciting just by occupying this picturesque cottage, by seducing themselves with those old travel books in the library, searching for a certain angled light with which to romance themselves, to locate what had been conjured only as a tale to tell before the Royal Geographic Society, when the author returned to give a talk accompanied by sherry and a scrolled certificate of honor prized with gold for an exploration of the far Himalayan kingdoms – but far from what? Exotic to whom? It was the center for the sisters, but they had never treated it as such.
>
> Parallel lives were being led by those … for whom there was no such doubleness or self-consciousness, while Lola and Noni indulged themselves in the pretense of it being a daily fight to keep up civilization in this place of towering, flickering green. They maintained their camping supplies, their flashlights, mosquito netting, raincoats, hot water bottles, brandy, radio, first-aid kit, Swiss army knife, book on poisonous snakes. These objects were talismans imbued with the task of transforming reality into something otherwise, supplies manufactured by a world that equated them with courage. But, really, they were equivalent to cowardice.
>
> (pp.247–8)

The centrality of things, commodities, and the social worlds they embodied, comes through: for Noni and Lola, the Swiss Army knife and the hot-water bottles allow them the fantasy of camping in the Lake District or in the northern reaches of Scotland whilst still living in Kalimpong. They are objects animated by lives lived elsewhere.

If the 'elsewhere' for Jemubhai and the sisters proved difficult to either forget or to incarnate, Biju, the illegal alien in New York City, was finding that other than Bollywood songs and movies – in other words, precisely that which the likes of Jemubhai held in contempt – there was little to commend India in the eyes of his fellow illegal aliens. Biju is himself an equal-opportunity-hater, and especially detests Muslims and the dark-skinned while revering the whites. Biju's education into the status of his nation in the subterranean world of New York's illegal labourers is swift:

> In Tanzania, if they could, they would throw them out like they did in Uganda.
> In Madagascar, if they could, they would throw them out.
> In Nigeria, if they could, they would throw them out.
> In Fiji, if they could, they would throw them out.
> In China, they hate them.
> In Hong Kong.
> In Germany.
> In Italy.
> In Japan.
> In Guam.
> In Singapore.
> Burma.
> South Africa.
> They don't like them.
> In Guadeloupe – they love us there?
> No.
>
> (p.173)

Meanwhile, Sai and Gyan are distanced from each other by class, ethnicity and their degrees of separation from the desired international. Like the doomed marriage of Chacko and Margaret in Roy's novel, their brief romance collapses as Gyan discovers his own ethnicity and Sai's alienness in the north-east as the insurgency grows, and Sai discovers the poverty and provinciality of Gyan's life. While it is precisely such 'mystery' that constituted their desire for each other in the first place, it rapidly becomes the reason for their falling out of love in the second. As Desai works it out in a compelling passage, Gyan contemplates betraying the Judge and his granddaughter Sai and enlisting on the side of the ethnic insurgents:

> Why should he not betray Sai? She who could speak no language but English and pidgin Hindi, she who could not converse with anyone outside her tiny social stratum. She who could not eat with her own hands; could not squat down on the ground on her haunches to wait for a bus; who had never been to

a temple but for architectural interest; never chewed a paan and had not tried most sweets in the mithaishop, for they made her retch; she who had left a Bollywood film so exhausted from emotional wear and tear that she walked home like a sick person and lay in pieces on the sofa; she who thought it vulgar to put oil in your hair and used chapter to clean her bottom; felt happier with so-called English vegetables, snap peas, French beans, spring onions, and feared – *feared* – loki, tinda, kathal, kaddu, patrel, and the local saag in the market.

Eating together they had always felt embarrassed – he, unsettled by her finickiness and her curbed enjoyment, and she, revolted by his energy and his fingers working the dal, his slurps and smacks. The judge ate even his chapattis, his puris and parathas with knife and fork. Insisted that Sai, in his presence, do the same.

Still Gyan was absolutely sure that she was proud of her behavior; masqueraded it about as shame at her lack of Indianness, maybe, but it marked her status. Oh yes, it allowed her that perverse luxury, the titillation of putting yourself down, criticizing yourself and having the opposite happen – you did not fall, you mystically rose.

(pp.176–7)

The Inheritance of Loss ends with a desolateness that is hard and incredibly heartless. Biju has endeared himself to the reader by his feistiness and his wildly irreverent sense of humour even while being put upon by just about everyone he encounters in New York. Riven by guilt about having left behind his father and realizing that the pot of gold at the end of the American rainbow was a mirage, he decides to come back home to Kalimpong. He gathers up all his precious savings and after spending a fair amount on commodities similar to that of the returning Gulf labourers at Cochin airport in Roy's novel, he tucks the bulk of the money beneath the insoles of his shoes.

As Biju completes a complicated multi-leg trip back home, he falls victim to the same ethnic insurgency movement that has blighted the lives of Noni, Lola and all the rest. The militants strip him of all his money, his baggage, and literally every stitch of clothing on his body including his foreign underwear. In his desperation, Biju can find only a bedraggled pink nightgown cast away by someone. In the gloam of rapidly falling night in Kalimpong, his figure approaches the bungalow of Jemubhai where his father still toils but with hope that his son is going to make it in faraway New York and rescue him from this drudgery any day now. Desai spares us the anguish of their reunion as the novel ends with Biju's pink-nightie-clad apparition nearing the bungalow's gates. I wonder if it's because the utter desolation of that scene is beyond her imagination to write – and ours to comprehend. As with Velutha's murder in Roy's novel, the distribution of the sensible in their subaltern world is closed to us: whether or not the subaltern can speak has always seemed to me less important than the fact that if they did, as they surely do, we would be amongst the last to understand. 'Our' novels, like 'our' nations, are literally closed books to them.

Conclusion

Amidst the tortured journeys of the various characters in *The Shadow Lines*, *The God of Small Things* and *The Inheritance of Loss*, to me, N's stands out for the growing wisdom with which he understands the dialectic of movement between inside and outside, the home and the world, one's own culture and nation and the desired space of the foreign and international, and the fact of their irresolution. His realization that there was no destination to be reached, no place of overcoming, seems to contain in it not the possibility of resolution or redemption, but that of living with and living through. His ideas of selfhood had always been mediated through the outside, there had never been any prelapsarian purity from which he emerged and to which he could possibly return.

> I thought of how much they all wanted to be free; how they went mad wanting their freedom; I began to wonder whether it was I that was mad because I was happy to be bound: whether I was alone in knowing that I could not live without the clamour of the voices within me.
>
> (p.89)

I am not suggesting that Ghosh offers a way out of postcolonial melancholia or narcissism. On the contrary I am suggesting that he invites us to see ourselves in such a distribution of the sensible, and mines it for all it has to offer by way of insight into who we are and how we are formed by our desires for elsewheres, while resisting the quest for that moment of overcoming, or closure, or redemption.

The troubling class distinctions, and delineations between the cosmopolitan and the vernacular, that inhabit all these novels are also the delineations that underlie our attachment to some of the characters and our relative indifference to the pain and violence visited on some others, or our incapacity to describe it with something bordering empathy or authenticity. What makes fiction intriguing, to me at any rate, is that these authors seem to hew to a greater responsibility to literature understood as a realistic or authentic distribution of the sensible than as a moralistic act of overcoming. Ghosh evades the depiction of the inner world of the subaltern because none of the characters in *The Shadow Lines* falls into that category; Desai comes to the brink of such an encounter, as we saw in the final scene of the novel, but retracts; Roy forges forward but her description of the mental landscape of Velutha sounds thin in comparison with that of Rahel or others. These authors' inability or unwillingness to redistribute the sensible of their milieu to include the subaltern is matched by 'our' inability to empathize with their depictions of subaltern tragedy beyond a point. The postcolonial world remains as riven and serrated as ever, and the promise of national becoming or arrival remains as distant as ever.

The partial and class-riven construction of the nation in these novels contrasts with the method of IR which is to freeze its analytical units so that we can better understand them in their immobile facticity, and their assumed and unalienated totality.

The nation is viewed as an ontological entity within IR discourse, one that is formed and constituted prior to the encounter. From that vantage, IR becomes the actions of such prefabricated entities in an anarchic milieu. Such a form of abstraction is analytically explicable given that the main purpose of IR discourse as currently constituted is to energize the quest for an unattainable security. What these postcolonial novels sensitize us to is the fact that nations are not comprehensible in their ontic solidity but rather in their performative fragility. The nation does not envelop all within its realm, not in the postcolony and not in the 'West'. It is a fiction, a structure of feeling that is incomplete in its sway but real in the ways it hierarchizes various groups, classes, ethnicities and other rubrics in terms of their affiliation with or distance from such an idea. Postcolonial novels liquefy the nation; they follow the injunction that one can understand concepts only in their mobility, their deployment, their performativity, their life, in other words. The nation is lived as much in mental landscapes as it is on the ground – in the rules and regimes of security, development, travel, emigration, war, diplomacy and trade. Neither is more important nor less real than the other: reminding ourselves of that may be a good thing to do.

Notes

1 I thank Cheryl Naruse, Kirin Narayan, Angharad Closs-Stephens, Sanjay Seth, audiences at the International Studies Association meetings and the English Department at the University of Hawai'i at Manoa for their generous and insightful comments on previous drafts of this chapter.
2 See Gayatri Chakravorty-Spivak, *A Critique of Postcolonial Reason: toward a history of the vanishing present* (Cambridge, MA: Harvard University Press 1999), 191 for an elaboration of the idea of a 'culture of imperialism'. I have discussed Spivak and the constitution of postcolonial middle classes in terms of their facility with the culture of imperialism in my *Globalization and Postcolonialism: hegemony and resistance in the 21st century* (Lanham, MD: Rowman and Littlefield 2009), 98–104.
3 Jacques Rancière, *The Politics of Aesthetics: the distribution of the sensible*, trans. Gabriel Rockhill (London: Continuum 2004).
4 I deliberately use the term 'IR discourse' instead of phrases like 'IR theory' or 'IR literature' or even just 'IR' to highlight the power of social constructions of the worlds we inhabit. For more on this distinction between 'discourse' and 'description/narrative/theory' see my 'Race, Amnesia, and the Education of International Relations', *Alternatives*, 26 (2001), 401–24.
5 Pierre Bourdieu, 'Structures, Habitus, Power', in his *Outline of a Theory of Practice*, trans. Richard Nice (Cambridge, UK: Cambridge University Press 1977), 167.
6 Amitav Ghosh, *The Shadow Lines* (Delhi: Ravi Dayal 1988).
7 Kalpana Seshadri-Crooks has persuasively argued that the postcolonial desire for whiteness is not merely epidermal, though one should never underestimate the power of that longing. Rather, 'whiteness' signifies a combination of attributes: economic, cultural, symbolic, racial and social capital; a certain ease of disposition as the world seems to be made for one's travels; an absence of alienation or of split selves as part of one's habitus. From a postcolonial standpoint, to desire whiteness is to desire to be seen as within, constitutive of, and constituted by, the culture of imperialism without the tethered shadow of self-doubt. See Seshadri-Crooks, *Desiring Whiteness: a Lacanian analysis of race* (London: Routledge 2000).

8 See Paul Gilroy, *Postcolonial Melancholia* (New York: Columbia University Press 2005) for a meditation on how contemporary England is in many ways a place trapped in nostalgia for its imperial past and unable to reconcile itself to a multiracial present.
9 I cannot elaborate on Ghosh's use of the term 'middle class' here for reasons of space. I have done so at some length in two recent essays of mine, however: see 'The Social Life of a Bomb: India and the Ontology of an "Overpopulated" Society', in Itty Abraham (ed.), *South Asian Cultures of the Bomb: Atomic Publics and the State in India and Pakistan* (Bloomington: Indiana University Press 2009), 68–88 and 'The Bomb, Biography, and the Indian Middle Class', *Economic and Political Weekly*, XLI: 23 (10 June 2006), 2327–31, Mumbai, India.
10 Arundhati Roy, *The God of Small Things* (New York: Random House 1997).
11 Kiran Desai, *The Inheritance of Loss* (New York: Grove Press 2006).

8 The 'Bandung impulse' and international relations

Mustapha Kamal Pasha

> We drove past the conference building and saw the flags of twenty-nine participating nations of Asia and Africa billowing lazily in the weak wind; already streets were packed with crowds and their black and yellow and brown faces looked eagerly at each passing car ... it was the first time in their downtrodden lives that they'd seen so many of their color, race and nationality arrayed in such aspects of power, their men keeping order, their Asia and their Africa in control of their destinies. Imperialism was dead here, and as long as they could maintain their unity, organize and conduct international conferences, there would be no return to imperialism.
>
> Wright, *The Color Curtain*

Any historical account, Michel-Rolph Trouillot proposes in *Silencing the Past*,[1] is 'a particular bundle of silences' produced by power. A principal consequence of the process of *silencing* is the evacuation of others from history. Trouillot's perceptive undoing of conventional historiography casts an uncanny presence on International Relations (IR), a discipline remarkably parochial in its assumed promise to capture the world. Despite many reflexive 'turns' to expand its post-Westphalian horizon, to inject multivocality, or to embrace alternative methodologies, IR has remained a soundly Euro-American intellectual and political enterprise.[2] The cultural substratum of IR gets concealed in its claim of universality.

To contextualize, disciplinary IR has shown remarkable heterogeneity, reflexivity and flux in recent years. From its institutionalization as an autonomous field in Western social science (bearing an elective affinity with the consolidation of US hegemony at the end of the Second World War) to growing multivocality (linked to a multidimensional crisis of that hegemony) at the dawn of the new century, IR has seen a radical transformation. Against the backdrop of the various 'turns' (linguistic, aesthetic, multicultural, affective), neither the self-evident verities of Realism (Classical and Structural) seem sustainable, nor the hubris of a self-congratulatory Liberalism. The arrival of 'terrible simplifiers'[3] in catchphrases like the 'end of history'[4] or the 'clash of civilizations'[5] has not curtailed the revolt against orthodoxy, allowing IR to become sensitized to multiple vernaculars (feminist, poststructuralist, postcolonial). The seeming reflexivity of IR, however, is not *sui generis*; it bears close affinity to mutations of the worlds it seeks to comprehend. These mutations are reflected in the new vocabulary that readily circulates in both the academy and popular consciousness. Growing multivocality within the discipline gives IR a picture of malleability and self-learning. Those exercising firm attachments to particular vernaculars can celebrate, not only for effectively gaining greater representation, albeit in the name of marginality, subalternity or difference, but in the belief that claims of marginality and difference in themselves *constitute* politics. Multivocality, however, rests on brittle foundations. Despite the adoption of multiple languages within IR to interpret the world, its horizon remains trapped within the antinomies of tacit background assumptions confirming the hegemony of the West.

Broadly speaking, IR is structured around two seemingly opposing invented traditions helping to shape the fiction of continuity, coherence and self-identity for the field. The first follows a civilizational storyline dotted with epochal moments of transcendence – stretching from a pre-Westphalian world of religious wars and Providence to the promised modern land of secular reason and sovereignty. This is a familiar chronicle centred on the myth of Westphalia and the world conjured up in its name. On this myth, IR is a declaration of independence from religious hegemony and 'the expansion of international society'[6] in space and time. Underwriting both processes is the liberal political order realized as the distinctive achievement of Western civilization. IR, however, is not merely an account of the world, but a normative ideal presented for emulation to those 'outside' international society.

The second narrative presents a less cheerful picture of the international, a world characterized by anarchy, fear, violence and insecurity, on the one side, and order, freedom, peace and security on the other. Only a part of humanity, the story goes, can taste the fruits of orderly governance, prosperity and freedom; the rest is condemned to perpetual states of insecurity or war. Built on a fictionalized Hobbesian tale of the state of nature, the principal task of IR on this assignment is to secure order, which is the chief burden for civilization. History is essentially a narrative of civilizing those who are unable to procreate orderliness and, as an effect, powerless to engender material prosperity.

In essence, these apparently competing narratives are two parts of the same story, assembled in relation to an 'outside' that resists civilization, a world irremediably attached to irrational passion, unable and unwilling to enter international society. The two narratives are connected with a 'conventional developmental understanding of humanity'.[7] (Both presume the threshold of a modernity that divides the past from the present, the West from the Rest.) Once the colonial, now the postcolonial, this 'outside' remains peripheral to IR's spatio-temporal gaze. Yet, without this exterior, IR has no self-image. Only from different sites and other locales do other accounts become intelligible. Hence, the story of the rise of the West is also the story of coloniality; civilization that of erasure; and decolonization, not as 'expansion', but the restructuring of international society.

The modern 'outside' of the international is the Third World; its history largely silenced in the larger compendium featuring Western civilization. Predictably, the universal storyline of international history congeals principally Euro-American pathologies; only *their* staging into the global public sphere provides content and meaning to the flow of time. The silencing of the postcolonial non-West is materialized quite expressively in the subsumption of decolonizing moments under the civilizing tropes of either the 'expansion of international society'; or modernization and development; or state-building and democratization. Unable to produce its own futures, the postcolonial world can merely mimic political and economic forms already on offer. This normalized gaze is best illustrated in the fleeting memories of the Afro-Asian Conference held in Bandung, Indonesia in 1955, an event now firmly relegated to the distant regions of nostalgia. Like other epochal moments in a largely under-reported narrative of Afro-Asian political decolonization, Bandung can scarcely match the triumphal story of Western civilization. This essay revisits Bandung as a small exploration into the paradoxical link between the expansion of IR and the marginalization of postcolonial histories, and especially the silencing of decolonizing narratives. Despite its assumed openness to difference, the essay suggests, IR has failed to recognize decolonization as rupture. Instead, the political awakening of the ex-colonial world has been subsumed into an account of the socialization of newcomers into the established norms and practices of the international.

There are compelling reasons to accept socialization as a vital facet of connectivity across borders. Intersubjectivity produces compliance. The incorporation of those outside the international into History is an integral part of IR's autobiography. Equally salient is the willing acquiescence of postcolonial elites to the expectations of hegemony. The benefits of submission seem to outweigh those of dissent or deviance. Notwithstanding the lure of inclusion, however, socialization is also another name for silencing 'decolonial' possibilities. These possibilities still remain pertinent. The ascendancy and consolidation of neo-liberal orthodoxy on a global scale lends greater urgency to an exploration of the decolonial option. Bandung, I argue, encodes decolonial possibilities, albeit, with all the tensions and ambivalences associated with postcoloniality. For narrower purposes explored here, the Bandung impulse is a durable challenge to the provincial, if hegemonic, self-understanding of IR. To stress, hegemonic accounts see the Bandung Conference only as a subaltern facet of the international – anti-colonial discontent in the name of a formative 'Third World' – rather than as a *discontinuous* moment in the universal story recounted at the behest of IR. In interpreting Bandung, therefore, the hegemonic modern re-enactment of the international (or IR theory by another name) follows a well-known script: one of the formation, consolidation and expansion of civilized or Western society, a script in which Bandung appears as a cathartic anti-Western whimper, that merely confirms the marginality of the postcolonial world to IR. This is not the view from the margins,[8] but with the waning of Third Worldism, Bandung's significance as history has become increasingly questionable. Only as memory can it retrieve its historical salience.

Situating Bandung within the field of IR's subaltern histories is not without aporias. The postcolonial world does not have a separate, self-subsistent or monadic presence in world politics. Postcoloniality is a creation of hegemony. No aspect of the postcolonial world has remained untouched by the dialectic of colonial domination/subordination. Attempts to retrieve Bandung as Third World history can, therefore, merely reinforce established hierarchies. Released from the prison-house of History, however, the postcolonial world can seek other meanings or alternative futures. As memory of 'decoloniality',[9] Bandung can speak to the 'colonial' present—a racialized order of difference, asymmetry and exclusion. This essay explores the implications of this intuition. Specifically, it sees Bandung as a perpetual challenge to a normalized world order in which the questions of racial equality and inclusion of marginalized populations have been abandoned in favour of a fictitious totem pole of development. For that reason, revisiting Bandung is to provoke IR into examining its own assumptions concerning the constitution of international society or a yet-to-be-formed inclusive global political community.

Subaltern histories

> What they meant was simple: that the colonized world had now emerged to claim its space in world affairs, not just as an adjunct of the First or Second World, but as a player in its own right. Furthermore, the Bandung spirit was a refusal of both economic subordination and cultural suppression – two of the major policies of imperialism. The audacity of Bandung produced 'its own image.'[10]

From a 'decolonial'[11] perspective, Bandung remains a defining moment in twentieth-century international history, in vivid contrast to its marginalization in IR's self-accountings. Barring a few exceptions, the inaugural meeting of newly independent nations at Bandung has escaped any sustained engagement in Western IR scholarship. This is unsurprising against the backdrop of the field's filial attachments to a largely Anglo-American cartography. Extending Trouillot's language, IR is marked by both 'erasure and trivialization' in equal measure. The 'general silence' in IR emanates from 'the incapacity to express the unthinkable'[12] including the possibility (indeed actuality) of recently independent postcolonial nations forging emblematic unity. Bandung's symbolic message lies principally in repudiating the belief that 'The West' alone is the maker of history, the idea that 'the world has a permanent geographical center and a permanent periphery: an Inside and an Outside. Inside leads, Outside lags. Inside innovates, Outside imitates!'[13]

What is the relevance of Bandung? A milestone in the emergence of the Third World for those outside History, Bandung is often recognized in postcolonial circles as an event that brings common awareness of coloniality and its legacy; heightens the politics of Afro-Asian solidarity; and revives fleeting memories of the non-aligned movement – a non-hegemonic constellation of states seeking to be a part of international society, but *on their own terms*. On the face of it, Bandung is merely an acknowledgement of decolonization, as arrival and promise. A convention of delegations representing 29 independent and newly independent Asian and African countries was unlikely to revolutionize world politics. Conferences follow predictable pathways; they are rarely world-transforming happenings. Yet, in its audacity, as Prashad notes, Bandung produced an image that continues to persist. Its audacity lies in its unrealized promise of *perpetual decolonization*.

Bandung itself did not come out of a historical void. Colonial subjects had long recognized the importance of inverting hegemonic rituals to their advantage. Several Pan-African Congresses took place beginning in 1900: in particular, the 1911 Universal Races Congress in London, the League against Imperialism held in Brussels in 1927, and the two Pan-Asian People's Conferences held in Nagasaki (1926) and Shanghai (1927). Notably, the Asian Relations Conference, held in Delhi in 1947, set the stage for the Bandung meeting in 1955. These conferences served a twofold purpose: linking awareness of colonial subjection horizontally and raising consciousness of the ravages of colonialism in the metropolis. Bandung, however, presented a more self-confident picture in a complex global context, one that marked the political achievement of producing an alternative space for postcolonial nations unhinged from superpower rivalry. Significantly, though, from a postcolonial standpoint, Bandung underscored the dawn of a new era in world history, one marked by the irreversible march of decolonization. Yet, it also exposed the fissure between *de jure* and de facto decolonization.

From the vantage point of Third World romanticism, Bandung underscores the political possibility of non-alignment through 'Third World solidarity'.[14] In Bandung's shadow, the 'Third World' was no longer viewed as a pejorative term, but as a positive marker and virtue, a political alternative to colonialism and the hegemonic grasp of the two superpowers – the United States and the Soviet Union. With hindsight, Bandung becomes the progenitor of the Nonaligned Movement (NAM). In symbolic terms, however, Bandung helps relocate 'the darker nations'[15] within a racial economy of representation. Organized by intellectuals and leaders of colour, this is not insignificant in itself. The conference's five sponsors, Indonesia, India, Ceylon (Sri Lanka), Burma (Myanmar) and Pakistan all grew out of the colonial experience. The self-awareness that the conference was a 'coloured' affair was not far from the stated rhetoric of 'non-alignment'.

Bandung offered a new form of socialization based on equality and mutual respect, not 'the standard of civilization'. The Secretary General of the Bandung conference, Roselan Abdulghani, sums up this sentiment in untailored terms:

> The purpose of the Conference was 'to determine ... the standards and procedures of present-day international relations' and to contribute to 'the formulation and establishment of certain norms for the conduct of present-day international relations and the instruments for the practical application of these norms.'[16]

The 'universal' code of conduct reserved for certain nations was now available for diffusion among the newly independent countries. Bandung stressed a *normative* basis for the conduct of international relations between the great powers and the new nations themselves. The principle of sovereignty was not abandoned, but recast as the preferred source of preserving the political independence of weaker states. A major achievement of Bandung was to disallow ideology as a pretext to subvert sovereignty. Undergirding this feat was the acceptance of the principles of non-interference and diplomacy to advance state sovereignty. While deliberations at Bandung were never without controversy or intensity, the collective mood prevailing amongst the delegates mitigated against the advancement of parochial sentiment.

It would, however, be naïve to neglect the crooked course of decolonization, a key aspect of postcolonial global politics. Decolonization was never a straightforward movement from coloniality to postcoloniality. Multiple currents, often mutually incompatible, infused decolonization. Chakrabarty nicely captures the context in which the contradictory career of decolonization becomes explicable:

> Ideas regarding decolonization were dominated by two concerns. One was development. The other I will call 'dialogue'. Many anticolonial thinkers considered colonialism as something of a broken promise. European rule, it was said, promised modernization but did not deliver on it.[17]
>
> But there was also another side to decolonization that has received less scholarly attention. Anticolonial thinkers often devoted a great deal of time to the question of whether or how a global conversation of humanity would genuinely acknowledge cultural diversity without distributing such diversity over a hierarchical scale of civilization – that is to say, an urge toward cross-cultural dialogue without the baggage of imperialism. Let me call it the dialogical side of decolonization.[18]
>
> [Decolonization] was not a simple project of cultivating a sense of disengagement with the West. There was no reverse racism at work in Bandung. If anything, the aspiration for political and economic freedom that the Conference stood for entailed a long and troubled conversation with an imagined Europe or the West.[19]

Chakrabarty ably captures the indivisible structuring horizon of modernity *and* decolonization. However, within the institutional setting of the international and geopolitics afforded by the Cold War, the 'dreamers'[20] in Bandung faced special constraints: the desire to reconcile acceptance in the international community with a repudiation of the pitfalls of alignment with either of the two superpowers. Rival political pressures were working at the time of the conference. Chakrabarty, however, reads the decolonizing impulse operative at Bandung in fairly traditional terms. Undoubtedly, the discourse and politics of decolonization in the nations that met in Bandung often displayed an uncritical emphasis on modernization. Sustaining this attitude was a clear and conscious desire to 'catch up' with the West. Whilst the 'catching up' aspiration has been central to all modernization projects, Chakrabarty overstates his case by decontextualizing Bandung – without sufficient attention to the nature of the international. Bandung voiced a subaltern aspiration for *coevalness* within a historically produced hegemonic international order. The modernization narrative only dovetailed the imaginary of the nation-state, itself a product of the international. Misrecognition of the centrality of the international allows Chakrabarty to conflate the Bandung impulse and the structuring logic of the (hegemonic) international:

> This emphasis on development as a catching-up-with-the-West produced a particular split that marked both [sic] the relationship between elite nations and their subaltern counterparts as well as that between elites and subalterns within national boundaries. Just as the emergent nations demanded *political* equality [emphasis in original] with the Euro-American nations while wanting to catch up with them on the economic front, similarly their leaders thought of their peasants and workers simultaneously as people who were *already* full citizens – in that they had associated rights – but also as people who were not quite full citizens in that they needed to be educated in the manners of citizens. This produced a style of politics on the part of the leaders that could only be called pedagogical.[21]

The key question facing the Bandung delegates was to find a pathway between anti-imperialism and neo-imperialism. This objective was (and continues to be) fraught with grave pitfalls, accentuating the impossibility of escaping the international. In a sense, the challenges faced by the Bandung member states have only been exacerbated with the consolidation of the institutional apparatus of the international. Despite summoning the arrival of a post-Westphalian moment through the auspices of a global civil society, cosmopolitan democracy, or globalization, the constraining logic of the international has only been fortified, not weakened. Bandung is a reminder of the inescapability of the international. It also reveals the aporetic nature of the international, not merely the derivative nationalist discourse of postcolonial elites. Clearly, against the force of linear history and the disintegration of old polarities, Bandung appears increasingly anachronistic, an historic addendum. Bandung and political subjectivities summoned in its name speak vernaculars; not languages. On a purely historicist reading, the salience of Bandung to international history is easily diminished with the demise of the Third World and triumph of global neo-liberal social engineering. Detached from historicism, however, other interpretative options open up. The competing claims of History and Memory are clearly exposed in the case of Bandung. The latter allows Bandung to unmask the ideological character of liberal cartographies of the international.

The Bandung 'impulse'

As a memory of anti-colonial struggles and a call for greater equality, the Bandung 'impulse' provides a vital source for political decolonization, conceived as a condition of active contestation and challenge to a normalized world order in which colonial rationality passes as civilization. The language of 'impulse' repudiates the teleological gaze in genealogies of decolonization. On this reading, three principal elements are significant. First, Bandung does not merely serve as an event or phase in the long march towards decolonization, either in the formation of Third World consciousness or (even) the Nonaligned Movement (NAM). Doubtless, both Third World solidarity and the awareness of postcolonial alterity within West-dominated structures of world politics are linked quite effortlessly to the Bandung spirit. In familiar linear textbook accounts of IR, Bandung is an inescapable cipher. Yet, linearity conflates *histoire événementielle* [22] with *decolonization as rupture.* Bandung is an important event in the history of decolonization, but 'events history' is too limited a field of vision to fully recognize Bandung's importance and meaning to IR. The spatio-temporal horizon of (international) politics resides less in the linearity of data than in the repositories of meaning produced in struggles for recognition. Bandung gestures towards the latter – the presence of discrete political desires, commitments and aspirations that are ever-present.

Second, the terminology of 'impulse' points towards the unfinished history of decolonization. Impulse connotes both the nagging absence of the 'Third World' in the imaginings of mainstream IR, but also marginalization of a *particular* kind of disquiet expressed at Bandung. This disquiet relates not only to the differential character of power, but to the persistence of a racialized world order. Bandung is a reminder that decolonization is an impulse, not an event. It seeks to show the *colonial* character of the international. The silencing of race in IR generally, but especially in liberal imaginaries of the international – cosmopolitanisms of various hues; global civil society; global democracy; or globalization – conceals *coloniality* or the durable existence of structures of racial distinction and incorporation.

Third, implicit in the expression 'impulse,' is recognition of repressed history,[23] an acknowledgement of other registers to hegemonic IR. These include a different understanding of temporality conceived outside the prison-house of Westphalia; real political decolonization not as the 'transfer of power' from the metropolis to the colony, but as the demise of *coloniality* – a coloniality that remains the defining feature of the international. As rupture, the Bandung 'impulse' speaks to both. Approaching Bandung outside historicist frames is to initially recognize that its salience depends not so much on its political achievements, in helping forge particular global alignments, but rather in giving shape to a particular vision of inclusiveness and parity with durable affective and symbolic effects. Positivist strictures erase these dimensions in any meaningful sense. Bandung bares the disconnection between history and memory: the Bandung 'impulse' is about the present and its living and lived memory in which a specific form of political consciousness resides.

Hence, as a cipher of Third World consciousness, identity and politics, Bandung can only represent a subordinate tier of the international and its histories; it cannot materialize as an integral part of the constitution of the international.

The disconnection between its salience for many, but real marginality for some, insinuates postcolonial sensibilities, both addressing the structure of IR thought and the place of non-Euro-American histories in the 'universal' canon. Bandung is clearly not absent in the official story, but it surfaces only as a subplot involving non-hegemonic players of its time. Epistemic marginalization ensures ontological subordination.[24] This is not an aberration.

During the entire period of the Cold War, the world outside Euro-America remained tangential to mainstream IR, serving as its 'outside', a zone for intervention, intrusion, or manipulation. Despite the centrality of this (Third) world to the performativity of the Cold War in proxy conflicts, sustained violence, dislocation and counter-revolution – the actual theatre of superpower rivalry – it could only stand in the shadows of the Cold War. In mainstream historical recollection, this location has remained unchanged. Rather, Bandung has further slipped in significance in 'textbook' retellings of IR. Although references to the 1955 Bandung Conference are an obligatory ritual in more recent IR textbooks,[25] it pales into insignificance relative to Westphalia, the Treaty of Maastricht, or the fall of the Berlin Wall. Reduced to the dictates of 'events history' as a prisoner of historicism, Bandung rarely transcends its own time.

To attend to Bandung, not as datum, but as aspiration drawn from memories of anti-colonial struggles now spurned in official narratives, is to basically confront ambivalences of the condition of postcoloniality. This encounter brings to the surface lost traces, genealogies and counter-memories[26] of the colonial past to help interrogate the 'colonial present'.[27] The end product is a re-description of the past, not as the pre-history of History, but as alter-history. This is not a simple undertaking as real limits emerge. The world of Bandung has long gone; the principals are no longer on the horizon of politics to inspire vision, protest, or resistance against the inexorable advance of neo-liberal globalization; the 'three-world' map[28] has been replaced by a deterritorialized Manichean universe of privilege and destitution;[29] the certainties of capitalism or socialism are enfeebled by perennial crises in the former, and political homelessness in the latter. Against these currents, Bandung seems irrelevant: merely a romantic saga unable to resonate with the political or psychic demands of the present. Not only do the inheritors of imperial hubris now find comfort in the disappearance of the 'Bandung Spirit', but so do the political children and grandchildren of the first generations of the postcolonials. The memory of Bandung confirms the scale of the historic compromise and acquiescence. Eager to reach the Promised Land of plenty and advantage, the only secure path is a willing embrace of Davos consciousness – the enclaved, mediatized, securitized sector of the global political economy standing in direct contrast to the vast and growing swamps of global impoverishment.

Bandung as memory[30]

One of the more remarkable features of Western IR is the continual silencing of marginalized populations in its mappings. Memory of empire metamorphoses typically as nostalgia, not as enactment of coloniality. Calls to decolonize IR are mere gesturing without recognizing coloniality as a durable feature of the international; before a new inventory of politics can be produced, engagement with coloniality is necessary. Catherine Hall conveys the wider context of this undertaking, one that applies with equal force to IR:

> Many Europeans, concerned to forget the past, look to a future which focuses on Europe and discards the uncomfortable memories of colonialism. Perhaps before we can embark on the construction of new myths we need to do some 'memory work' on the legacy of Empire. Memory, as we know, is an active process which involves at one and the same time forgetting and remembering.[31]

The problem, however, is that a 'memory place'[32] is only accessible as partial memory; memory can never be complete and whole.[33] This directly relates to Bandung. Since 1955, world politics has travelled great distances: from alternative pathways of building worlds to a present world increasingly appearing as a world without alternatives; from the exuberance of political decolonization to neo-liberal capitulation. The world is unrecognizable from its past, yet utterly familiar. Coloniality remains embedded in postcoloniality. If memory provides an access to the experiential aspects of social processes and situations, Bandung connects present consciousness with past reality. Alternatively, memory allows reconstructing the past from the vantage point of the present. Memory gestures towards human consciousness; it is a part of the past which animates living aspirations. In postcoloniality's collective memory, the promise of Bandung is unavoidable.

Disciplinary IR privileges history over memory. In the canon, the history is a linear account linking the rise of the West to its universalization. In this game of retrieval, however, there is very little room for actual memory, except the nostalgia of empire. Klein's distinction between history and memory, though marred by essentialist assumptions, helps situate the hegemonic thinking in Western IR.

As Klein notes, 'Memory appeals to us partly because it projects an immediacy we feel has been lost from history'.[34]

Against the above image, Bandung's location in 'event history'[35] is problematic, a moment of surface, yet deceptive, effects. Event history reduces Bandung to a datum on a linear trajectory of decolonization. However, Bandung is itself a decolonizing move, an utterance of muted revolt against the past. In its cathartic quintessence, Bandung registers a 'structure of feeling' associated with the injuries and violence of colonialism; it is a reminder that the past occluded in the memory of international society rests on a burial ground. Speaking through the agency of elite ventriloquism represented at Bandung, ex-colonials sought to reveal the ellipses marking the constitution of international society. On this reading, the conscious attempt of the Bandung delegates to overcome ideological straightjackets in favour of 'Afro-Asian' solidarity becomes intelligible. Bandung's affective resonance as a 'decolonial' moment was inseparable from its politics. The convention offered a different promise of the future premised on subaltern solidarity forged through anti-colonial struggles. From the privileged location of postcolonial critique, the failure to transform postcolonial aspirations of independence into reality lies in the 'derivative discourse' of the nationalism which informed it. The main reasons for the eventual diminution of the Bandung spirit, however, as with many subsequent effects, including the largely reformist New International Economic Order, are traceable to the nature of postcolonial sovereignty and the latter's entanglements with Western modernity.

Bandung was initially a protest against Western arrogance, but its aspirations could only materialize in the idiom of modernity: nation, sovereignty, human rights, or development. While these terms did not enjoy fixed meanings, they presented different things to the Bandung interlocutors. The 'revolt against the West'[36] was neither indifferent to the inheritance of modernity nor animated towards the pre-modern. It was ultimately addressed to the *shape* and *content* of the international: the former recognizing a more egalitarian framework of recognition; the latter actualizing equality itself. The disconnection between the symbolism of Bandung and its materiality affirms the incongruity embodied in the postcolonial condition.

In actuality, the principal problem of an obvious incongruity between the two registers of Bandung is situated in the ambivalent nature of the international. A modern construct, the international does not exhaust modernity. IR speaks for the modern and, in its reflexive moments, for its others. Yet, it speaks only in the language of the modern. The subaltern climbs to the surface as protest, yet often articulated only in the language of modernity. Marginality acquires speech, but only by adopting the rituals and syntax of hegemony. The subaltern does speak, but speaks in the idiom of hegemony. Outside hegemony, it has silence; no existence. Hence, the chief aporias of IR, evidenced at Bandung, belong to the recognition that the marginality of postcolonial nations can only be articulated in the implicit language of hegemony. Provincializing modernity only hegemonizes it.

These pitfalls do not justify analytical capitulation; they only underscore the problematic nature of postcoloniality. Bandung demonstrates the effective impossibility of escaping modernity while declining its productions; of fully embracing the language of modernity, while recognizing its silences and erasures; of actively participating in worlds conjured up by modernity, but seeking alternatives to these worlds. The postcolonial predicament plays itself out in the aporias of sovereignty. Bandung captures these aporias: an ambivalent condition of being and nothingness, of affirmation and negation, of inclusion and marginalization. Caught in between the promise of freedom and the limit of structure, Bandung is a commentary on the international present.

The new nations and nations-in-waiting represented at the Bandung Conference were all progenies of colonial or semi-colonial political orders. They all spoke the language of sovereignty: its denial under colonialism, or of its promise under political independence. But these nations were also cognizant of the great divide between the formal accoutrements of sovereignty and its real expressions. Operating within a world of Western hegemony (albeit partitioned into two ideological camps at that time), they were well aware that the principle of national sovereignty also made them vulnerable to asymmetrical power. This could only be compensated with 'Third World Solidarity'. A more durable passageway to *real* sovereignty lay in modernization, precariously situated in an international economic order sustained by Western hegemony. Bandung anticipated subsequent battles over the 'new international economic order' waged within the reformist United Nations framework in the early 1970s. Today, with the ascendancy of neo-liberalism worldwide, and the collapse of the socialist project in the European East, even reformist agendas appear immensely radical, and are usually dismissed with disdain and contempt.

The awkward link between postcolonial sovereignty and modernization illustrates the contradictory aspirations of Bandung (and the present order). Modernization was a dreamworld produced both within colonial modernity (as absence) and metropolitan modernity (as aspiration). The 'dreamers'[37] in Bandung were moderns without modernity. Bandung was not a revolt against modernity, but a revolt against its 'childlike' instantiation in the colony. The postcolony sought a mature articulation of modernity in the hope of attaining parity. This aspiration was not necessarily the principal item on the agenda, but it clearly reflected the structure of feeling animating ex-colonials. Reminiscent of earlier anti-colonial critiques which condemned colonialism, not simply for its denial of agency to the 'natives', but for not failing to fully modernize the colony,[38] Bandung echoed a similar sentiment. No alternatives were available on the international horizon except for 'development'. The ideological divide never questioned the legitimacy of development, but sought alternative routes to attain it. Bandung did not have any Gandhi or Aurobindo to suggest a different destination; the 'leaders' represented at Bandung were mostly westernized elites. More to the point, Bandung was not even about 'development', but decolonization, sovereignty, and the spectre of nuclear war that permeated world politics.

For Chakrabarty, the ideal of modernization visualized at Bandung embodies the figure of the engineer. In more expanded terms, it is not merely the engineer who casts her long shadow on postcolonial experience, but the Western metaphysics that accompanies all derivative discourses.[39] As Venn proposes:

> With the discourse of modernity… the static temporality describing the Christian journey through life to salvation or otherwise, and the determining unilateral agency of an unknowable God is replaced by the linear, progressive temporality of modernity and the agency of the modern, rational, unitary, self-present subject, the logocentric subject. The displacement in the foundation of the subject-agent proceeds from a transcendent God to other transcendentals, namely, History, Reason, Science.[40]

In embracing modernity, Bandung was an implicit acceptance of a new transcendental order – apparently the only available option at the time. Yet, the groundwork for this acceptance had already been laid by colonialism. Notably, the imposition of the nation-state as the modular form of political community derived unswervingly from the colonial institutional impact. The political form was not the natural outgrowth of indigenous processes, nor imagined in the colony, but imposed by the colonial international. Bandung expressed this ambivalence: rejecting the colonial international, yet accepting its political form. Bandung does not initiate an alternative modernity or suggest multiple modernities. Rather, as Partha Chatterjee proposes in another context, it advances the right to 'our modernity'[41] expressed as a collective voice by the Afro-Asian ex-colonial nations.

The main item on the Conference's agenda was the menacing reverberation of the Cold War – a civil war within Northern hegemony, which had spread to Asia, particularly with mounting tensions between the United States and China. Bandung promised a way out of this civil war in the shape of a radically new idea: non-alignment. The nations represented at Bandung were not non-aligned in any meaningful way: several states were fully integrated into security pacts with the United States, or appeared to be 'proxies' of the Soviet Union. However, this did not lead the participant members to abandon the claims of decolonization, sovereignty or autonomy. Operating within the existing framework of international society and its alignment with the United Nations, remonstrations could be articulated that sounded familiar. The Articles of the United Nations Charter were 'universal principles', as the Bandung leaders saw them, but there was no hermeneutic closure to those principles. Elements that secured the autonomy of the postcolonial world were privileged. The impudence of Bandung lay in the public acknowledgement that another world was possible, without necessarily spelling out the contours of that world. With the conceit of hindsight, Bandung's aspirations appear excessive, more fiction than fact, more romance than truth. On the other hand, lifted out of the historicist iron cage, Bandung stands out as a defining moment of dissidence against 'superpower' arrogance. Calls for Third World solidarity were not an expression of postcolonial moral outrage but an early intimation of the desire for sovereignty. The new nations (and those seeking to replicate them) were expressing an *experiential,* not merely rational, aspiration of sovereignty; not a case of *ressentiment,* but an awakening occasioned by memories of colonialism.

Clearly, the individual motivations of the 29 participating nations were neither uniform nor adjustable to a common denominator. Each brought with it particular historical baggage, interests and expectations. Beneath the idea of solidarity, rivalries simmered. Ideology and alignments, combined with individual ambition, were not easily dispelled. Yet, despite internal differences, a 'common' vision was forged. Mignolo offers a useful summary of the mixed motivations behind the conference:

> The conference reflected the five sponsors' [Indonesia, Burma (Myanmar), Ceylon (Sri Lanka), India and Pakistan] dissatisfaction with what they regarded as a reluctance by the Western powers to consult them on decisions affecting Asia; their concern over the tension between the People's Republic of China and the United States; their desire to lay firmer foundations for China's peaceful relations with themselves and the West; their opposition to

colonialism, especially French influence in North Africa, and Indonesia's desire to promote its case in the dispute with the Netherlands over western New Guinea (Irina Jaya). Major debate centred upon the question whether Soviet policies in Eastern Europe and Central Asia should be censured along with Western colonialism. A consensus was reached in which 'colonialism in all of its manifestations' was condemned, implicitly censuring the Soviet Union, as well as the West.[42]

In postcolonial memory, Bandung presents the hope of transcendence. Bandung signalled, as Walter Mignolo puts it, 'a decolonial moment'.[43] Mignolo defines the decolonial option as one that 'opens up a way of thinking that delinks from the chronologies of new epistemes or new paradigms (modern, postmodern, altermodern, Newtonian science, quantum theory, theory of relativity, etc)'. Reading the significance of that event not in terms of the Western story of the international, but in challenging that story, Mignolo recognizes the hidden meaning of Bandung:

> [D]ecoloniality has its historical grounding in the Bandung Conference of 1955 ... the main goal of the conference was to find a common ground and vision for the future that was neither capitalism nor communism. That way was 'decolonization'. It was not 'a third way' à la Giddens, but a delinking from the two major Western macro-narratives.[44]

Perhaps, Mignolo offers an embellished account of Bandung in stressing the aspiration of 'delinking', but he seems to correctly show the limits of Bandung that emanate from its attachments to the Western episteme:

> The most enduring legacy of the Bandung Conference was delinking: delinking from capitalism and communism, that is, from Enlightenment political theory (liberalism and republicanism – Locke, Montesquieu) and political economy (Smith) as well as from its opposition, socialism-communism.[45]

For Mignolo, Bandung was not

> daring in its specific modelling of the future, but its repudiation of the restrictive field produced by colonialism and the ideological straightjacket of the Cold War. Neither the past nor the present were acceptable options. The splendour of the Bandung conference was precisely to show that another way was possible. Its limit was to remain within the domain of political and economic delinking. The epistemic question was not raised.[46]

This issue was only raised subsequently by Dependency Theory, which was 'a response to the fact that the myth of development and modernization was a myth

158 *Performance*

to hide the fact that Third World countries cannot develop and modernize under imperial conditions'.[47] Bandung revealed the dilemmas of postcoloniality (including postcolonial IR): despite the desire for autonomy, decolonial vernaculars remain fragile, unable to free themselves from hegemonic modes of epistemic authorization.

Indeed, if Mignolo's provocation that 'modernity is not an ontological unfolding of history but the hegemonic narrative of Western civilization', or 'as a narrative not as ontology', is taken in any meaningful sense, the aporias of Bandung cannot be transcended in attempts to provincialize Europe,[48] but by bypassing it altogether. Neither Bandung nor extant postcolonial thinking embraces that prospect. 'Alternative or subaltern modernities claiming their right to exist reaffirm the imperiality of Western modernity disguised as universal modernity,' Mignolo cautions.[49] Yet, unlike the ambivalence of lived and living memories of anti-colonial struggles embedded in Bandung, postcolonial theory does not face any of those challenges;[50] its antinomies are alienated from the life-worlds of those it claims to represent.

Revolt against imperial time

The retreat from Bandung is not merely the repudiation of the promise of an alternative pathway to national selfhood, but the return of civilizational hierarchies in the subtler jargon of conditionalities of modern state-building: good governance, democracy, or civil society. Lacking in these assets and other credentials, states can quickly enter the zone of indeterminacy: quasi-statehood, rogueness, failure, or collapse. The international, under these conditions, no longer serves as a site of incorporation, but of closure and exclusion; the international appears increasingly fluid: states can enter *and* exit, a process over which they have little control. The fate of states resides in quenching the insatiable Kantian thirst for civilizational commensurability. This is a scenario Bandung opposed, not in denying the international, but by seeking to reconfigure it.

Trapped in the Westphalian imaginary, the Bandung nations were not seeking a cosmopolitan exemption to dissolve the burgeoning 'international society of states'.[51] Rather, they were rejecting the terms of incorporation into that society. These terms vitiated the potential for either the realization of sovereignty or recognition. Colonialism, in all its disguises, effectively removed vast populations from international society, denied equality and prevented the realization of freedoms. In repudiating the architecture and colonial operational code, Bandung was audaciously challenging 500 years of 'world history' and the Enlightenment narrative of progress. Bandung's reliance on Westphalia to make the case for decolonization by invoking the vocabulary of sovereignty was inescapable. Outside the international, there was little solace. Recovering from the despoiling effects of colonial plunder and violence, a radically different world order could only be a distant aspiration. The relentless condemnation of colonialism 'in all its forms' at the Bandung Conference, yet *without* a clear blueprint of an alternative order, becomes explicable. The specificity of the historical conjuncture also clarifies the commitment to the secular nation-state seeking modernization and development. The singularity of this political form promised a passage to the international.

Bandung defied the colonial assertion that the Third World was still in its infancy with regard to the conduct of diplomacy. The sheer fact that a conference of such scale, 'representing' a large and hitherto unrepresented part of the world could even take place, much less attain the results that it did, repudiated established prejudice. As a clearing-ground to articulate grievance and vision, hopes and misgivings, Bandung consolidated the sentiment that produced the non-aligned movement. Notwithstanding its antinomies, this movement staged a persistent reminder of the limits of hegemony.

Several key aspects of these limits confer on Bandung a timelessness untamed by historicist constructions. As a rupture in imperial time and the cognitive verities associated within its compass, Bandung brings forth memories of previous struggles against empire. Viewed through the prism of the current international order, these struggles can appear feeble. Yet, what would be the shape of the world without Bandung and the historical sequence it provoked? There are no firm answers to this rhetorical question, but it is a plausible conjecture that the colonial operational code could have lasted longer. At any rate, there is no doubt that the experience of coloniality has shaped the contours of the international with mixed legacies. What is less controversial is that the experience of coloniality acquired a concrete articulation in Bandung. The affective and experiential facets of Third World consciousness are unimaginable without the intrusion of the Bandung moment.

In the purely experiential realm, Bandung makes the world appear more proximate to its realness: a diverse and multicoloured habitation of peoples, political desires, cultures and hopes. The political awakening of the non-Western 'darker nations' also means the *colouration of the international*. Unlike the colonial spatiality of the international in which only a bifurcated world[52] can be imagined, Bandung anticipates a more heterodox world of identity and difference. The epithet 'Afro-Asian' is only the initial marker of a more diverse world to follow.[53] In colonial cartography, the 'coloured' world is relegated to the 'outside' of the international, one that makes the imperial 'inside' possible. With Bandung, these lines appear less definite. Yet, there is no linearity in this awareness. Colonial mappings return as do civilizational hierarchies – all in the name of the 'standard of civilization'. Bandung plays hide-and-seek, ensuring the suspicion that the linear script of civilizational process can easily lend itself to involution or implosion. The royal road to maturity invents new infantile creatures seeking redemption in the march of history.

The 'standard of civilization' still remains a critical feature for acceptance in international society. Cast as a requirement sanctioned by a global community, it easily conceals a Euro-American cultural imperative of statehood and sovereignty, rights and obligations. This is not to suggest that elements of this standard have not 'expanded' beyond the North Atlantic cultural zone. Ideas, institutions and practices travel. However, it is only their ideal Euro-American form that is regarded as legitimate. The selective deployment of the standard of civilization, in turn, is yet another critical issue that echoes the Bandung moment.

In repudiating imperial time, Bandung was rejecting the Euro-American standard of civilization. This becomes particularly obvious in deliberations over decolonization. Colonization is neither sanctioned as a necessary passage to modernity nor denied its essential brutality. The language of human rights is invoked to affirm the humanity of all races and peoples. Similarly, the discussion over disarmament underlines rejection of the Euro-American 'death wish' in the garb of security. The emphasis on 'peaceful' conduct of relations is not seen by the Bandung nations as a subordinate principle to the logic of 'self-help' or deterrence, but as an alternative way to organize international society. Against the backdrop of colonialism, the two world wars and the bloody conflict in the Korean Peninsula, the immediacy of this alternative pathway was more real than romance.

The end of the 'Third World' has also meant the evacuation of the symbolic relevance of coloniality as an intrinsic feature of the world order despite its materialization under different guises. Coloniality acquires an historical address of the past, albeit entangled with modernity, leaving behind structures and practices. Yet it is not only the 'end of the Third World' that underscores the apparent irrelevance of coloniality to IR, but the absence of alternatives to a Manichean world of privilege and deprivation. The triumph of neo-liberalism on a global scale, despite repeated exposure of its fragility as an ordering principle of social life, strengthens the case against Bandung – and its promise of a different architecture of international practice.

Conclusion

Mixed impulses are readily noticeable in the actual proceedings of the conference, but especially in its aftermath. With hindsight, 'non-alignment' turns out to be merely a comforting tale of relative collective autonomy in a world divided by ideology, suspicion and uncertainty, punctured both by the imperatives of global political economy and geopolitics. The horizon of development, of 'catching up' with the West, is safely ensconced within predictable linear vectors. Fanon's admonishment of the perils of imitation confirms the failure of the postcolonial world imagined at Bandung.[54] In recognizing these limits, it is also important to outline that Bandung was a product of a world created by empire and colonialism, not postcoloniality.

A key message of Bandung is the recognition that the terms of incorporation into international society are partial and unjust. Whilst the postcolonial nations are willing to eschew delinking in favour of incorporation, they enter the field with the expectation that the colonial order would be a thing of the past. Decolonization – albeit partial and wholly incomplete at the time of Bandung – was accompanied by the ominous presence of a Cold War – an arrogant ideological undertaking with the potential to trample the quest amongst burgeoning ex-colonial nations to give their respective peoples the minimal fruits of independence.

From the positionality of hegemony, Bandung merely symbolizes desperate attempts at Third World solidarity charged with the trope of resentment which culminate in calls for a New Economic International Order (NIEO). Lineages to the emergence of a 'Third World' bloc, especially within the confines of the United Nations, can be traced to Bandung. However, Bandung is principally about alternative principles of international order and practice. The exceptional feature of these alternative principles lies in an unabashed and unambiguous embrace of sovereignty as the principle of global order, but eschewing the conceit of anarchy. Rather, it is cooperation, not anarchy that appears as the preferred principle of the world order. Within this optic, the stress is on multilateralism, not bilateralism. The imposing shadow of the Cold War between rival ideological camps provided the backdrop for multilateralism. Bandung also enshrines mutual respect, not competition or coercion, as the operative logic of conduct in international relations.

Above all, Bandung congeals the aporias of the international: an arena of mutuality and contestation; of formal equality and hierarchy; of participation and marginality. In a word, Bandung underscores the antinomies of postcolonial sovereignty. Current postcolonial criticism generally embraces an unsympathetic relation to the past. Anti-colonial struggles appear deficient, inadequate, romantic, derivative, westernized, and modern. In extreme cases, those leading the charge are reckoned as subjectivized individuals, boldly parading as freedom fighters, yet haplessly collaborating with the imperial power in deed and diction. Operating with and within parameters drawn by the Western imaginary of the nation or the state, anti-colonialism is seen to be trapped in the cartographic straitjacket of modernity characterized by colonial institutional forms of governance and rule. The 'modular' nation remains a dreamworld, inevitably aspiring to replicate the metropolitan original. Against this stark image, Bandung can at best advance a romantic desire for autonomy; at worst a cathartic eruption of the meek.

The Bandung Principles do not merely echo the United Nations Charter, but reinterpret the principle of sovereignty in light of the postcolonial predicament. On the one hand, the five Bandung principles (mutual respect of all nations for sovereignty and territorial integrity; non-aggression; non-interference in internal affairs; equality and mutual benefit; and peaceful coexistence) reinforce the theme of sovereignty. On the other hand, there is an implicit recognition of the difficulty of forging a world order defined by mutuality; absence of foreign intervention; unequal relations between the dominant and subaltern powers; and belligerence. The ambivalences captured in Bandung underline particular genealogies of the international viewed from an alternative vantage point.

A source of these ambivalences lies in the character of nationalism itself, which inspired struggles for independence. Without exception, the movements to win political independence shared the modernist dream characterized by developmentalism, industrialization, economic progress, and an urban bias. All anti-colonial movements aimed to build a 'nation-state' with an imagined, albeit homogenized, political community overriding porous identities. National self-determination centred on the idea of 'national' sovereignty, notwithstanding the multi-ethnic character of postcolonial populations. The limiting horizon of the 'nation-state' ensured reduced recognition of internal difference – a legacy that continues to haunt postcolonial futures. While Bandung sought political decolonization for all of Asia and Africa, it could not anticipate how the institution of modernization, often under authoritarian rule or the lure of secular nationalism, would diminish prospects to build alternative social and political orders. The dreamworld of political decolonization eclipsed the compulsion of conceiving an alternative register of political economy unhinged from the prevailing ideological hegemony of the Cold War.

Another crucial source of these ambivalences lies in the conception of decolonization itself, not as a pathway to autonomy or independence, but as admission into existing hegemonic structures with their own requirements and protocols. The Bandung representatives principally sought equitable representation in the world order, but did not seek redistribution and restructuring of world order. This produced a basic contradiction between the claims of procedural and substantive justice, one that continues to plague the shape of the international. The context of the Bandung impulse becomes apparent: the continual relevance of the question of substantive justice in a world increasingly reproducing a colonial cartography. Yet, few voices today speak of the Bandung spirit, Afro-Asian solidarity or Third World consciousness. Those seeking transcendence from the prevailing imperial constellation speak instead in the language of globalization or cosmopolitanism, reaching for new orders beyond the strictures of the nation-state. To stress, there are two aspects to the imperial project: pedagogy of violence and pedagogy of civilization. The former has an established genealogy from the Cold War to global militarism. On this image, the war on terror, which rests on an imperial prerogative or the power to declare the colonial exception, consolidates the colonial mode. The latter rests on a standard of civilization which demarcates the lines between insiders and outsiders.

The memory of Bandung produces normative ideals that reappear in new global sites. However, without a collective political agency to articulate and materialize those ideals, Bandung can only produce affective and symbolic effects, now diminished, but not vanquished. Above all, Bandung underscores the ambivalences of postcoloniality: the desire for decolonization within largely inescapable global structures of capitalism and Westphalia. On the one hand, the Bandung impulse suggests an alternative cartography of international relations, based upon recognition both of the racialized nature of world order, and the incompleteness of the project of decolonization. On the other hand, Bandung is also tacit acknowledgement of the difficulty, if not desirability, of realizing sovereignty within extant structures. Apparently, the two tendencies are inherently irreconcilable against the legacy of empire, domination and violence.

Notes

1 Michel-Rolph Trouillot, *Silencing the Past* (Boston: Beacon Press 1995).
2 Turan Kayaoğlu, 'Westphalian Eurocentrism in International Relations Theory', *International Studies Review*, 12: 2 (2010), 193–217.

3 Jacob Burckhardt, 'Letter to Friedrich von Preen', in A. Dru (ed.), *The Letters of Jacob Burckhardt* (London: Routledge & Kegan Paul (1955) [1889]), 220.
4 Francis Fukuyama, *The End of History and the Last Man* (London: Penguin 1992).
5 Samuel P. Huntington, *The Clash of Civilizations and the Remaking of World Order* (London: Simon & Schuster 1996).
6 Hedley Bull and Adam Watson (eds) *The Expansion of International Society*. Oxford: (Clarendon Press 1984).
7 Barry Hindess, 'The Past is Another Culture', *International Political Sociology*, 1 (2007), 325–38.
8 Roselan Abdulghani, *The Bandung Connection: The Asia-Africa Conference in Bandung in 1955*, trans. by Molly Bondan (Singapore: Gunung Agung 1981); George McTurnan Kahin, *The African-Asian Conference: Bandung, Indonesia, April 1955* (Ithaca: Cornell University Press 1956); David Kimchie, *The Afro-Asian Movement: Ideology and Foreign Policy of the Third World* (New York: Halstead Press 1973); Carlos P. Romulo, *The Meaning of Bandung* (Chapel Hill: University of North Carolina Press 1956); Richard Wright, *The Color Curtain: A Report of the Bandung Conference* (Jackson: University of Mississippi Press 1995 [1955]) and See Seng Tan and Amitav Acharya (eds), *Bandung Revisited: The Legacy of the 1955 Asian-African Conference for International Order* (Singapore: National University of Singapore 2008).
9 Walter D. Mignolo, 'Geopolitics of Sensing and Knowing: On De (Coloniality), Border Thinking and Epistemic Disobedience', *Postcolonial Studies*, 14: 3 (2011), 273–83.
10 Vijay Prashad, *The Darker Nations: A People's History of the Third World* (New York: The New Press 2008).
11 Mignolo, 'Geopolitics of Sensing and Knowing'.
12 Trouillot, *Silencing the Past*, 97.
13 J. M. Blaut, *The Colonizer's Model of the World: Geographical Diffusionism and Eurocentric History* (New York and London: The Guilford Press 1993), 1.
14 Prashad, *The Darker Nations*, 45–46.
15 Ibid.
16 Abdulghani, *The Bandung Connection*, 72, 103.
17 Chakrabarty cites Césaire in his *Discourse on Colonialism* to make his point: '[I]t is the indigenous peoples of Africa and Asia who are demanding schools, and colonialist Europe which refuses them ... it is the African who is seeking ports and roads, and colonialist Europe which is niggardly on this score ... it is the colonized man who wants to move forward, and the colonizer who holds things back.' Dipesh Chakrabarty, 'The Legacies of Bandung: Decolonization and the Politics of Culture', in Christopher J. Lee, *Making a World after Empire: The Bandung Moment and Its Afterlives*, (Athens, OH: Ohio University Press, 2010), 46.
18 Ibid. 46–47.
19 Ibid. 48.
20 Fouad Ajami, 'The Fate of Nonalignment', *Foreign Affairs*, 59: 2 (1980), 366–85.
21 Chakrabarty, 'The Legacies of Bandung', 53–4.
22 Fernand Braudel, *The Mediterranean and the Mediterranean World in the Age of Philip II* (London: Collins 1972).
23 Ashis Nandy, 'History's Forgotten Doubles', *History and Theory*, 34 (1995), 44–66.
24 Walter D. Mignolo and Arturo Escobar (eds), *Globalization and the Decolonial Option* (London: Routledge 2010).
25 John Baylis, Steve Smith and Patricia Owens (eds), *The Globalization of World Politics: An Introduction to International Relations* (Oxford: Oxford University Press 2011).
26 Michel Foucault, *Language, Counter-Memory, Practice*, Donald F. Bouchard (ed.) (Ithaca, NY: Cornell University Press 1977).

27 Derek Gregory, *The Colonial Present: Afghanistan, Palestine, Iraq* (Malden, MA; Oxford: Blackwell 2004).
28 Mark Berger, 'After the Third World? History, Destiny and the Fate of Third Worldism', *ThirdWorld Quarterly*, 25 (2004), 9–39.
29 Mike Davis, *Planet of Slums* (London: Verso 2006).
30 On memory, see Dipesh Chakrabarty, 'Postcoloniality and the Artifice of History: Who Speaks for "Indian" Pasts?', *Representations*, 37 (1992),1–26; Paul Connerton, *How Societies Remember* (Cambridge: Cambridge University Press 1989); David Lowenthal, *The Past is a Foreign Country* (Cambridge: Cambridge University Press 1985); Joanne Rappaport, *The Politics of Memory* (Cambridge: Cambridge University Press 1990); and Trouillot, *Silencing the Past*. For classic statements, see Maurice Halbwachs, *On Collective Memory*, edited, translated, and with an introduction by Lewis A. Coser (Chicago and London: University of Chicago Press 1992); Frances Amelia Yates, *The Art of Memory* (Harmondsworth: Penguin 1969) and Frederic C. Bartlett, *Remembering: A Study in Experimental and Social Psychology* (Cambridge: Cambridge University Press 1932). For a more recent intervention, see Jan Assmann, 'Globalization, Universalism, and the Erosion of Cultural Memory', in Aleida Assmann and Sebastian Conrad (eds), *Memory in a Global Age: Discourses, Practices and Trajectories* (Palgrave Macmillan 2010).
31 Catherine Hall, 'Histories, Empires and the Post-Colonial Moment', in Iain Chambers and Lidia Curti (eds), *Post-Colonial Question: Common Skies, Divided Horizon* (Florence, KY: Routledge 1996), 66.
32 Yates, *The Art of Memory*; Pierre Nora, 'Between Memory and History: Les Lieux de Mémoire', *Representations*, 26 (1989), 7–24.
33 Halbwachs, *On Collective Memory*.
34 Kerwin Lee Klein, 'On the Emergence of Memory in Historical Discourse', *Representations*, 69 (Winter 2000), 129.
35 Braudel, *The Mediterranean*.
36 Bull and Watson (eds), *The Expansion of International Society*.
37 Ajami, 'The Fate of Nonalignment'.
38 Aimé Césaire, *Discourse on Colonialism*, trans. Joan Pickham (New York: Monthly Review Press 2000).
39 Partha Chatterjee, *Nationalist Thought and the Colonial World: A Derivative Discourse* (Minneapolis: University of Minnesota Press 1986).
40 Couze Venn, 'Altered States: Post-Enlightenment Cosmopolitanism and Transmodern Socialities', *Theory, Culture & Society*, 19: 1–2 (2002), 68.
41 Partha Chatterjee, *Our Modernity*. South-South Exchange Programme for Research on the History of Development (SEPHIS) and the Council for the Development of Social Science Research in Africa (CODESRIA) (Rotterdam/Dakar; Kuala Lumpur: Vinlin Press 1997).
42 Mignolo, 'Geopolitics of Sensing and Knowing', 282–3.
43 Ibid., 274.
44 Ibid., 273.
45 Ibid., 275.
46 Ibid., 296.
47 Ibid., 276.
48 Dipesh Chakrabarty, *Provincializing Europe: Postcolonial Thought and Historical Difference*. (Princeton and Oxford: Princeton University Press, 2000).
49 Mignolo, 'Geopolitics of Sensing and Knowing', 279.
50 Ibid., 280.
51 Hedley Bull, *The Anarchical Society: A Study of Order in World Politics*. (London: Macmillan 1977).
52 Frantz Fanon, *The Wretched of the Earth* (Harmondsworth: Penguin 1967).

53 As Bull notes: 'The solidarity of non-whites against whites has been one of the principal elements making for the cohesion of the loose coalition of states and movements, to which we refer as the Third World' (Bull and Watson, *The Expansion of International Society*, 221).
54 'Come, then, comrades, the European game has finally ended; we must find something different. We today can do everything, so long as we do not imitate Europe, so long as we are not obsessed by the desire to catch up with Europe'(Fanon, *The Wretched of the Earth,* 312).

9 The spirit of exchange

Robbie Shilliam

Introduction: a maddening generosity[1]

In the feverish weeks of aid giving that followed the Haitian earthquake on 12 January 2010, Guyana emerged as the most generous donor of the international community. The Guyanese government had given US$1,000,000, private companies and church groups had raised almost US$900,000, and the Guyana Red Cross had collected approximately 7.2 million Guyanese dollars.[2] Guyana's GDP per capita is one of the lowest in the Americas and easily in the bottom third worldwide. So although absolute contributions from the USA dwarfed that of Guyana, in relative terms the latter's donation was 0.088 per cent of its overall GDP while that of the former stood at only 0.0011 per cent.[3]

A story to warm the sympathetic heart of any Kantian idealist, or a maddening generosity if one were looking through the Hobbesian lens of diffidence and self-survival. Indeed, more realistic minds could always take comfort in the remorseless self-interest at work in Guyanese politics disguised in the rhetoric of moral commitment. For example, President Bharrat Jagdeo felt it expedient that the bulk of the money from faith groups and NGOs should be channelled through an ostensibly non-partisan government organ, The National Haiti Relief Effort, headed by the human services minister Priya Manickchand. Very soon into the effort Manickchand chastised the Guyana Red Cross Society for making a separate appeal for aid.[4] At least one political commentator declared more trust for the Red Cross than for a government charged with multiple cases of corruption, and besides, local and general elections were looming, the campaigns of which required heavy financing.[5] Additionally, President Jagdeo began to use the Haitian situation as a proxy for regional geopolitiking.[6] Finally, self-interested – or at least communitarian – sentiments started to usher forth from some of the Guyanese population: it was poverty at home that should be addressed first, argued some, and it was rich countries that had the prime responsibility for addressing the needs of Haitians.[7]

Yet, if one listened carefully enough, a sense of obligation and responsibility was being broadcast in Guyana that ran deeper than the wavelengths of expedient philanthropy, moral blame or power politics. The Minister of Health, Dr Bheri Ramsaran, spoke of Haiti's revolutionary history, the lead that its peoples had taken in ridding the Americas of slavery to become in 1804 the first postcolonial, post-slaving state in the Americas, and the debt of 150 gold francs that Haitians were forced to incur in 1825 by the old colonial power France for loss of its colony. 'In CARICOM', argued Ramsaran, 'we tend not to give Haiti its true position; it took a long time for them to be included in the first place [and] when we look at that [it] is a slap in the face of the people who first shed their blood to show us the way.'[8] Similar sentiments of indebtedness were expressed outside of government by Andaiye, a long-time social activist from Red Thread, a Guyanese women's grassroots organization.[9] Her sentiments predated the earthquake. In August 2009 she had spoken out against the violence meted to Haitian citizens by the UN peacekeeping forces and had criticized the passivity of the regional powers who let this happen. Arguing for principled engagement by Caribbean organizations, Andaiye warned, '[i]t is wrong for us not to pay our debt to Haiti, if we don't, we will regret it.'[10]

Exchange theory, IR and social anthropology

In examining this maddening generosity, it becomes more and more apparent that the obligation felt by many Guyanese to 'repay' the Haitians for gifts previously given is not easily explained by either a liberal idealism predicated upon abstracted moral imperatives or a realist world view grounded in self-interest, disguised or blatant. But these are still the dominant explanatory frameworks in the field of International Relations (IR) used to explore the relationship between morality and power.

Nevertheless, the discipline has by no means ignored the phenomenon of gift giving. At some point in the 1970s, American political scientists started to look beyond the 'security dilemma' towards forms of social behaviour that were predicated upon norms of equivalence and/or obligation. How could these behaviour patterns, manifested in practices of burden-sharing, foreign aid giving and trade negotiations, be explained as part of an international system that principally operated in terms of self-interest and self-help? In other words, how might economic exchange be understood as social behaviour that implicated the pursuit of political power?[11]

Exchange theory helped to answer this question by defining reciprocity as a form of power understood as the rational pursuit of interest based on cost–benefit analyses, but one that legitimized itself by reference to a normative framework of equity and obligations. By this definition reciprocity could be understood as a power relation of quid pro quo, a morally inflected competition to foster unequal obligations. Perhaps Joseph Nye's 'soft power' or Hilary Clinton's 'smart power' are contemporary incarnations of this theoretical approach.

The sources of exchange theory in IR are multiple, but the field is probably most indebted to prior discussions within American sociology.[12] We should further note that George Homans, widely seen as the father of exchange theory in American sociology, asserted that heretofore the only explicit theoretical work on the subject was to be found in a social anthropology text from the 1920s,

Essay on the Gift by Marcel Mauss.[13] Indeed, when exchange theory has been utilized in contemporary IR, Mauss's text is often cited; and even if done only in a cursory fashion this, in effect, confirms its canonical importance.[14]

I want to dwell on this influence, even if it is understated, because, in the wider field, the application of a sociological lens to the anthropological investigation of the 'native' has played an important but underestimated role in the development of IR theory. Specifically, social anthropology has provided an influential analogical mode of thought that allows for international relations to be conceived of as a socially constituted sphere of human interaction.[15] In this analogical imagination, anarchy in the international realm is to be understood not as the absence of governance but rather the presence of 'primitive' forms of governance that exhibit weak, multiple and diffused political hierarchies and obligations. In this imagination, more advanced – or 'civilized' – forms of governance are related to the inside of states in terms of the hierarchical political relationship between government, law and the citizen.[16]

In this respect it is important to recognize that, as a field, IR inherits the founding methodological and political tendency of social anthropology to fit variegated societies and peoples into a hierarchical status binary of being either primitive/traditional or civilized/modern.[17] By virtue of colonial intervention, ethnographers representing civilized/modern peoples set themselves up as active observers and collectors of the knowledge of primitive/traditional peoples who were imagined only to be passive repositories of this knowledge. In other words, the ethnographer-observer of the civilized world would reveal to the primitive-observed the meaning and value of their own life world through the application of sociological method to ethnographic interpretation. With these epistemological assumptions, social anthropology, especially in the early twentieth century, promoted a colonial division of humanity between those who produced valid knowledge of the human condition and those who were unable to do so and could only provide raw data.

I will return to the significance of this colonial division of intellectual labour presently. But, having made some links between current exchange theory in IR and sociology to the colonial science of social anthropology, let us now turn in more detail to Marcel Mauss, nephew to the great don of sociology Emile Durkheim, and specifically to Mauss's influential social-anthropological text *The Gift,* and in particular the most controversial section of Mauss's text, 'The Spirit of the Thing Given'.[18]

The spirit of the gift

Mauss was somewhat of a dissenter to the model that justified a colonial division of intellectual labour, as described above. He argued that 'archaic societies' should not be examined as 'undeveloped' but rather as 'total social phenomena'. That is to say, for Mauss, 'native' societies not only incorporated the religious and moral dimensions of social interaction but also those dimensions usually associated with modern/civilized societies, especially the legal and the 'economic'.

Through this approach, Mauss wished to show that, while seemingly voluntary, exchange made by means of gifts in archaic societies were in fact reciprocal obligations that included not just goods but peoples, values and relations.[19] As a number of commentators have noted, Mauss, similar to his contemporary Karl Polanyi, hoped that his anthropological investigations of exchange and the economy would validate the European socialist alternative pursued in the interwar years.[20]

The controversial section of Mauss's text rotates around a discussion of the practices of the indigenous peoples of Aotearoa New Zealand, the Māori, and in particular the exchange of gifts from the forest. The main source that Mauss uses is a set of letters exchanged between a Māori *tohunga* (sage),[21] Tamati Ranapiri of Ngāti Raukawa, and Elsdon Best, a New Zealand administrator and ethnographer of European descent who translated the thoughts of his interlocutor into English. Copies of the letters were found by Mauss when he posthumously edited the works of his colleague Robert Hertz.[22]

Mauss presented the guiding question of his inquiry as 'What is the principle whereby the gift received has to be repaid? What force is there in the thing given which compels the recipient to make a return?'[23] In order to address this question Mauss discusses at length a hypothetical scenario that Ranapiri conveys to Best concerning the appropriate use of the *taonga (*gifts) of the forest. One person gives a gift to another who, after time has passed, makes of this a gift to yet another. After more time has passed this last person decides to reciprocate by giving another gift to the second person who must pass this gift back to the person who first gave a gift. To not reciprocate the gift in this way is to invite death.

I will go into more detail with this passage presently. For now, however, it is enough to note that what Mauss finds crucial in this text is the obligation that remains with the receiver even after the gift has been passed on. Mauss understands this obligation as arising from the workings of a spiritual power articulated in the Māori language as *hau*. His interpretation of Ranapiri's scenario by reference to this power deserves to be quoted at length:

> For the *taonga* [gift] is animated with the *hau* of its forest, its soil, its homeland, and the *hau* pursues him who holds it. It pursues not only the first recipient of it or the second or the third, but every individual to whom the *taonga* is transmitted. The *hau* wants to return to the place of its birth, to its sanctuary or forest and clan and to its owner. The *taonga* or its *hau* – itself a kind of individual – constrains a series of users to return some kind of *taonga* of their own. [24]

Mauss then typifies these exchange relations as:

> first and foremost a pattern of spiritual bonds between things which are to some extent parts of persons, and persons and groups that behave in some measure as if they were things.[25]

170 *Performance*

Subsequent receptions of Mauss, no matter how sympathetic, have tended to criticize precisely his interpretation of *hau* as a form of spiritual power to the extent that it mystifies the power that binds exchange relations through obligation and reciprocity.[26] And, in light of the tendency I ascribed to twentieth-century social anthropology to work within a colonial division of intellectual labour, it is instructive to now examine some of these critiques.

The critique of Mauss

Social anthropological critiques of Mauss have mostly sought to disassemble the implicit cosmology behind his notion of *hau* – glossed as spiritual power – so as to rearticulate this form of power as a variant of either material, ideological or symbolic power. For example, Raymond Firth, a New Zealand-born anthropologist who became a leading figure in the English school of social anthropology, complains that Mauss's interpretation ignored the fact that *hau* required human agency to move.[27] For Firth it would seem that a notion of spiritual power cannot incorporate a critical (and implicitly emancipatory) understanding of human agency. Firth is one example of the project of de-spiritualizing – or *making profane* – Mauss's interpretation of the *hau* of the gift. By exploring the critiques of two other notable anthropologists I will show how this endeavour supports a colonial division of labour that impels practitioners in the Western academy to decipher particular 'native' forms of knowledge production in order to reveal a putatively universal body of profane social scientific knowledge.

Marshal Sahlins's critique provides a clear and influential example of this practice. For Sahlins, *hau* is better understood as meaning 'return on', and in this respect Sahlins argues that Mauss's use of the term 'spirit' should be replaced with the term 'profit'.[28] In fine, Sahlins believes that the set of exchanges described by Ranapiri are best interpreted as the workings of a profane moral economy. Through this lens, Sahlins interprets the main obligation in this kind of economy to be the handing over of the yield (productiveness) on any gift to the original donor: 'one man's gift should not be another man's capital, and therefore the fruits of a gift ought to be passed back to the original holder.'[29] In this act of interpretation Sahlins deciphers *hau* as an expression of animatism – an impersonal power over which humans can have partial control. Therefore, *hau* does not refer to a spiritual quality per se, as Mauss seemed to have suggested by 'individualizing' it. Rather, *hau* functions ultimately as a quality associated uniquely with fecundity and, at a higher level of understanding, an imperative to exploit the natural and social world in a sustainable fashion.[30]

What I want to note here is that Sahlins's interpretation is based upon a categorical distinction between the spiritual and social-material dimensions. Hence, the core function of obligation and reciprocity in exchange relations is to morally moderate material exploitation by and between social beings. The residue of this explanation is that social beings must be educated to be moral despite their profane human nature. Thus, for Sahlins, exploitation and its moral solution – reciprocity – are ontologically material and not spiritual phenomena; in short, the spiritual has been transmogrified into a profane morality. But if Sahlins makes the particular exchange relations described by Ranapiri profane for social anthropological analysis, Lévi-Strauss renders profane Te Ao Māori (the world of Māori) entirely.

Lévi-Strauss reminds the reader that Mauss delineates the extent of his inquiry as nothing less than 'total social phenomena'. However, he charges Mauss with falling short of his own aim. The challenge of this form of interpretation, argues Lévi-Strauss, lies in arriving at an objective understanding of a totality from the outside but at the same time managing to incorporate the subjective understanding of living within this totality.[31] In effect, he claims that the method of 'total social phenomena' demands that the anthropologist incorporate 'native' subjectivity into a social-scientific objective account. Moreover, Lévi-Strauss assumes that such a challenge can only be supplied in the language of outsiders.[32] Who are these outsiders? They are, of course, the ethnographers who, unlike the native, can presumably break the cardinal rule of total social analysis when they come to interpret their own European-modern societies as having supplied the profane standpoint from which the cultural world can be approached in both subjective and objective terms. In other words, the objective social-scientific account is only accessible from a particular epistemological-cultural standpoint.

Lévi-Strauss claims that structural linguistics is the best tool available to allow the ethnographer to work from such a standpoint. Structural linguistics makes spiritual power (Lévi-Strauss calls it 'magic'[33]) profane by articulating that which can be felt but not seen – i.e. structure – as a symbolic realm distinct from ideology (i.e. belief systems) and material relations. In this realm a 'deep grammar' determines the position of each signifying element to the whole, and in so doing the grammar produces the meanings of various practices. For Lévi-Strauss, the structure of this grammar rests upon the relation between the unconscious and conscious planes. The 'fundamental phenomena of mental life' are to be found on the plane of the unconscious because we do not realize our essential self on this plane, but rather, we uncover symbolic activity that is both ours (conscious self) and not ours (unconscious other). Understanding this activity holds the potential to let us 'win back our estranged selves'.[34] Once this is realized, Lévi-Strauss claims that it is simply an act of transposition to apply the same principles to the self-as-ethnographer and the other-as-native.[35]

In this way, structural linguistics, when applied to anthropology, provides a universal language of communication that incorporates subjective interpretation (unconscious self/native) into objective analysis (conscious self/ethnographer). Yet this transposition effectively relegates *both* the conscious and unconscious elements of the lived experience of the 'native' into the sphere of unconsciousness, and concomitantly promotes both the unconsciousness and consciousness of the observer into the sphere of consciousness. In other words, Lévi-Strauss supports an effective mingling of unreflexivity with that which is observed, and a gluing of sufficient reflexivity to the observer.

Precisely through this reasoning, Lévi-Strauss charges Mauss with mystifying Te Ao Māori by confusing a subjective belief system – *hau* as spiritual power – with

172 *Performance*

an objective explanation of the underlying reality of exchange. For Lévi-Strauss this reality cannot be explained in the formulations of insiders (i.e. the cosmology of the Māori sage), but in the rendering objective of these beliefs by structural linguistic analysis:

> Hau is not the ultimate explanation for exchange, it is the conscious form whereby men of a given society, in which the problem had particular importance, apprehended an unconscious necessity whose explanation lies elsewhere.[36]

It is not necessary to go into what ultimate explanation Lévi-Strauss provides for exchange using this method, except to say that he renders spiritual power as a floating signifier necessitated by the inability of the finite human condition to allocate totality to a signified.[37] But what we should take from this discussion is that in Lévi-Strauss's critique of Mauss, the 'native' is not allowed to possess an adequate self-reflexivity – i.e. a conscious articulation – of their own belief system. Rather, the particular consciousness of the 'native' must be transmogrified into a universal unconsciousness that can then only be adequately translated through the profane world view of the ethnographer.

Spiritual revolution

It would be trite to charge Sahlins or Lévi-Strauss with being colonizers. But their creative efforts to render profane Mauss's explanation of the *hau* of the gift must be understood as part of an epistemological policing on behalf of social anthropology. The coloniality of power operates in the sphere of epistemology when spiritual power cannot be allowed to hold any explanatory power in and of itself but must be consistently transmogrified into a profane form of power, whether symbolic, moral or ideological. This policing of epistemology cannot be divorced from the broader colonially-induced disciplinary nature of the relationship between the ethnographer – the observer – and the 'native' – the observed. In other words, spirituality, when it is entwined with explanatory frameworks, must be taken only as a sign of the primitiveness, or in more polite terms, unreflexivity of the native. The profaning of their explanation is the civilizing of their being.

Against such civilizing missions, Ashis Nandy makes the following plea:

> Must a society always choose between materialism and spiritualism, between hard realities and unreal dreams? Or is the perception of such a choice itself a product of [the] imperial mission?[38]

Let us be sensitive to this plea. Let us consider how attributing explanatory value to the spiritual dimension undermines the hierarchical divide between the observing ethnographer and observed native. I say this not to make a normative argument for the goodness of spirituality – or at least religion – per se, but in order to promote an epistemological intervention that seeks to decolonize the conditions of knowledge production in the Western Academy.[39] In other words, we should not assume that exploring the human condition as a profane condition produces a higher, more advanced truth of said condition; rather we must remember that such activity has usually promoted a particular project of domination in thought and practice.

With this in mind, let us briefly return to that contested section of Mauss's text, *The Gift*. Manuka Henare has recently pointed out the significance of a mistranslation of Ranapiri's letter introduced by his interlocutor, Best. It occurs when Ranapiri discusses the repayment of the gift from the third to the second person. When considering whether to pass this gift back to the original giver, Best's text (the source for the various translations utilized by Mauss, Sahlins, Lévi-Strauss and others) states:

> Now, that article that he gives to me is <u>the hau of the article</u> I first received from you and then gave to him.

I have underlined the contentious part. Henare notes that the grammar of Ranapiri's text does not use the definite article 'the' – in *Te Reo Māori* (the Māori language) 'te'; rather, it uses the possessive article 'your' – 'tō'. The correct translation given by Henare is:

> Now that gift which was given to me, is your life force in your gift given to me before.[40]

Henare explains that the Māori language makes a fundamental distinction between temporary possession articulated as a location, and ownership articulated as possession.[41] It is the latter that Ranapiri alludes to in the text.

The significance of this reinterpretation, for Henare, is that Ranapiri is referring to the *hau* (which Mauss glosses as spiritual power) *of the original donor* and not only of the object that is donated by her/him. In fine, this *hau* is associated with the original ownership of the gift and travels with it. To my mind this corrected translation highlights the purposeful and inescapable weave of spiritual, social and natural forces within exchange relations in Māori cosmology. Henare represents this weave in terms of a matrix – rather than hierarchy – of values of which *hau* acts as one of a number of cardinal points.[42] I might add that Best's translation always laid the way open for an unweaving of the spiritual from the social-natural world to the extent that the second gift in his translation is described as a depersonalized (fetishized?) object that simply substitutes for the original object.[43] In this translation, the embeddedness of spiritual power in relations of social-natural exchange is diluted, hence leading the way to a profaning of the entire exchange relationship by for example Sahlins, Lévi-Strauss and others. Henare observes that this is a trap that Mauss, despite the mistranslation he worked with, seems to intuitively avoid when he explains exchange as:

> first and foremost a pattern of spiritual bonds between things which are to some extent parts of persons, and persons and groups that behave in some measure as if they were things.[44]

In light of these observations, let us, if not for the sake of a decolonial politics then for the sake of the best tradition of European-modern experimentation, follow Mauss's intuition and dare to relax the imperial disciplines of the social sciences. So, in what follows, I shall glean some knowledge of the *hau* of the gift from what is provided within Māori cosmology, spiritualism and all.

The three baskets of knowledge

A detailed knowledge of Māori cosmology would, in the past, have been esoteric (and probably in many ways still is). Nevertheless, in taking the first uninitiated steps we are not faced with an untranslatable or entirely mystical/mystified world view, rather, one that requires long periods of slow, careful and compassionate translation/edification. First, the weaving of the spiritual, natural and social dimensions in Māori cosmology must be studied so that we can better understand exchange relationships in the terms presented by Ranapiri. For this purpose, I depend upon the writings of the Reverend Māori Marsden, a noted twentieth-century *tohunga,* and also on the more recent work of Henare.[45]

Henare has proposed a new definition of Māori cosmology (his term is 'metaphysics') as a philosophy of vitalism and humanism rooted in the belief that there is an original and singular source of life that, as a force, 'imbues and animates all forms and things in the cosmos'.[46] The ultimate reality of life and the cosmos is therefore the spirit or, as Marsden calls it, *wairua*.[47] Social beings are both human (natural) and divine because the cosmos is an open system into which the spiritual dimension impinges; and being open, it is also possible for social beings to discern the spirituality of processes.[48]

While the ultimate reality may be spiritual, there are many facets to the experience of this reality that are woven into the originating impulse, key of which for Marsden seems to be the material, psychical and symbolic. Moreover, the weave takes on many shades, intensities, relationalities and sequences. In this respect, three dimensions of the cosmos seem to be crucial for Marsden: the world of potential, symbolized by Te Korekore (begotten, not created); the world of becoming, symbolized by Te Pō (the world of nights); and the world of being, symbolized by Te Ao Mārama (the world of light).[49]

As Marsden makes clear, the mindset of social anthropology is in many ways a burden to apprehend Māori cosmology to the extent that it constantly seeks to collapse the varied dimensions of human existence into a narrow analytic of the profane symbolic, ideological and material. Indeed, as I have shown above, this is effectively what Sahlins and Lévi-Strauss do in their reinterpretations of Mauss. Alternatively, Marsden allows the dimensions to function in their specificity except that this specificity is not interrogated through a methodological individualist approach but rather is folded back into a relational-pluralistic reality woven together by spiritual forces. In this way, the material can be material *and* spiritual, whereas in the social anthropological understanding that is predicated upon making the social and natural world profane, the spiritual must be ontologically transmogrified *into* material cause (or ideology or symbol).

Moreover, it seems that Marsden uses the symbolic realm (so beloved of Lévi-Strauss) more as a medium to help draw out a deeper spiritual reality than as the ultimate language of reality.[50] Marsden comments that poetic imagery, especially when tied into narratives, facilitates understanding of Māori cosmology much more than social-anthropological approaches.[51] Following Marsden's advice, I shall use the framework provided by the story of Tane, the progenitor of humankind and forest life. Tane ascended through the varied worlds of existence to arrive at the ultimate world occupied by Io-Matua-Kore (the supreme parentless god). There he obtained three baskets of knowledge, with which he descended back into the world of humanity.

Knowledge in these three baskets relates to the conditions of potential, becoming and being. In one basket lies knowledge of Te Ao Tua-ātea – the world beyond space-time. This is the transcendent and eternal world of the spirit, of potential, of the first cause – Io-taketake – and a world towards which the cosmos as a whole is tending. It is, in short, the ultimate reality.[52] In another basket is knowledge of Tua-uri, the real world, but a world of darkness (*te pō*) that exists behind the natural world of sense perception. It is the 'seed bed of creation' wherein space-time is gestated, evolves and is refined into the various and specialized manifestations of the natural world. It is in this world of becoming that four related concepts are manifested: *mauri*, the life force that 'interpenetrates all things to bind and knit together, creating unity in diversity'; *hihiri*, a pure energy refined from *mauri* that manifests as radiant light; *mauri-ora*, the 'life principle', a bonding force that further refines energy to make life possible; and *hau-ora*, the 'breath or wind of spirit which is infused into the process of birth to animate life'.[53] As Marsden puts it, '*hau-ora* begat shape, shape begat form, form begat space, space begat time and time begat Rangi and Papa.'[54] Ranginui – the sky father – and Papatūānuku – the earth mother – embraced each other in this world of becoming until their children, including Tane, forced their separation and birthed Te Ao Mārama – the world of light. In this respect, Papa refers to land from beyond the veil, that is to say it is the personified form of *whenua* – the natural earth.[55] This, then, leads us to the final basket of knowledge of Te Aro-nui, the natural world of being that can be apprehended through our senses in terms of events, sequences, cycles, regularities and, in general, chains of cause and effect.[56]

Having sketched out the basic constituency of the cosmos, it is now possible to better understand the manipulation of the environment in which human beings live. And through this endeavour it will be possible to glean the importance of *hau*, the concept that is so central to Māori cosmology yet has been so difficult to grasp in its fullness.[57]

The *hau* of the gift revisited

Marsden makes an important distinction between the material-natural, psychic (emotional and intellectual) and spiritual aspects of human existence. For example, willpower (*ihi*) is not spiritual but psychic power.[58] Hence, in Marsden's recounting of Māori cosmology, the will to power that is invoked in realist explanations of exchange is in no way denied but is clearly differentiated from the channelling of spiritual power. This is also an important distinction to note because it pre-empts the strategy used in social anthropological explanations to transmogrify the spiritual to the affective and/or ideological.

Alternatively, Marsden works with a relational plurality of forces and effects/affects: the natural refers to basic needs; the psychological to cultural values of sharing, caring and obligation; and the spiritual (always beyond the full grasp of mortal humans) to the achievement of divinity (*atuatanga*).[59] In this ultimate spiritual endeavour, which has the deepest influence upon the human environment, two qualities are decisive: *mana* (authority/power) and *tapu* (sacredness). I will focus here on *mana*, except to say with regards to *tapu* that it does not work as the moral opposite (taboo) of *mana*, and that it might be best to describe *tapu* as the latent form of *mana*.[60]

Marsden defines *mana* as 'that which manifests the power of the gods', that is to say, 'lawful permission delegated by the gods to their human agents and accompanied by the endowment of spiritual power to act on their behalf and in accordance with their revealed will'.[61] *Mana* incorporates relationships through time and space, for example in relation to the spiritual powers of ancestors, and is manifested through action.[62] In affective economies such as those operating within and between various Māori corporate entities,[63] *mana* is pursued as a practice of reciprocating and balancing with others (*utu*) over the long run, but in ways that tend to reproduce an inequality of obligations.[64]

The pursuit of *mana* might be confused with the social-scientific articulation of exchange as the pursuit of self-interest by other means, e.g. the 'soft power' competition to foster unequal obligations. While it would be trite to deny that this *ihi*-powered pursuit is undertaken by real-existing human beings, Marsden makes clear that the human is never the source of *mana* (unlike psychic forces such as *ihi*); rather, she/he is the agent and channel of the gifts of the gods – and *mana* is a gift that can be rescinded. *Mana* therefore remains a spiritual power manifested in pursuit of divinity through actions that (imperfectly) pursue the integrity of things. This integrity is forged through the gradual intensification of *mauri* in Te Pō (the worlds of becoming) and manifested in Te Ao Mārama (the natural world). That its human pursuit in the material-natural world might be inflected through the will to war, as much as guided by the moral compass of compassion, is a given. *Mana* therefore has to be associated with respecting and upholding the *mauri* that is immanent within all things in the natural world and the *hau ora* (breath of life) through which *mauri* is most clearly manifested.

There is, in this respect, a subtle but important distinction that Marsden makes between inanimate and animate objects: when referring to the latter, *mauri ora* and *hau ora* are synonymous; when applied to the former, *mauri* does not have its qualifying adjective *ora* (life). Moreover, human life is the expression of *mauri ora* in its highest principle.[65] What can be gleaned from these subtle distinctions is that even when working within a cosmology that posits spiritual power as the ultimate reality, and even when this potential power is taken to be imbued and woven into all things from their becoming to their being, it is still possible to entertain distinctions – *but not of the categorical kind* – between the spiritual, natural and the social-natural world. Again, and recalling the discussion above of Sahlins's critique, such subtle distinctions are not possible in the profane world of social anthropology.

More importantly, these subtle distinctions lead me to think that, because the breath of life (*hau ora*) that animates human beings operates as the highest instantiation and refinement of spiritual power, it is also the most critical element to attend to in terms of balance and obligation, i.e. in terms of the integrity of the weave of the cosmos itself. In this respect, it is important to relate a subtle distinction that Henare makes between *mauri* and *hau*: while both are fundamentally spiritual phenomena, the former can be understood as the cement that binds body and spirit together, while the latter is that which determines outcomes especially in terms of relationships.[66] This special significance given to *hau* also seems to be affirmed in a part of the Māori creation stories. *Hau* was a gift from Hauora, a child of Rangi and Papa. The children argued over the rights and wrongs of separating their parents – i.e. of creating the natural world – and in the course of argument each tried to destroy the *hau* of the others.[67] Implicated in this story of creation, 'the spiritual impulse that is *hau* urges reciprocity in human relations with nature and in relations with other people.'[68] Indeed, as I have mentioned already, Henare notes that *tikanga hau* forms one of the cardinal ethics and virtues – the 'ethic of the spiritual power of obligatory reciprocity in relationships with nature, life, force, breath of life'.[69]

We might, then, propose the following understanding of exchange as it emerges from Māori cosmology. The materiality of exchange lies in unequal relations of reciprocity pursued indefinitely in a world of cause and effect; the morality of exchange lies in the imperative to ensure that wilful actions (*ihi*) do not fundamentally disturb the balance of the natural world in which – and as part of which – human beings must exist; the symbolism of exchange provides a narrational medium through which we might glean the spirituality of exchange; and the spiritual power underlying exchange seeks to ensure that the weave of the cosmos retains an integrity that supports the manifestation of its divine potential. This framework of understanding is not mono-causal: the spiritual has a distinct agency that should not be confused or conflated with the material, moral or symbolic. But neither is the framework simply multi-causal: spiritual power is the ultimate reality precisely because it alone weaves its way through *all* these other intervening aspects of human existence. It now remains to apply this understanding to the obligation that many Guyanese felt they owed to Haitians after the earthquake in 2010.

Conclusion: the spirit of the Haitian Revolution

Atlantic slavery was a practice that sought to destroy the spiritual integrity of enslaved Africans and their descendants. Slave plantations in the Americas were built on the (near) eradication of indigenous peoples, the exhaustion of their *whenua*, and the death-by-labour of imported workers. Platitudes aside, the enslaved were not treated as human beings but rather as things – material factors of production for the accumulation of super-profits. The plantation system effectively turned Te Ao Mārama – the world of being – into a living death, especially for the enslaved Africans.

But when the sun set, the enslaved would gather clandestinely, and with drums, song and dance reach out into Te Ao Pō – the dark world of becoming – to pick up once more the threads of spirituality begotten in Te Korekore – the realm of potential. In so doing, the enslaved would allow the spirits of their African ancestors and gods to animate their living-dead slave bodies with *hau ora*. Out of such Vodou circles in Saint-Domingue would burst forth the insurrectionary Kongo militias. Blessed with *hau*, filled with *ihi*, these militias would on pain of mortal death fight the French, Spanish and British for more than a bloody decade between 1791 and 1804.[70] This spiritual war would, in the name of cosmic balance (*utu*) and for the redemption of the *mana* of the African ancestors, leave inscribed for posterity a moral commandment in the first constitution of the Empire of Haiti, a commandment that all the revolutions of slave-holding powers had heretofore left unwritten: 'Slavery is forever abolished.'

The struggle to ensure a meaningful freedom continued after independence as social forces from both within (the predatory elites) and without (the surrounding slave-holding powers and their sympathizers) sought to impoverish and neutralize the *mauri* of the Haitian peoples. France demanded payment for the loss of its colony, attempting to transmogrify the *utu* of the Revolution into a profane pecuniary sum.[71] Throughout the twentieth century, but initially in order to protect its own investments and its own racialized division of labour, the United States regularly intervened, destabilizing and undermining further the *mana* of independent Haiti in the name of balancing interests in the Western hemisphere. The last coup mounted against President Aristide is the latest episode in this long story.

And yet, Haiti was at the same time a beacon of light to the other Americas and Americans. It was the independent southern republic of Haiti that Simon Bolivar fled to in 1815 for protection from colonial forces. From there Bolivar returned to the mainland to pursue the wars of independence with Haitian troops given on condition that, wherever he went, Bolivar would ensure the abolition of slavery. But more than anything else, the Revolution made it impossible for the slaving and slave-holding powers to presume that the many and regular insurrections of the enslaved were the actions of unthinking brutes. This revelation engendered shock, guilt, confusion, curiosity, even incredulity… but, above all, fear. A mortal blow was thus dealt to Atlantic slavery far more powerful than any given by Quakers and abolitionists or, indeed, the 'new' economics of the industrial age.[72]

The Haitian Revolution was, therefore, a *taonga* (a gift) to the enslaved of the Americas and their descendants of the most *tapu* (sacred) kind: it was, quite literally, the gift of *hau ora* – a spiritual breath that would animate the slaves with their own life. In this respect, the Haitian Revolution was at the same time also a gift of humanism to all in the Americas and beyond, borne out of the inhuman Atlantic triangular trade that had unbalanced three continents in its pursuit of material accumulation.

Imbued with the life blood of its givers, the *hau* of the Haitians travels with the gift of liberation. And this *hau* wants to return to the place of its birth. The gift must be reciprocated so that the spiritual weave of the cosmos retains an integrity that supports the manifestation of its divine potential. To not return the gift would be to invite, as Ranapiri prophesied, a 'consequence of death,'[73] that is, to vindicate the treatment of humans in general – but non-Europeans especially – as living dead. Perhaps Andaiye feels the *tapu* nature of the calling of the original gift when she issues her urgent warning: '[i]t is wrong for us not to pay our debt to Haiti, if we don't, we will regret it.' In the glare of such sacredness, self-interest and soft power (while all too real attributes of the Te Ao Mārama) take on a pallid hue. They are revealed as inadequate explanations for the generosity of the Guyanese people.

As I was writing this chapter, an earthquake of the same magnitude as that suffered in Haiti hit Christchurch in the South Island of Aotearoa New Zealand. Almost immediately, the Prime Minister of the Kingdom of Tonga launched an appeal fund. The Honourable Dr Feleti Vakauta Sevele, who had completed his secondary, undergraduate and graduate education in Christchurch, stated:

> The Government and the people of New Zealand are always amongst the first to come to our assistance in our time of need so I urge the people of Tonga to give generously to this appeal fund. I also appeal for the Tongan public's moral support and prayers for the people of Christchurch.[74]

Within less than a month, a staggering donation of NZ$634,500 was raised and the message that accompanied the donation read:

> Please accept this small gift from all the People and the Government of the Kingdom of Tonga. This gift is tiny and insignificant but it comes from the depths of our hearts. With it comes our prayers and hopes that with God's help, you will continue to rebuild and recover from the devastating earthquake.[75]

Is there no end to this maddening generosity?

Notes

1 My thanks to the editor for his suggestions. Special thanks to Manuka Henare for his comments and guidance. Thanks also to Clinton Hutton for illuminating discussions regarding the Haitian Revolution. This chapter was written during a stay at the Centre for Caribbean Thought, University of West Indies. I thank the Centre for its hospitality. Ngā mihi nui ki a koutou katoa.

2 ReliefWeb, *Haiti Funding 2010*, 2010, available at: http://www.reliefweb.int/rw/fts.nsf/doc105?OpenForm&rc=2&emid=ACOS-635P2K; 'Guyana Red Cross nets $7.2M for Haiti', *Kaieteur News*, 31 January 2010, http://www.kaieteurnewsonline.com/2010/01/31/guyana-red-cross-nets-72m-for-haiti/.

3 David McCandless, 'Haiti Earthquake: Who's Given What?', *Information is Beautiful*, 26 January 2010, available at: http://www.informationisbeautiful.net/2010/haiti-earthquake-whos-given-what/. Ghana was the second most generous donating country at 0.018%.

4 'Controversy in Guyana over Haiti Aid Efforts; Others Rush Relief to Survivors', *Caribbean*, 360, 14 January 2010, available at: http://www.caribbean360.com/index.php/news/17535.html.

5 Freddie Kissoon, 'I am Giving my Haitian Money to the Red Cross', *Guyana Observer*, 16 January 2010, available at: http://www.guyanaobservernews.org/content/view/2467/1/.

6 'Guyana's President Says US an Obstacle to Efforts to Help Haiti', *Caribbean Net News*, 22 January 2010, available at: http://www.caribbeannetnews.com/article.php?news_id=21008.

7 For example, Rayvonne Bourne, 'Guyana Is in No Position to Resettle People from Haiti', *Stabroek News*, 23 January 2010, available at: http://www.stabroeknews.com/2010/letters/01/23/guyana-is-in-no-position-to-resettle-people-from-haiti/.

8 Guyana Government Information Agency, 'Panel Discussion Addresses Haiti Disaster and Future of Country', 18 January 2010, available at: http://www.gina.gov.gy/archive/daily/b100118.html.

9 Ibid.; for background, see Alissa Trotz, 'Red Thread: The Politics of Hope in Guyana,' *Race & Class*, 49: 2 (2007), 71–79.

10 'Region Must Save Haiti – Andaiye', *Stabroek News*, 5 August 2009, available at: http://www.stabroeknews.com/2009/stories/08/05/region-must-save-haiti-andaiye/.

11 See especially David A. Baldwin, 'Power and Social Exchange', *The American Political Science Review*, 72: 4 (1978), 1229–42; Robert O. Keohane, 'Reciprocity in International Relations,' *International Organization*, 40: 1 (1986), 1–27.

12 See especially D. A. Baldwin, 'Exchange Theory and International Relations', *International Negotiation*, 3: 2 (1998), 139–49.

13 George C. Homans, 'Social Behaviour as Exchange,' *The American Journal of Sociology*, 63: 6 (May 1958), 597–8.

14 See for example, Baldwin, 'Exchange Theory and International Relations', 139, 144; Keohane, 'Reciprocity in International Relations', 6; Tomohisa Hattori, 'The Moral Politics of Foreign Aid,' *Review of International Studies*, 29: 2 (April 2003), 232–4.

15 For a summary of these issues see R Shilliam, 'Modernity and Modernization', in B. Badie, D. Berg-Schlosser and L. Morlini (eds), *IPSA Encyclopedia of Political Science*, 8 vols (London: Sage 2010).

16 An important work in this vein, influencing both Kenneth Waltz and Hedley Bull, is Roger D. Masters, 'World Politics as a Primitive Political System', *World Politics*, 16: 4 (1964), 595–619. An acute analysis of these influences can be found in Aaron B. Sampson, 'Tropical Anarchy: Waltz, Wendt, and the Way We Imagine International Politics', *Alternatives*, 27 (2002), 429–57.

17 Of course, over the last 40 years anthropology has done much to reflect critically on its colonial roots. In fact, the discipline is increasingly taking Western institutions to be its object of inquiry. In a world where the materiality of Western power is fast being spread out amongst non-Western powers, is classical anthropology fast becoming an impossibility?

18 See in general Lygia Sigaud, 'The Vicissitudes of The Gift', *Social Anthropology*, 10: 3 (2002), 335–58.

19 See Marcel Mauss, *The Gift: Forms and Functions of Exchange in Archaic Societies*, trans. Ian Cunnison (London: Routledge & Kegan Paul 1966), 1–3.

20 David Graeber, *Toward an Anthropological Theory of Value: The False Coin of Our Own Dreams* (Basingstoke: Palgrave Macmillan 2001), 153–5; Keith Hart, 'Marcel Mauss: In Pursuit of the Whole. A Review Essay', *Comparative Studies in Society and History*, 49: 2 (2007), 5–8.

21 More than an 'expert' a tohunga is a 'person chosen or appointed by gods to be their representative and agent by which they manifested their operations in the natural

The spirit of exchange 181

world by signs of power accurately'; Māori Marsden, 'God, Man and Universe: A Māori View', in Te Ahukaramū Charles Royal (ed.), *The Woven Universe: Selected Writings of Rev. Māori Marsden* (Masterton: The Estate of Rev. Māori Marsden 2003), 14.
22 Graeber, *Toward an Anthropological Theory of Value: The False Coin of Our Own Dreams*, 169.
23 Mauss, *The Gift: Forms and Functions of Exchange in Archaic Societies*, 1.
24 Ibid., 9–10.
25 Ibid., 11.
26 See Manuka Arnold Henare, 'The Changing Images of Nineteenth Century Māori Society – From Tribes to Nation' (DPhil thesis, Victoria: University of Wellington 2003), 92.
27 See Joan Metge, 'Returning the Gift – "Utu" in Intergroup Relations: In Memory of Sir Raymond Firth', *The Journal of the Polynesian Society*, 111: 4 (2002), 319–20.
28 Marshall Sahlins, 'The Spirit of the Gift', in *Stone Age Economics* (London: Tavistock 1974), 159–60.
29 Ibid., 160.
30 Ibid., 165–6.
31 Claude Lévi-Strauss, *Introduction to the Work of Marcel Mauss* (London: Routledge & Kegan Paul 1987), 28–30.
32 Ibid., 31.
33 Ibid., 35.
34 Ibid.
35 Ibid., 36.
36 Ibid., 48.
37 Ibid., 61–2.
38 Ashis Nandy, *The Intimate Enemy: Loss and Recovery of Self Under Colonialism* (Delhi: Oxford 1983), 80.
39 See Enrique D. Dussel (ed.), *Coloniality at Large; Latin America and the Post Colonial Debates* (Durham: Duke University Press 2008).
40 Henare, 'The Changing Images of Nineteenth Century Māori Society', 105.
41 Ibid., 103.
42 Personal communication with Henare, 16 January 2011.
43 As a general point, see David Thompson, 'The Hau of the Gift in its Cultural Context', *Pacific Studies*, 11: 1 (1987), 63–79. For a cognate critique of the Western misunderstanding of indigenous thought and practice regarding worldly 'objects' in the Americas, see Rodolfo Kusch, *Indigenous and Popular Thinking in America* (Durham: Duke University Press 2010), chs 13–14.
44 Mauss, *The Gift: Forms and Functions of Exchange in Archaic Societies*, 11.
45 That Marsden was also Christian in no way de-authenticates him as an 'expert' of Māori cosmology unless we assume that the cosmology of Christianity, a religion emerging from the cultural crossroads of Africa and the Levant, is as exclusionary and *sui generis* an intellectual artefact as Western social science!
46 Henare, 'The Changing Images of Nineteenth Century Māori Society,' 47.
47 Māori Marsden, 'The Natural World and Natural Resources: Maori Value Systems and Perspectives', in Te Ahukaramū Charles Royal (ed.), *The Woven Universe: Selected Writings of Rev. Māori Marsden* (Masterton: The Estate of Rev. Māori Marsden 2003), 33.
48 Māori Marsden, 'Kaitiakitanga: A Definitive Introduction to the Holistic World View of the Māori', in Te Ahukaramū Charles Royal (ed.), *The Woven Universe: Selected Writings of Rev. Māori Marsden* (Masterton: The Estate of Rev. Māori Marsden 2003), 65.
49 Marsden, 'God, Man and Universe', 20.
50 Marsden, 'Kaitiakitanga', 62.

51 Marsden, 'God, Man and Universe', 23.
52 Marsden, 'Kaitiakitanga', 63.
53 Ibid., 60–61.
54 Ibid., 62.
55 Marsden, 'The Natural World and Natural Resources', 44.
56 Marsden, 'Kaitiakitanga', 61.
57 Henare, 'The Changing Images of Nineteenth Century Māori Society', 51; Metge, 'Returning the Gift', 320.
58 Marsden, 'The Natural World and Natural Resources', 41.
59 Marsden, 'God, Man and Universe', 5; Marsden, 'The Natural World and Natural Resources', 39–40.
60 Marsden, 'God, Man and Universe', 6; Henare, 'The Changing Images of Nineteenth Century Māori Society', 48–50.
61 Marsden, 'God, Man and Universe', 4.
62 Henare, 'The Changing Images of Nineteenth Century Māori Society', 49.
63 Ibid., 153.
64 Metge, 'Returning the Gift', 317.
65 Marsden, 'God, Man and Universe', 6; Marsden, 'The Natural World and Natural Resources', 44.
66 Personal communication with Henare, 16 January 2011.
67 Henare, 'The Changing Images of Nineteenth Century Māori Society', 52–3.
68 Ibid., 151.
69 Ibid., 90.
70 On this interpretation see Clinton Hutton, *The Logic and Historic Significance of the Haitian Revolution and the Cosmological Roots of Haitian Freedom* (Kingston: Arawak 2007).
71 In Te Reo, *utu* is a term that should not be used to indicate an instrumental commercial transaction.
72 Robin Blackburn, *The Overthrow of Colonial Slavery, 1776–1848* (London: Verso 1988).
73 Henare, 'The Changing Images of Nineteenth Century Māori Society', 105.
74 Prime Minister's Office, 'Prime Minister Launches Christchurch Earthquake Appeal Fund', 16 September 2010, available at: https://www.pmo.gov.to/prime-minister-launches-christchurch-earthquake-appeal-fund.html.
75 Prime Minister's Office, 'NZ$634,500 Donated to Red Cross Christchurch Earthquake Appeal', 17 October 2010, available at: https://www.pmo.gov.to/nz634500-donated-to-red-cross-christchurch-earthquake-appeal.html.

Bibliography

Abbott, Jason P. (ed.). 2002. *Critical Perspectives on International Political Economy.* Basingstoke: Palgrave Macmillan.
Abdulghani, Roselan. 1981. *The Bandung Connection: The Asia-Africa Conference in Bandung in 1955,* trans. by Molly Bondan. Singapore: Gunung Agung.
Abraham, Itty (ed.). 2009. *South Asian Cultures of the Bomb: Atomic Publics and the State in India and Pakistan.* Bloomington: Indiana University Press.
Abu-Lughod, J.L. 1989. *Before European Hegemony.* Oxford: Oxford University Press.
Abu-Lughod, Lila. 2006 (1991). 'Writing against culture', in Henrietta L. Moore and Todd Sanders (eds), *Anthropology in Theory.* Oxford: Blackwell.
Adas, Michael. 1979. *Prophets of Rebellion: Millenarian Protest Movements against the European Colonial Order.* Chapel Hill, NC: University of North Carolina Press.
Ajami, Fouad. 1980. 'The Fate of Nonalignment', *Foreign Affairs,* 59: 2, 366–85.
Anderson, Benedict. 1983. *Imagined Communities.* London: Verso.
Anderson, Benedict. 2006. *Imagined Communities: on the Origin and Spread of Nationalism.* London: Verso, 2nd (revised) edition.
Anderson, Fred. 2001. *The Crucible of War.* New York: Vintage Books.
Anghie, Antony. 2005. *Imperialism, Sovereignty and the Making of International Law.* Cambridge: Cambridge University Press.
Anghie, Antony. 2006. 'Decolonizing the Concept of "Good Governance"', in Branwen Gruffydd Jones (ed.), *Decolonizing International Relations.* Lanham, MD: Rowman and Littlefield.
Appadurai, Arjun. 1988. 'Putting hierarchy in its place', *Cultural Anthropology,* 3: 1, 36–49.
Arendt, Hannah. 1959. 'Reflections on Little Rock', *Dissent,* Winter.
Arendt, Hannah. 1965. *On Revolution.* New York: Faber and Faber.
Armstrong, Tim. 2003. 'Slavery, insurance and sacrifice in the Black Atlantic', in Bernhard Klein and Gesa Mackenthun (eds), *Sea Changes: Historicizing the Ocean.* New York: Routledge.
Ashley, Richard. 1995. 'The Powers of Anarchy: Theory, Sovereignty, and the Domestication of Global Life', in James Der Derian (ed.), *International Theory: Critical Investigations.* London: Macmillan.
Ashton, T.H. and C.H.E. Philpin (eds). 1985. *The Brenner Debate.* Cambridge: Cambridge University Press.
Assmann, Aleida and Sebastian Conrad (eds). 2010. *Memory in a Global Age: Discourses, Practices and Trajectories.* London: Palgrave Macmillan.

Bibliography

Assmann, Jan. 2010. 'Globalization, Universalism, and the Erosion of Cultural Memory', in Aleida Assmann and Sebastian Conrad (eds), *Memory in a Global Age: Discourses, Practices and Trajectories*. London: Palgrave Macmillan.

Badie, B., D. Berg-Schlosser and L. Morlini (eds). 2010. *IPSA Encyclopedia of Political Science*, 8 vols. London: Sage.

Bakan, Elazar and Ronald Bush (eds). 1995. *Prehistories of the Future: The Primitivist Project and the Culture of Modernism*. Stanford, CA: Stanford University Press.

Bala, A. 2006. *The Dialogue of Civilizations in the Birth of Modern Science*. Houndmills: Palgrave Macmillan.

Baldwin, David A. 1978. 'Power and Social Exchange', *The American Political Science Review*, 72: 4, 1229–42.

Baldwin, D.A. 1998. 'Exchange Theory and International Relations', *International Negotiation*, 3: 2, 139–49.

Barkawi, Tarak. 2001. 'War Inside the Free World: the Democratic Peace and the Cold War in the Third World', in Tarak Barkawi and Mark Laffey (eds), *Democracy, Liberalism and War: Rethinking the Democratic Peace Debates*. Boulder, CO: Lynne Rienner.

Barkawi, Tarak and Mark Laffey (eds). 2001. *Democracy, Liberalism and War: Rethinking the Democratic Peace Debates*. Boulder, CO: Lynne Rienner.

Barkawi, Tarak and Mark Laffey. 2006. 'The Postcolonial Moment in Security Studies', *Review of International Studies*, 32: 4, 329–52.

Bartlett, Frederic C. 1932. *Remembering: A Study in Experimental and Social Psychology*. Cambridge: Cambridge University Press.

Bartov, Omer. 1992. *Hitler's Army*. Oxford: Oxford University Press.

Baucom, Ian. 2001. 'Specters of the Atlantic', *The South Atlantic Quarterly*, 100: 1, 61–82.

Baucom, Ian. 2005. *Specters of the Atlantic: finance capital, slavery, and the philosophy of history*. Durham, NC: Duke University Press.

Baucom, Ian. 2009. '"Signum rememorativum, demonstrativum, prognostikon": Slavery and Finance Capital', in Nancy Henry and Cannon Schmitt (eds), *Victorian Investments: New Perspectives on Finance and Culture*. Bloomington and Indianapolis: Indiana University Press.

Baylis, John, Steve Smith and Patricia Owens (eds). 2011. *The Globalization of World Politics: An Introduction to International Relations*. Oxford: Oxford University Press.

Bayly, Christopher and Tim Harper. 2004. *Forgotten Armies: The Fall of British Asia, 1941–1945*. London: Allen Lane.

Bayly, Christopher and Tim Harper. 2008. *Forgotten Wars: The End of Britain's Asian Empire*. London: Penguin.

Benjamin, Walter. 1968 [1940]. 'Theses on the Philosophy of History', in *Illuminations: Essays and Reflections*, edited and with an Introduction by Hannah Arendt, trans. by Harry Zohn. New York: Schocken Books.

Berger, Mark. 2004. 'After the Third World? History, Destiny and the Fate of the Third Worldism', *Third World Quarterly*, 25: 9–39.

Berlin, Isaiah. 1969. *Four Essays on Liberty*. Oxford: Oxford Paperbacks.

Bhabha, Homi. 1984. 'Of Mimicry and Man: The Ambivalence of Colonial Discourse', *October*, 28 (Spring), 125–33.

Bhabha, Homi. 1994. *Nation and Narration*. New York: Routledge.

Bhabha, Homi. 1994. *The Location of Culture*. London: Routledge.

Bhabha, Homi. 2004. *The Location of Culture*. London and New York: Routledge, 2nd edition.

Bhambra, Gurminder. 2007. *Rethinking Modernity: Postcolonialism and the Sociological Imagination*. Basingstoke: Palgrave Macmillan.
Bin Wong, Roy. 1997. *China Transformed: Historical Change and the Limits of Western Experience*. Ithaca, NY: Cornell University Press.
Black, Jeremy. 1998. *War and the World: Military Power and the Fate of Continents 1450–2000*. New Haven: Yale University Press.
Black, Jeremy. 2004. *Rethinking Military History*. London: Routledge.
Blackburn, Robin. 1988. *The Overthrow of Colonial Slavery, 1776–1848*. London: Verso.
Blackburn, Robin. 1997. *The Making of New World Slavery: From the Baroque to the Modern, 1492–1800*. London and New York: Verso.
Blaney, David L. and Naeem Inayatullah. 2006. 'The savage Smith and the temporal walls of capitalism', in Beate Jahn (ed.), *Classical Theory in International Relations*. Cambridge: Cambridge University Press.
Blaney, David L. and Naeem Inayatullah. 2009. *Savage Economics: Wealth, Poverty and the Temporal Walls of Capitalism*. London: Routledge.
Blaut, J.M. 1993. *The Colonizer's Model of the World: Geographical Diffusionism and Eurocentric History*. New York and London: The Guilford Press.
Bourdieu, Pierre. 1977. *Outline of a Theory of Practice*, trans. by Richard Nice. Cambridge, UK: Cambridge University Press.
Bourne, Rayvonne. 2010. 'Guyana Is in No Position to Resettle People from Haiti', *Stabroek News*, 23 January. Available at: http://www.stabroeknews.com/2010/letters/01/23/guyana-is-in-no-position-to-resettle-people-from-haiti/.
Bowden, B. 2009. *The Empire of Civilization*, Chicago: Chicago University Press.
Brantlinger, Patrick. 1996. *Fictions of State: Culture and Credit in Britain, 1694–1994*. Ithaca, NY: Cornell University Press.
Braudel, Fernand. 1972. *The Mediterranean and the Mediterranean World in the Age of Philip II*. London: Collins.
Brenner, R. 1985. 'The Agrarian Roots of Capitalism', in T.H. Ashton and C.H.E. Philpin (eds), *The Brenner Debate*. Cambridge: Cambridge University Press.
Brewer, John. 1989. *The Sinews of Power: War, Money and the English State 1688–1783*. New York: Knopf.
Broadie, Alexander (ed.). 2003. *The Cambridge Companion to the Scottish Enlightenment*. Cambridge: Cambridge University Press.
Brown, Chris. 1991. 'Hegel and International Ethics', *Ethics and International Affairs*, 5: 1.
Brown, Chris. 2000. 'Cultural Diversity and International Political Theory: From the Requirement to "Mutual Respect"?', *Review of International Studies*, 26: 2 (April).
Browning, Christopher. 1992. *Ordinary Men*. New York: HarperCollins.
Bryan, Dick and Michael Rafferty. 2005. *Capitalism With Derivatives: A Political Economy of Financial Derivatives, Capital and Class*. Basingstoke: Palgrave Macmillan.
Bucholz, Arden. 1985. *Hans Delbrück and the German Military Establishment*. Iowa City: University of Iowa Press.
Buck-Morss, Susan. 1995. 'Envisioning Capital: Political Economy on Display', *Critical Inquiry*, 21, 434–67.
Buck-Morss, Susan. 2009. *Hegel, Haiti, and Universal History*. Pittsburgh, PA: University of Pittsburgh Press.
Bull, Hedley. 1977. *The Anarchical Society: A Study of Order in World Politics*. London: Macmillan.

Bibliography

Bull, Hedley and Adam Watson (eds). 1984. *The Expansion of International Society*. Oxford: Clarendon Press.
Bull, Hedley and Adam Watson. 1984. 'Introduction', in Hedley Bull and Adam Watson (eds), *The Expansion of International Society*. Oxford: Clarendon Press.
Burch, Kurt. 1997. 'Constituting IPE and modernity', in Kurt Burch and Robert Allen Denemark (eds), *Constituting International Political Economy*. Boulder, Colo.: Lynne Rienner. International Political Economy Yearbook, vol. 10.
Burckhardt, Jacob. 1955 [1889]. 'Letter to Friedrich von Preen', in A. Dru, *The Letters of Jacob Burckhardt*. London: Routledge & Kegan Paul.
Burckhardt, Jacob. 1960. *The Civilization of the Renaissance in Italy*, trans. by S.C.G. Middlemore. New York: Mentor.
Burke, Edmund. 1961. 'Letter to William Robertson, 9 June 1777', in T.W. Copeland (ed.), *Edmund Burke: Correspondence, Volume 3*. Cambridge: Cambridge University Press.
Buzan, Barry and Richard Little. 2000. *International Systems in World History: Remaking the Study of International Relations*. Oxford: Oxford University Press.
Buzan, Barry and Lene Hansen. 2009. *The Evolution of International Security Studies*. Cambridge: Cambridge University Press.
Caporaso, James A. and David P. Levine. 1992. *Theories of Political Economy*. Cambridge: Cambridge University Press.
Caribbean 360. 2010. 'Controversy in Guyana over Haiti Aid Efforts; Others Rush Relief to Survivors', *Caribbean 360*, 14 January. Available at: http://www.caribbean360.com/index.php/news/17535.html
Caribbean Net News. 2010. 'Guyana's President Says US an Obstacle to Efforts to Help Haiti', *Caribbean Net News*, 22 January. Available at: http://www.caribbeannetnews.com/article.php?news_id=21008
Carlyle, Thomas. 1849. 'Occasional Discourse on the Negro Question', *Fraser's Magazine,* reproduced as 'West India Emancipation' in *The Commercial Review of the South and West*, June 1850, 527–38.
Césaire, Aimé. 2000. *Discourse on Colonialism*, trans. by Joan Pickham. New York: Monthly Review Press.
Chakrabarty, Dipesh. 1992. 'Postcoloniality and the Artifice of History: Who Speaks for "Indian" Pasts?', *Representations,* 37,1–26.
Chakrabarty, Dipesh. 1998. 'Minority Histories, Subaltern Pasts'*, Postcolonial Studies,* 1: 1, 15–29.
Chakrabarty, Dipesh. 2000. *Provincializing Europe: Postcolonial Thought and Historical Difference*. Princeton: Princeton University Press.
Chakrabarty, Dipesh. 2005. 'The Legacies of Bandung: Decolonization and the Politics of Culture', *Economic and Political Weekly*, 40: 46 (12 November), 45–68.
Chakravorty-Spivak, Gayatri. 1999. *A Critique of Postcolonial Reason: toward a history of the vanishing present*. Cambridge, MA: Harvard University Press.
Chambers, I. and L. Curti (eds). 1996. *The Post-Colonial Question*. Florence, KY: Routledge.
Chatterjee, Partha. 1986. *Nationalist Thought and the Colonial World: A Derivative Discourse*. Minneapolis: University of Minnesota Press.
Chatterjee, Partha. 1997. *Our Modernity*. South-South Exchange Programme for Research on the History of Development (SEPHIS) and the Council for the Development of Social Science Research in Africa (CODESRIA), Rotterdam/Dakar. Kuala Lumpur: Vinlin Press.

Clavin, Matthew. 2010. *Toussaint Louverture and the American Civil War*. Philadelphia: University of Pennsylvania Press.
Clendinnen, Inga. 1991. '"Fierce and unnatural cruelty": Cortes and the conquest of Mexico', *Representations*, 33, 65–100.
Connerton, Paul. 1989. *How Societies Remember*. Cambridge: Cambridge University Press.
Conrad, Joseph. 1973 [1902]. *Heart of Darkness*. Harmondsworth: Penguin.
Cooper, Randolf G.S. 2005. 'Culture, Combat and Colonialism', *The International History Review*, 27: 3, 536–8.
Cooper, Randolf G.S. 2005. *The Anglo-Maratha Campaigns and the Contest for India: The Struggle for Control of the South Asian Military Economy*. Cambridge: Cambridge University Press.
Crapanzano, Vincent. 1995. 'The moment of prestidigitation: magic, illusion, and mana in the thought of Emile Durkheim and Marcel Mauss', in Elazar Bakan and Ronald Bush (eds), *Prehistories of the Future: The Primitivist Project and the Culture of Modernism*. Stanford, CA: Stanford University Press, pp.95–113.
Crawford, Neta. 2002. *Argument and Change in World Politics: Ethics, Decolonization and Humanitarian Intervention*. Cambridge: Cambridge University Press.
Cromer, L. 1908. 'The government of subject races', *Edinburgh Review*, 207, 1–27.
Cubitt, Geoffrey. 2007. *History and Memory*. Manchester: Manchester University Press.
D'Aguiar, Fred. 1997. *Feeding the Ghosts*. London: Chatto and Windus.
Davis, Mike. 2006. *Planet of Slums*. London: Verso.
Dawson, Doyne. 2008. 'The Return of Military History?', *History and Theory*, 47.
Delbrück, Hans. 1990. *History of the Art of War*, 4 vols. Lincoln: University of Nebraska Press.
Der Derian, James (ed.). 1995. *International Theory: Critical Investigations*. London: Macmillan.
Derrida, Jacques. 1985. *Margins of Philosophy*. Chicago: University of Chicago Press.
Desai, Kiran. 2006. *The Inheritance of Loss*. New York: Grove Press.
Dobb, Maurice. 1973. *Theories of Value and Distribution Since Adam Smith: Ideology and Economic Theory*. Cambridge: Cambridge University Press.
Du Bois, William Edward Burghardt. 1996 [1946]. *The World and Africa: An Inquiry into the Part Which Africa has Played in World History*. New York: International Publishers.
Dumont, Louis. 1970. *Homo Hierarchicus: the Caste System and its Implications*. Chicago: University of Chicago Press.
Dumont, Louis. 1986 [1983]. *Essays on Individualism*. Chicago: University of Chicago Press.
Durkheim, Emile. 1965. *The Elementary Forms of the Religious Life*. New York: Free Press.
Durkheim, Emile. 1975 [1898]. 'Individualism and the intellectuals', in W.F.S. Pickering (ed.), *Durkheim on Religion*. Routledge and Kegan Paul: London and Boston, pp.59–73.
Durkheim, Emile. 1984 [1893]. *The Division of Labour in Society*. Basingstoke: Macmillan.
Dussel, Enrique D. (ed.). 2008. *Coloniality at Large; Latin America and the Post Colonial Debates*. Durham, NC: Duke University Press.
Engelhardt, Tom. 1998. *The End of Victory Culture*. Amherst: University of Massachusetts Press.

Bibliography

Fabian, Johannes. 1983. *Time and the Other. How Anthropology Makes its Object*. New York: Columbia University Press.
Fahmy, Khaled. 2002. *All the Pasha's Men*. Cairo: The American University in Cairo Press.
Falola, Toyin (ed.). 2000. *Africa, Vol.1: African history before 1885*. Chapel Hill, Carolina: Carolina Academic Press.
Fanon, Frantz. 1967. *The Wretched of the Earth*. Harmondsworth: Penguin.
Fasolt, Constantin. 2004. *The Limits of History*. Chicago: University of Chicago Press.
Final Communiqué of the Asian-African Conference held at Bandung from 18–24 April 1955, *Interventions*, 11: 1, 94–102.
Flynn, D.O. and Giráldez, A. 1994. 'China and the Manila Galleons', in A.J.H. Latham and H. Kawakatsu (eds), *Japanese Industrialization and the Asian Economy*. London: Routledge.
Foucault, Michel. 1970. *The Order of Things*. London: Tavistock.
Foucault, Michel. 1977. *Language, Counter-Memory, Practice*, edited by Donald F. Bouchard. Ithaca, NY: Cornell University Press.
Foucault, Michel. 2007. *Security, Territory, Population. Lectures at the Collège de France 1977–1978*, edited by Michel Senellart, trans. by Graham Burchell. Basingstoke: Palgrave Macmillan.
Frank, Andre Gunder. 1998. *ReOrient: Global Economy in the Asian Age*. Berkeley: University of California Press.
Fry, Greg and J. O'Hagan (eds). 2000. *Contending Images of World Politics*. London: Macmillan.
Fukuyama, Francis. 1992. *The End of History and the Last Man*. London: Penguin.
Gandhi, Leela. 1998. *Postcolonial Theory: A Critical Introduction*. St Leonards, NSW: Allen and Unwin.
Gathii, James. 2006. 'Dispossession through International Law: Iraq in Historical and Comparative Context', in Branwen Gruffydd Jones (ed.), *Decolonizing International Relations*. Lanham, MD: Rowman and Littlefield.
Gathii, James. 2009. *War, Commerce, and International Law*. Oxford: Oxford University Press.
Geertz, Clifford. 1993. *The Interpretation of Cultures*. New York: Fontana Press.
Germain, Randall D. (ed.). 2000. *Globalization and its Critics: Perspectives from Political Economy*. Basingstoke: Macmillan.
Ghosh, Amitav. 1988. *The Shadow Lines*. Delhi: Ravi Dayal.
Giddens, A. 1985. *The Nation-State and Violence*. Cambridge: Polity.
Gill, Stephen and David Law. 1988. *The Global Political Economy: Perspectives, Problems and Policies*. London: Harvester Wheatsheaf.
Gilpin, R. 1981. *War and Change in World Politics*. Cambridge: Cambridge University Press.
Gilroy, Paul. 2005. *Postcolonial Melancholia*. New York: Columbia University Press.
Girard, Rene. 1977. *Violence and the Sacred*. Baltimore: Johns Hopkins University Press.
Glendinnen, Inga. 1991. '"Fierce and unnatural cruelty": Cortes and the conquest of Mexico', *Representations*, 33, 65–100.
Glubb, John. 1966. 'The Conflict Between Tradition and Modernism in the Role of Muslim Armies', in Carl Leiden (ed.), *The Conflict of Traditionalism and Modernism in the Muslim Middle East*. Austin, Texas: University of Texas Press.
Goody, Jack. 1996. *The East in the West*. Cambridge: Cambridge University Press.
Goody, Jack. 2004. *Islam in Europe*. Cambridge: Polity.
Graeber, David. 2001. *Toward an Anthropological Theory of Value: The False Coin of Our Own Dreams*. Basingstoke: Palgrave Macmillan.

Greenhalgh, Susan. 1996. 'The social construction of population science: an intellectual, institutional, and political history of twentieth-century demography', *Comparative Studies in Society and History*, 38: 1, 26–66.

Gregory, Derek. 2004. *The Colonial Present: Afghanistan, Palestine, Iraq*. Malden, MA; Oxford: Blackwell.

Grovogui, Siba N. 2002. 'Regimes of Sovereignty: International Morality and the African Condition', *European Journal of International Relations*, 8: 16.

Grovogui, Siba N. 1996. *Sovereigns, Quasi Sovereigns and Africans: Race and Self-determination in International Law*. Minneapolis: University of Minnesota Press.

Grovogui, Siba N. 2006. 'Mind, Body, and Gut!: Elements of a Postcolonial Human Rights Discourse', in Branwen Gruffydd Jones (ed.), *Decolonizing International Relations*. Lanham, MD: Rowman & Littlefield.

Grovogui, Siba N. 2009. 'Counterpoints and the Imaginaries Behind Them', *International Political Sociology*, 3: 3.

Gruffydd Jones, Branwen (ed.). 2006. *Decolonizing International Relations*. Lanham, MD: Rowman & Littlefield.

Guha, Ranajit. 1999. *Elementary Aspects of Peasant Insurgency in Colonial India*. New Delhi: Oxford University Press.

Guha, Ranajit. 1996. *Subaltern Studies: Writings on South Asian History and Society*. Oxford: Oxford University Press.

Guyana Government Information Agency. 2010. 'Panel Discussion Addresses Haiti Disaster and Future of Country, 18 January. Available at: http://www.gina.gov.gy/archive/daily/b100118.html

Halbwachs, Maurice. 1992. *On Collective Memory*, edited, trans. and with an introduction by Lewis A. Coser. Chicago and London: University of Chicago Press.

Hall, Catherine. 1996. 'Histories, Empires and the Post-Colonial Moment', in Iain Chambers and Lidia Curti (eds), *Post-Colonial Question: Common Skies, Divided Horizon*. Florence, KY: Routledge.

Hall, Stuart. 1996. 'When Was "The Post-Colonial": Thinking at the Limit', in I. Chambers and L. Curti (eds), *The Post-Colonial Question*. Florence, KY: Routledge.

Halperin, Sandra. 2007. 'Re-Envisioning Global Development: Conceptual and Methodological Issues', *Globalizations*, 4: 4, 547–61.

Hanson, Victor Davis. 1989. *The Western Way of War*. New York: Oxford University Press.

Hanson. 2002. *The Western Way of War: Carnage and Culture*. New York: Anchor Books.

Harkin, Maureen. 2005. 'Adam Smith's missing history: primitives, progress and problems of genre', *ELH*, 72, 429–51.

Hart, Keith. 2007. 'Marcel Mauss: In Pursuit of the Whole. A Review Essay', *Comparative Studies in Society and History*, 49: 2, 473–85.

Hartley, Lesley P. 1958. *The Go-Between*. London: Penguin.

Hartog, Francois. 1988. *The Mirror of Herodotus. The representation of the Other in the Writing of History*. Berkeley and Los Angeles: University of California Press.

Hattori, Tomohisa. 2003. 'The Moral Politics of Foreign Aid', *Review of International Studies*, 29: 2, 229–47.

Hegel, G.W.F. 1857. *Philosophy Of History*, trans. by J. Sibree. Kitchener, Ontario: Batoche Books.

Hegel, G.W.F. 1991. *Elements of the Philosophy of Right*, edited by Allen W. Wood. Cambridge: Cambridge University Press.

Heller, Thomas C., Morton Sosna and David E. Wellbery (eds). 1986. *Reconstructing Individualism*. Stanford: Stanford University Press.

Helliwell, Christine and Barry Hindess. 2005. 'The temporalizing of difference', *Ethnicities*. 5: 3, 414–18.
Helliwell, Christine and Barry Hindess. Forthcoming. 'Kantian cosmopolitanism and its limits'.
Henare, Manuka Arnold. 2003. 'The Changing Images of Nineteenth Century Māori Society – From Tribes to Nation', DPhil thesis. Victoria: University of Wellington.
Henry, Nancy and Cannon Schmitt (eds). 2009. *Victorian Investments: New Perspectives on Finance and Culture*. Bloomington and Indianapolis: Indiana University Press.
Herbig, Katherine. 1989. 'Chance and Uncertainty in *On War*', in Michael Handel (ed.), *Clausewitz and Modern Strategy*. London: Frank Cass.
Hindess, Barry. 2001.'The liberal government of unfreedom', *Alternatives*. 26 (2): 93–111.
Hindess, Barry. 2007. 'The past is another culture', *International Political Sociology*, 1: 4, 325–38.
Hindess, Barry. 2008. 'Been there, done that', *Postcolonial Studies,* 11: 2, 201–13.
Hirst, Paul. 1994. 'The evolution of consciousness', *Economy & Society,* 23: 1, 47–65.
Hobbes, T. (1660) *The Leviathan*. Available at: http://oregonstate.edu/instruct/phl302/texts/hobbes/leviathan-contents.html
Hobson, J.M. 2004. *The Eastern Origins of Western Civilisation*. Cambridge: Cambridge University Press.
Hobson, J.M. 2010. 'The Myth of International Relations: Eurocentrism in International Theory, 1760–2010' (unpublished book manuscript).
Hobson, J.M. 2011. 'Orientalization in Globalization? Mapping the Promiscuous Architecture of Globalization, c.500–2010', in J.N. Pieterse and J. Kim (eds), *Globalization and Development in East Asia,* New York: Routledge.
Hobson, J.M. and Sharman, J.C. 2005. 'The Enduring Place of Hierarchy in World Politics: Tracing the Social Logics of Hierarchy and Political Change', *European Journal of International Relations*, 11: 1, 63–98.
Hodgson, M.G.S. 1993. *Rethinking World History*. Cambridge: Cambridge University Press.
Hoffman, Stanley. 1977. 'An American Social Science: International Relations', *Daedalus*, 106: 3, 41–60.
Hollander, Samuel. 1977. 'Adam Smith and the Self-Interest Axiom', *Journal of Law and Economics*, 20: 1, 133–52.
Homans, George C. 1958. 'Social Behavior as Exchange', *The American Journal of Sociology*, 63: 6 (May), 597–606.
Hont, Istvan. 2005. *Jealousy of Trade*. Cambridge, MA: Harvard University Press.
Hopkins, Stuart. 'Kant and the Morality of Anger'. Available at: http://www.philosophypathways.com/essays/hopkins2.html
Howard, Michael. 1962. *The Franco-Prussian War*. New York: Macmillan. Available at: http://www.correlatesofwar.org/
Howard, Michael. 2006. *Captain Professor*. London: Continuum.
Huntington, Samuel P. 1996. *The Clash of Civilizations and the Remaking of World Order*. London: Simon & Schuster.
Hutton, Clinton. 2007. *The Logic and Historic Significance of the Haitian Revolution and the Cosmological Roots of Haitian Freedom*. Kingston: Arawak.
Ileto, Reynaldo. 1989. *Pasyon and revolution: popular movements in the Philippines, 1840–1910*. Quezon City: Ateneo de Manila University Press.

Inayatullah, Naeem and David Blaney. 2004. *International Relations and the Problem of Difference*. New York: Routledge.
Inayatullah, Naeem and David Blaney. 2007. 'Shed No Tears: Wealth, Race, and Death in Hegel's Necro-Philosophy'. Panel on Hegel and International Relations, 48th annual meeting of the International Studies Association, Chicago, 28 February–3 March 2007.
Inikori, Joseph E. 1979. 'The slave trade and the Atlantic economies 1451–1870', in UNESCO (ed.), *The African Slave Trade from the Fifteenth to the Nineteenth Century*. Paris: United Nations Educational, Scientific and Cultural Organization.
Inikori, Joseph E. 1981. 'Market Structure and the Profits of the British African Trade in the Late Eighteenth Century', *Journal of Economic History*, 41: 4, 745–76.
Inikori, Joseph E. 1987. 'Slavery and the Development of Industrial Capitalism in England', *Journal of Interdisciplinary History*, 17: 4, 771–93.
Inikori, Joseph E. 1990. 'The credit needs of the African trade and the development of the credit economy in England', *Explorations in Economic History*, 27, 197–231.
Inikori, Joseph E. 1992. 'Africa in world history: the export slave trade from Africa and the emergence of the Atlantic economic order', in Bethwell A. Ogot (ed.), *Africa from the Sixteenth to the Eighteenth Century*. Heinemann/ UNESCO/ University of California Press.
Inikori, Joseph E. 2000. 'Africa and the Trans-Atlantic Slave Trade', in Toyin Falola (ed.), *Africa, vol.1: African history before 1885*. Chapel Hill, Carolina: Carolina Academic Press.
Inikori, Joseph E. 2002. *Africans and the Industrial Revolution in England: A study in international trade and economic development*. Cambridge: Cambridge University Press.
Isin, Engin and Greg Nielsen. 2008. *Acts of Citizenship*, London: Zed Books.
Jabri, Vivienne. 1996. *Discourses on Violence*. Manchester: Manchester University Press.
Jackson, Robert H. 1994. *Quasi-states: sovereignty, international relations and the Third World*. Cambridge: Cambridge University Press.
Jackson, Robert. 2000. *The Global Covenant: Human Conduct in a World of States*. Oxford: Oxford University Press.
Jahn, Beate. 2000. *The Cultural Construction of International Relations*. Houndmills: Palgrave.
Jahn, Beate (ed.). 2006. *Classical Theory in International Relations*. Cambridge: Cambridge University Press.
James, C.L.R. 2001 [1938]. *The Black Jacobins: Toussaint L'Ouverture and the San Domingo Revolution*. London: Penguin.
Jeffords, Susan. 1989. *The Remasculinization of America*. Bloomington: Indiana University Press.
Jones, E.L. 1981. *The European Miracle*. Cambridge: Cambridge University Press.
Kahin, George McTurnan. 1956. *The African-Asian Conference: Bandung, Indonesia, April 1955*. Ithaca, NY: Cornell University Press.
Kaieteur News. 2010. 'Guyana Red Cross nets $7.2M for Haiti', *Kaieteur News*, 31 January. Available at: http://www.kaieteurnewsonline.com/2010/01/31/guyana-red-cross-nets-72m-for-haiti/
Kamtekar, Indivar. 2002. 'A Different War Dance: State and Class in India 1939–1945', *Past and Present*, 176: 1, 187–221.
Kant, Immanuel. 1970. 'Idea for a universal history', in H. Reiss (ed.), *Kant's Political Writings*. Cambridge: Cambridge University Press, pp.41–53.

Karl, Rebecca. 2002. *Staging the World*. Durham, NC: Duke University Press.
Kaviraj, Sudipta. 2001. 'In search of civil society', in Sudipta Kaviraj and Sunil Khilnani (eds), *Civil Society History and Possibilities*. Cambridge: Cambridge University Press.
Kayaoğlu, Turan. 2010. 'Westphalian Eurocentrism in International Relations Theory', *International Studies Review*, 12: 2, 193–217.
Keane, John. 1996. *Reflections on Violence*. London: Verso.
Keegan, John. 1978. *The Face of Battle*. London: Penguin.
Keegan, John. 1989. 'Introduction' in Victor Davis Hanson, *The Western Way of War*. New York: Oxford University Press.
Keene, Edward. 2002. *Beyond the Anarchical Society: Grotius, Colonialism and Order in World Politics*. Cambridge: Cambridge University Press.
Kennedy, Valerie. 2000. *Edward Said: A Critical Introduction*. Cambridge: Polity.
Keohane, R.O. (ed.). 1986. *Neorealism and its Critics*. New York: Columbia University Press.
Keohane, Robert O. 1986. 'Reciprocity in International Relations', *International Organization*, 40: 1, 1–27.
Kimchie, David. 1973. *The Afro-Asian Movement: Ideology and Foreign Policy of the Third World*. New York: Halstead Press.
Kissoon, Freddie. 2010. 'I am Giving my Haitian Money to the Red Cross', *Guyana Observer*, 16 January. Available at: http://www.guyanaobservernews.org/content/view/2467/1/
Klein, Bernhard and Gesa Mackenthun (eds). 2003. *Sea Changes: Historicizing the Ocean*. New York: Routledge.
Klein, Kerwin Lee. 2000. 'On the Emergence of Memory in Historical Discourse', *Representations* (Winter), 127–150.
Kolff, Dirk. 1990. *Naukar, Rajput, and Sepoy: The Ethnohistory of the Military Labour Market in Hindustan, 1450–1850*. Cambridge: Cambridge University Press.
Kramer, Paul. 2006. *The Blood of Government*. Chapel Hill: University of North Carolina Press.
Krishna, Sankaran. 2001. 'Race, Amnesia, and the Education of International Relations', *Alternatives*, 26, 401–24.
Krishna, Sankaran. 2006. 'The Bomb, Biography, and the Indian Middle Class', *Economic and Political Weekly, XLI:* 23 (10 June 2006), 2327–31.
Krishna, Sankaran. 2009. 'The Social Life of a Bomb: India and the Ontology of an "Overpopulated" Society', in Itty Abraham (ed.), *South Asian Cultures of the Bomb: Atomic Publics and the State in India and Pakistan*. Bloomington: Indiana University Press.
Krishna, Sankaran. 2009. *Globalization and Postcolonialism: hegemony and resistance in the 21st century*. Lanham, MD: Rowman and Littlefield.
Kusch, Rodolfo. 2010. *Indigenous and Popular Thinking in America*. Durham, NC: Duke University Press.
LaCapra, Dominick. 1996. *Representing the Holocaust: History, Theory, Trauma*. Ithaca, NY: Cornell University Press.
Latham, A.J.H. and H. Kawakatsu (eds). 1994. *Japanese Industrialization and the Asian Economy*. London: Routledge.
LeBon, Gustave. 1960. *The Crowd*. New York: Viking.
Lee, Benjamin and Edward LiPuma. 2002. 'Cultures of circulation: the imaginations of modernity', *Public Culture*, 14, 191–214.

Leiden, Carl (ed.). 1966. *The Conflict of Traditionalism and Modernism in the Muslim Middle East.* Austin, Texas: University of Texas Press.

Lemkin, Raphael. 2005. *Axis Rule In Occupied Europe: Laws Of Occupation, Analysis Of Government, Proposal for Redress.* Clark, NJ: The Lawbook Exchange Ltd.

Leung, Gil. 2010. 'What form would that extraction take now? The Otolith Group in Conversation with Gil Leung'. *Lux,* 2010. Available at: <http://lux.org.uk/blog/what-form-would-abstraction-take-now-otolith-group-conversation-gil-leung-part-1-3>

Lévi-Strauss, Claude. 1987. *Introduction to the Work of Marcel Mauss.* London: Routledge & Kegan Paul.

Linebaugh, Peter and Marcus Rediker. 2000. *The Many-Headed Hydra.* London: Verso.

Lipschutz, Ronnie D. 2003. 'Because People Matter: Studying Global Political Economy', *International Studies Perspectives*, 2: 4, 321–39.

LiPuma, Edward and Benjamin Lee. 2004. *Financial Derivatives and the Globalisation of Risk.* Durham, NC: Duke University Press.

Lobban, Michael. 2007. 'Slavery, Insurance and Law', *Journal of Legal History,* 28: 3, 319–28.

Locke, J. 2005 [1689]. *Two Treatises of Government,* edited by P. Laslett. Cambridge: Cambridge University Press.

Loomba, Ania. 2005. *Colonialism/Postcolonialism,* 2nd edition. London and New York: Routledge.

Lowe, Lisa. 1991. *Critical Terrains: French and British Orientalisms.* Ithaca, NY: Cornell University Press.

Lowenthal, David. 1985. *The Past is a Foreign Country.* Cambridge: Cambridge University Press.

Lukes, Steven. 2006. *Individualism.* Colchester: ECPR Press.

McCandless, David. 'Haiti Earthquake: Who's Given What?' *Information is Beautiful*, 26 January 2010. Available at: http://www.informationisbeautiful.net/2010/haiti-earthquake-whos-given-what/

McGrane, Bernard. 1989. *Beyond Anthropology: Society and the Other.* New York: Columbia University Press.

MacKenzie, John M. 1995. *Orientalism: History, Theory and the Arts.* Manchester: Manchester University Press.

McLean, Iain. 2006. *Adam Smith, radical and egalitarian: an interpretation for the twenty-first century.* Edinburgh: Edinburgh University Press.

MacLean, John. 2000. 'Philosophical Roots of Globalization and Philosophical Routes to Globalization', in Randall D. Germain (ed.), *Globalization and its Critics: Perspectives from Political Economy.* Basingstoke: Macmillan.

Macmillan, J. and Andrew Linklater (eds). 1995. *Boundaries in Question: New Directions in International Relations.* London: Pinter Publishers.

McNeil, William. 1982. *The Pursuit of Power.* Chicago: Chicago University Press.

McNeill, W.H. 1976. *Plagues and Peoples.* Garden City, NJ: Anchor.

Maine, Sir Henry Sumner. 1861. *Ancient Law.* London: John Murray.

Mandel, Ernest. 1986. *The Meaning of the Second World War.* London: Verso.

Manicas, P.T. 1987. *A History and Philosophy of the Social Sciences.* Oxford: Blackwell.

Mann, M. 1986. *The Sources of Social Power.* Cambridge: Cambridge University Press.

Mann, Michael. 1988. *States, War and Capitalism.* Oxford: Blackwell.

Marsden, Māori. 2003. *The Woven Universe: Selected Writings of Rev. Māori Marsden,* edited by Te Ahukaramū Charles Royal. Masterton: The Estate of Rev. Māori Marsden.

Marx, Karl. 2000 [1844]. 'On the Jewish Question', in *Karl Marx: Early Writings*, trans. by Rodney Livingstone and Gregor Benton. London: Penguin.
Marx, Karl. 1970 [1859]. *A Contribution to the Critique of Political Economy*. Moscow: Progress Publishers.
Marx, Karl. *Capital*, Vol. 1.1990 [1867]. London: Penguin.
Marx, Karl. *Capital*, Vol. 3.1991 [1894]. London: Penguin.
Masters, Roger D. 1964. 'World Politics as a Primitive Political System', *World Politics*. 16: 4. 595–619.
Mattingly, G. 1973. *Renaissance Diplomacy*. Harmondsworth: Penguin.
Mauss, Marcel. 1966. *The Gift: Forms and Functions of Exchange in Archaic Societies*, trans. by Ian Cunnison. London: Routledge & Kegan Paul.
Mayall, James. 1990. *Nationalism and International Society*. Cambridge: Cambridge University Press.
Meek, Ronald L. 1971. 'Smith, Turgot and the four stages "theory"', *History of Political Economy*, 3: 1, 9–27.
Meek, Ronald L. 1977. *Smith, Marx, and after: ten essays in the development of economic thought*. London: Chapman and Hall.
Mehta, Uday Singh. 1992. *The Anxiety of Freedom: Imagination and Individuality in Locke's Political Thought*. Ithaca: Cornell University Press.
Memmi, Albert. 1965. *The Colonizer and the Colonized*. New York: Penguin.
Metge, Joan. 2002. 'Returning the Gift – "Utu" in Intergroup Relations: In Memory of Sir Raymond Firth', *The Journal of the Polynesian Society*, 111: 4, 311–38.
Meyerson, Michael I. 2008. *Liberty's Blueprint*. New York: Basic Books.
Mignolo, Walter D. 2000. *Local Histories/Global Designs: Coloniality, Subaltern Knowledges, and Border Thinking*. Princeton: Princeton University Press.
Mignolo, Walter D. 2011. 'Geopolitics of Sensing and Knowing: On De (Coloniality), Border Thinking and Epistemic Disobedience', *Postcolonial Studies* 14: 3, 273–83.
Mignolo, Walter D. and Arturo Escobar (eds). 2009. *Globalization and the Decolonial Option*. London: Routledge.
Mill, John Stuart. 1850. *The Negro Question*. Littell's Living Age, XXIV, 465–9 (reproduced at http://cepa.newschool.edu/het/texts/carlyle/millnegro.htm).
Mill, John Stuart. 1977a [1859]. 'On Liberty', in John M. Robson (ed.), *Collected Works of John Stuart Mill, vol. xviii*. Toronto: University of Toronto Press; London: Routledge, pp.213–310.
Mill, John Stuart. 1977b [1861]. 'Considerations on Representative Government', in John M. Robson (ed.), *Collected Works of John Stuart Mill, vol. xix*. Toronto: University of Toronto Press; London: Routledge, pp.371–570.
Miller, Raymond C. (ed.). 2008. *International Political Economy: Contrasting World Views*. London: Routledge.
Mitchell, Timothy. 1988. *Colonising Egypt*. Cambridge: Cambridge University Press.
Moore, Henrietta L. and Todd Sanders (eds). 2006. *Anthropology in Theory*. Oxford: Blackwell.
Moore-Gilbert, Bart. 1997. *Postcolonial Theory: Contexts, Practices, Politics*. London: Verso.
Morillo, Stephen with Michael F. Pavkovic. 2006. *What is Military History?* Cambridge: Polity.
Morley, Neville. 1998. 'Political Economy and Classical Antiquity', *Journal of the History of Ideas*, 59: 1, 95–114.

Nandy, Ashis. 1983. *The Intimate Enemy: Loss and Recovery of Self Under Colonialism*. Delhi: Oxford.
Nandy, Ashis. 1995. 'History's Forgotten Doubles', *History and Theory*, 34, 44–66.
Needham, J., P.Y. Ho, G. Lu and L. Wang. 1986. *Science and Civilisation in China*, V. 7. Cambridge: Cambridge University Press.
Nietzsche, Friedrich. 2008 [1887]. *On the Genealogy of Morals*, trans. by Douglas Smith. Oxford: Oxford University Press.
Nora, Pierre. 1989. 'Between Memory and History: Les Lieux de Mémoire', *Representations*, 26, 7–24.
North, D.C. and R.P. Thomas. 1973. *The Rise of the Western World*. Cambridge: Cambridge University Press.
Nye, Robert. 1995. 'Savage crowds, modernism and modern politics', in Elazar Bakan and Ronald Bush (eds), *Prehistories of the Future: The Primitivist Project and the Culture of Modernism*. Stanford, CA: Stanford University Press.
Nyers, Peter (ed.). 2008. *Securitizations of Citizenship*. London: Routledge.
O'Brien, Robert. 1995. 'International Political Economy and International Relations: apprentice or teacher?', in J. Macmillan and Andrew Linklater (eds), *Boundaries in Question: New Directions in International Relations*. London: Pinter Publishers.
O'Brien, Robert and Marc Williams. 2010. *Global Political Economy: Evolution and Dynamics*, 3rd edition. Basingstoke: Palgrave Macmillan.
O'Gorman, E. 1961. *The Invention of America*. Bloomington: Indiana University Press.
Ogot, Bethwell A. (ed.). 1992. *Africa from the Sixteenth to the Eighteenth Century*. Heinemann/UNESCO/University of California Press.
Oldham, James. 2007. 'Insurance Litigation Involving the *Zong* and Other British Slave Ships, 1780–1807', *Journal of Legal History*, 28: 3, 299–318.
Osiander, A. 2001. 'Sovereignty, International Relations and the Westphalian Myth', *International Organization*, 55: 2, 251–87.
Pacey, A. 1991. *Technology in World Civilization*. Cambridge, MA: MIT Press.
Parker, Geoffrey. 1988. *The Military Revolution*. Cambridge: Cambridge University Press.
Pateman, Carole. 1988. *The Sexual Contract*. Stanford: Stanford University Press.
Pateman, C. and Mills C.W. 2007. *Contract and Domination*. Cambridge: Polity.
Peterson, V. Spike. 2003. *A Critical Rewriting of Global Political Economy: Integrating Reproductive, Productive and Virtual Economies*. London: Routledge.
Phillips, Nicola (ed.). 2005. *Globalizing International Political Economy*. London: Palgrave Macmillan.
Pickering, W.F.S. (ed.). 1975. *Durkheim on Religion*. London and Boston: Routledge and Kegan Paul.
Pieterse, J.N. and J. Kim (eds). 2012. *Globalization and Development in East Asia*, New York: Routledge.
Pluciennik, Mark. 2005. *Social Evolution*. London: Duckworth.
Pocock, J.G.A. 2005. *Barbarism and Religion*. Cambridge: Cambridge University Press.
Pollock, Sheldon. 2006. *The Language of the Gods in the World of Men: Sanskrit, Culture, and Power in Premodern India*. Berkeley: University of California Press.
Pomeranz, Kenneth. 2000. *The Great Divergence: China, Europe, and the Making of the Modern World Economy*. Princeton: Princeton University Press.
Porter, Roy (ed.). 1997. *Rewriting the Self*. London: Routledge.
Posen, Barry. 1993. 'Nationalism, the Mass Army, and Military Power', *International Security*, 18: 2, 80–124.

Bibliography

Prashad, Vijay. 2008. *The Darker Nations: A People's History of the Third World*. New York: The New Press.

Pratt, Mary L. 1995. 'Scratches on the Face of the Country: or, What Mr Burrow saw in the Land of the Bushmen', *Critical Inquiry*, 12: 1.

Prime Minister's Office. 2010. 'Prime Minister Launches Christchurch Earthquake Appeal Fund', 16 September. Available at: https://www.pmo.gov.to/prime-minister-launches-christchurch-earthquake-appeal-fund.html

Prime Minister's Office. 2010. 'NZ$634,500 Donated to Red Cross Christchurch Earthquake Appeal', 17 October. Available at: https://www.pmo.gov.to/nz634500-donated-to-red-cross-christchurch-earthquake-appeal.html

Ralston, David. 1990. *Importing the European Army*. Chicago: University of Chicago Press.

Rancière, Jacques. 2004. *The Politics of Aesthetics: the distribution of the sensible*, trans. by Gabriel Rockhill. London: Continuum.

Rappaport, Joanne. 1990. *The Politics of Memory*. Cambridge: Cambridge University Press.

Rawls, John. 1985. 'Justice as Fairness: Political Not Metaphysical', *Philosophy and Public Affairs* I, 14: 3.

Rawls, John. 1993. *Political Liberalism*. New York: Columbia University Press.

Rawls, John. 1999. *The Law of Peoples*. Cambridge, MA: Harvard University Press.

Reiter, Dan and Allan C. Stam. 2002. *Democracies at War*. Princeton: Princeton University Press.

ReliefWeb. 2010. *Haiti Funding 2010*. Available at: http://www.reliefweb.int/rw/fts.nsf/doc105?OpenForm&rc=2&emid=ACOS-635P2K

Renda, Mary. 2001. *Taking Haiti*. Chapel Hill: University of North Carolina Press.

Restall, Matthew. 2003. *Seven Myths of the Spanish Conquest*. Oxford: Oxford University Press.

Reus-Smit, C. 1999. *The Moral Purpose of the State*. Princeton: Princeton University Press.

Rogers, Clifford. 1995. *The Military Revolution Debate*. Boulder, CO: Westview.

Roll, Eric. 1992. *A History of Economic Thought*. London: Faber and Faber.

Romulo, Carlos P. 1956. *The Meaning of Bandung*. Chapel Hill: University of North Carolina Press.

Rose, Nikolas. 1995. 'Authority and the Genealogy of Subjectivity', in P. Heelas, S. Lash and P. Morris (eds), *Detraditionalization*. Wiley-Blackwell.

Rose, Nikolas. 1999. *Governing the Soul: Shaping of the Private Self*. London: Free Association Books, 2nd revised edition.

Rose-Ackerman, Susan. 1999. *Corruption and Government: Causes, Consequences and Reform*. Cambridge and New York: Cambridge University Press.

Rosenberg, J. 1994. *The Empire of Civil Society*. London: Verso.

Roy, Arundhati. 1997. *The God of Small Things*. New York: Random House.

Roy, Kaushik. 2005. 'Military Synthesis in South Asia: Armies, Warfare, and Indian Society, c.1740–1849', *The Journal of Military History*, 69 (July), 651–90.

Ruggie, J.G. 1983/1986. 'Continuity and Transformation in the World Polity: Towards a Neorealist Synthesis', in R.O. Keohane (ed.), *Neorealism and its Critics*. New York: Columbia University Press.

Ruggie, J. 1998. *Constructing the World Polity*. London: Routledge.

Sahlins, Marshall. 1974. 'The Spirit of the Gift', in *Stone Age Economics*. London: Tavistock, pp.149–84.

Said, Edward. 1979. *Orientalism*. New York: Vintage.
Sampson, Aaron B. 2002. 'Tropical Anarchy: Waltz, Wendt, and the Way We Imagine International Politics', *Alternatives*, 27, 429–57.
Scarry, Elaine. 1985. *The Body in Pain*. Oxford: Oxford University Press.
Schiller, Friedrich von 1972 [1789]. 'The nature and value of universal history', *History and Theory*, 11: 3, 321–34.
Semmel, Bernard. 1993. *The Liberal Ideal and the Demons of Empire: Theories of Imperialism from Adam Smith to Lenin*. New York: Johns Hopkins University Press.
Seshadri-Crooks, Kalpana. 2000. *Desiring Whiteness: a Lacanian analysis of race*. London: Routledge.
Seth, Sanjay. 1999. 'Rewriting Histories of Nationalism: The Politics of "Moderate Nationalism" in Colonial India, 1870–1905', *American Historical Review*, 104: 1.
Seth, Sanjay. 2000. 'A Postcolonial World?', in Greg Fry and J.O'Hagan (eds), *Contending Images of World Politics*. London: Macmillan.
Seth, Sanjay. 2001. 'Liberalism and the Politics of (Multi)Culture: or, Plurality is not Difference', *Postcolonial Studies*, 4: 1, 65–77.
Seth, Sanjay. 2004. 'Reason or Reasoning? Clio or Siva?', *Social Text*, 78, 85–101.
Seth, Sanjay. 2007. *Subject Lessons: The Western Education of Colonial India*. Durham, NC: Duke University Press.
Shaw, Martin. 1988. *Dialectics of War*. London: Pluto.
Shilliam, R. 2010. 'Modernity and Modernization', in B. Badie, D. Berg-Schlosser and L. Morlini (eds), *IPSA Encyclopedia of Political Science, 8 vols*. London: Sage.
Shils, Edward and Morris Janowitz. 1948. 'Cohesion and Disintegration in the Wehrmacht in World War II', *Public Opinion Quarterly*, 12: 2, 280–315.
Sigaud, Lygia. 2002. 'The Vicissitudes of The Gift', *Social Anthropology*, 10: 3, 335–58.
Skinner, Andrew S. 2003. 'Economic Theory', in Alexander Broadie (ed.), *The Cambridge companion to the Scottish Enlightenment*. Cambridge: Cambridge University Press.
Smith, Adam. *The Wealth of Nations*. 1979 [1776], edited by Andrew Skinner. Harmondsworth: Penguin Books,
Smith, Craig. 2006. *Adam Smith's Political Philosophy: The Invisible Hand and Spontaneous Order*. London: Routledge.
Smith, Steve. 2002. 'The United States and the Discipline of International Relations: Hegemonic Country, Hegemonic Discipline', *International Studies Review* , 4: 2.
Snyder, Claire. 1999. *Citizen Soldiers and Manly Warriors*. Lanham, MD: Rowman & Littlefield.
Solow, Barbara L. and Stanley L. Engerman (ed.). 1987. *British Capitalism and Caribbean Slavery: the Legacy of Eric Williams*. Cambridge: Cambridge University Press.
Spencer, Herbert. 1864. *Principles of Biology*. London: Williams and Norgate.
Spivak, Gayatri Chakravorty. 1999. *A Critique of Postcolonial Reason: Toward a History of the Vanishing Present*. Cambridge, MA: Harvard University Press.
Spruyt, H. 1994. *The Sovereign State and Its Competitors*. Princeton: Princeton University Press.
Stabroek News. 2009. 'Region Must Save Haiti – Andaiye', *Stabroek News*, 5 August. Available at: http://www.stabroeknews.com/2009/stories/08/05/region-must-save-haiti-andaiye/
Strachan, Hew. 2007. *Clausewitz's On War*. New York: Grove.
Strayer, J.R. 2005. *On the Medieval Origins of the Modern State*. Princeton: Princeton University Press.

Streets, Heather. 2004. *Martial Races*. Manchester: Manchester University Press.
Subrahmanyam, Sanjay. 1997. 'Connected Histories – Notes towards a Reconfiguration of Early Modern Eurasia', *Modern Asian Studies*, 31: 3.
Tan, See Seng and Amitav Acharya (eds). 2008. *Bandung Revisited: The Legacy of the 1955 Asian-African Conference for International Order*. Singapore: National University of Singapore.
Teschke, Benno. 2003. *The Myth of 1648: Class, Geopolitics and the Making of Modern International Relations*. London: Verso.
Tétreault, Mary Ann, Robert A. Denemark, Kurt Burch and Kenneth P. Thomas (eds). 2003. *Rethinking Global Political Economy: Emerging Issues, Unfolding Odysseys*. London: Routledge.
Thompson, David. 1987. 'The Hau of the Gift in its Cultural Context', *Pacific Studies*, 11: 1, 63–79.
Thornton, A. 2005. *Reading History Sideways. The Fallacy and Enduring Impact of the Developmental Paradigm on Family Life*. Chicago: University of Chicago Press.
Tilly, C. 1990. *Coercion, Capital and European States, AD 990–1990*. Oxford: Blackwell.
Todorov, T. 1984. *The Conquest of America*. New York: Harper & Row.
Tönnies, Ferdinand. 1887. *Gemeinschaft und Gesellschaft*. Leipzig: Fues's Verlag.
Trotz, Alissa. 2007. 'Red Thread: The Politics of Hope in Guyana', *Race and Class*, 49: 2, 71–9.
Trouillot, Michel-Rolph. 1995. *Silencing the Past*. Boston: Beacon Press.
Tse-tung, Mao. 2000. *On Guerrilla Wafare*. Urbana: University of Illinois Press.
Tuck, R. 1999. *The Rights of War and Peace*. Oxford: Oxford University Press.
Udovitch, A.L. 1970. *Partnership and Profit in Medieval Islam*. Princeton: Princeton University Press.
United States Holocaust Museum, *The Holocaust Encyclopedia*. Available at: http://www.ushmm.org/wlc/en/article.php?ModuleId=10007050
Venn, Couze. 2002. 'Altered States: Post-Enlightenment Cosmopolitanism and Transmodern Socialities', *Theory, Culture & Society*, 19: 1–2, 65–80.
Vitoria, F. di. 1991 [1539]. 'On the American Indians', in *Political Writings*, edited by A. Pagden and J. Lawrance. Cambridge: Cambridge University Press, pp. 231–92.
von Clausewitz, Carl. 1976. *On War*. Princeton: Princeton University Press.
Walcott, Derek. 1986. 'The sea is history', in *Collected Poems: 1948–1984*. New York: Farrar, Straus and Giroux.
Walker, R.B.J. 1992. *Inside/Outside: International Relations as Political Theory*. Cambridge: Cambridge University Press.
Walker, R.B.J. 1995. 'History and Structure in the Theory of International Relations', in James Der Derian (ed.), *International Theory: Critical Investigations*. London: Macmillan.
Walker, R.B.J. and Richard K. Ashley. 1990. 'Speaking the Language of Exile: Dissident Thought in International Relations', *International Studies Quarterly*, 34.
Wallerstein, I. 1974. *The Modern World-System*, I. London: Academic Press.
Walt, Stephen. 1991. 'The Renaissance of Security Studies', *International Studies Quarterly*, 35: 2.
Waltz, Kenneth. 1979. *Theory of International Politics*. New York: McGraw-Hill.
Watson, Adam. 1992. *The Evolution of International Society*. London: Routledge.
Watson, Alexander. 2008. 'Culture and Combat', *Historical Journal*, 51: 2.
Watson, Matthew. 2005. *Foundations of International Political Economy*. Basingstoke: Palgrave.

Webster, Jane. 2007. 'The *Zong* in the context of the eighteenth-century slave trade', *Journal of Legal History*, 28: 3, 285–98.
Williams, Eric. *Capitalism and Slavery*. 1987 [1944]. London: André Deutsch.
Winter, Jay. 1995. *Sites of Memory, Sites of Mourning*. Cambridge: Cambridge University Press.
Wolf, Eric. 1997. *Europe and the People Without History*. Berkeley: University of California Press.
Wood, Ellen Meiksins. 1995. *Democracy Against Capitalism: renewing historical materialism*. Cambridge: Cambridge University Press.
Wood, Ellen Meiksins. 1999. *The Origins of Capitalism*. New York: Monthly Review Press.
Wright, Richard. 1995 [1955]. *The Color Curtain: A Report of the Bandung Conference.* Jackson: University of Mississippi Press.
Yates, Frances Amelia. 1969. *The Art of Memory*. Harmondsworth: Penguin.
Young, Robert J.C. 2001. *Postcolonialism: An Historical Introduction.* Wiley-Blackwell.

Index

Abdulghani, Roselan 148
aboriginal peoples 76, 108–9
Abu-Lughod, Janet 35
Abu-Lughod, Lila 73
American Constitution 114
American Revolution 8, 22, 94, 116
Amerindians 41–4; *see also*
    Native Americans
anarchic character of international
    politics 16, 168
Anderson, Benedict 8, 24
Anderson, Fred 94, 103
Anghie, Antony 23
anthropology 11, 70–2, 101, 168–71, 174
Appadurai, Arjun 72
Arendt, Hannah 7–8, 106, 114–17, 121
Augsburg, Peace of (1555) 3, 19
Avicenna *see* Ibn Sīnā
Aztec civilization 75

Bacon, Sir Francis 37
Bandung Conference (1955) 10–11,
    146–63
Bartov, Omer 97
Baucom, Ian 50, 61–5
Berlin, Isaiah 117
Best, Elsdon 169, 173
'big bang theory' (BBT) 4, 32, 34, 41, 46
Black Death 39
Blaney, David 110, 112
Bolivar, Simon 178
Bourdieu, Pierre 125
Bowden, Brett 42
Brantlinger, Patrick 56–7
British Committee on the Theory of
    International Politics 16
British Empire 94
Brown, Chris 106, 110–15, 120
Browning, Christopher 97

Bruneschelli, Filippo 40
Buck-Morss, Susan 49
Bull, Hedley 18, 21, 23
Burch, Kurt 56
Burckhardt, Jacob 26
Burke, Edmund 72
Buzan, Barry 17, 21

capitalism 18–19; origins of 50–1;
    and slavery 5, 50–6
Chakrabarty, Dipesh 149–50, 155
Chatterjee, Partha 156
China 36, 93
civil rights movement 8, 116
Clausewitz, Carl von 90–2
Clavin, Matthew 95
Clinton, Hilary 167
coevalness 150; denial of 6, 70–1, 73
Cold War 10, 152, 156, 161–2
Collingwood, Luke 61–2
colonialism 49, 120, 159–60
colonization 21, 160
Columbus, Christopher 75
Conrad, Joseph 71
Copernicus, Nicolaus 40
Correlates of War (CoW) database 93
Cortes, Hernán 75
credit, provision of 54–7
Cromer, Lord 79
culture 21, 24, 73

decolonization 17–18, 93, 146–51,
    153, 157, 162
Defert, Daniel 19
dependency theory 157
derivatives, financial 63
Derrida, Jacques 108
Desai, Kiran 9, 124, 136, 141;
    see also The Inheritance of Loss

Index   201

development studies 59
diplomacy 4, 23–4, 159
division of labour 58
Du Bois, W.E.B. 53, 60–1, 65
Durkheim, Émile 77, 89

econometrics 59
Egypt 27, 38
Eisenhower, Dwight D. 114
English School of international relations studies 16–17, 21
Enlightenment thinking 58–9, 89
ethnography 171–2
Eurocentrism 3–5, 7, 15–18, 32–46, 87, 92–103
exchange theory 11, 167–77; *see also* market exchange

Fabian, Johannes 6, 70–3
Fanon, Frantz 161
Fasolt, Constantin 74–5
Ficino, Marsilio 40
financial institutions 54–5
financial investments 62–5
Firth, Raymond 170
Foucault, Michel 26, 75–6, 79, 98, 109
French Revolution 22
Freud, Sigmund 26

Galen 40
Gathii, James 23
Geneva Convention on war crimes 118
genocide 118–21
Gentili, Albert 44
Ghosh, Amitav 9, 124–6, 141; *see also The Shadow Lines*
gift-giving 11–12, 167–70
globalization see Oriental globalization
The God of Small Things 132–6, 140–1
Grotius, Hugo 44
gunpowder, use of 37
Guyana 11–12, 166–7, 179

Haiti 11, 52, 95, 110, 166–7, 177–9
Hall, Catherine 153
Hall, Stuart 1, 20–1
Hanson, Victor Davis 97–9
Harvey, William 40
Hegel, G.W.F. 7–8, 106–14, 120–1
Heidegger, Martin 114–15
Henare, Manuka 173–4
Hobbes, Thomas 28, 44, 108, 145, 166
Hodgson, Marshall 37
Holocaust, the 110–11, 117–20

Holy Roman Empire 74
Homans, George 167
Howard, Edward 62
Hume, David 58, 108
Husserl, Edmund 114–15

Ibn al-Haytham 40
Ibn al-Nafis 40
Ibn al-Shāṭir 40
Ibn Sīnā 40
imperialism 7, 9, 34, 41–6, 51, 79, 102, 124, 162
Inayatullah, Naeem 110, 112
India 27–8, 79, 94, 99, 102
individualism 73, 77–9
Indonesia 93
industrial revolution 17, 54
The Inheritance of Loss 136–41
Inikori, Joseph 53–4, 59–60, 65
insurance 55, 62–3
interaction between diverse political systems 3–4, 22
international law 4, 23–4, 42
international political economy (IPE) scholarship 5, 49–50, 56, 59, 64–5
international relations, descipline of 8, 11–12, 124–5, 167; *see also* English School of international relations studies
Iraq War 6
Italy 38–9

Jackson, Robert 21–4
Jagdeo, Bharrat 166
Jahn, Beate 41
James, C.L.R. 52
Jaspers, Karl 114–15
Jewish communities 110–12, 117
joint-stock companies 55

Kant, Immanuel (and Kantianism) 42, 72, 106–10, 113–18, 121, 158, 166
Karl, Rebecca 95
Kaviraj, Sudipta 27
Keegan, John 96
al-Khawārizmī 40
Klein, Kerwin Lee 153
knowledge, concepts of 4, 8, 15, 27
Kopenawa, Davi 76–7
Korean War 93, 95, 160
Kramer, Paul 95

Laffey, Mark 87
Lemkin, Raphael 106, 118–21
Lévi-Strauss, Claude 172–5

Index

liberal constitutionalists 112
liberalism, political 8, 22–8, 78, 114–17
Linebaugh, Peter 95
Little, Richard 17, 21
Little Rock incident (1957) 8, 114–16, 121
Locke, John 25–6, 44–5

McNeill, William 39
Manickchand, Priya 166
Mann, Michael 89
Mao Zedong 95
Māori cosmology 12, 173–7
market exchange 58; see also exchange theory
Marsden, Māori 174–6
Marx, Karl 22, 51–2, 60, 109
mathematics, development of 40
Mauss, Marcel 11, 167–74, 179; critique of 170–2
Mayflower Compact 116–17
Mehta, Uday 25–6
Mignolo, Walter 157–8
military institutions and the military revolution 36–7, 96–102
Mill, John Stuart 59, 77–9
Mitchell, Timothy 27
Montesquieu, Baron de 108
More, Thomas 44
Muhammad the Prophet 38
multivocality in international relations 145
Muslim communities 113

Nandy, Ashis 172
nation-states 7, 11, 24–8, 102–3, 156, 161
nationalism 24–5, 98, 103, 154, 162
Native Americans 113; see also Amerindians
Needham, J. 37
neo-liberalism 160
new international economic order (NIEO) 10, 154–5, 161
Nietzsche, Friedrich 26
Non-Aligned Movement (NAM) 10, 148, 151, 156, 160–1
novels, postcolonial 8–9, 124–42
Nye, Joseph 167

Oriental globalization 4, 34–5, 46
Oriental regionalization 34–5
Orientalism 97

Pan-African Congresses 148
Papacy, the 74
Pateman, Carole 45
Philippines, the 95

philosophy: analytic 109–10, 113; moral 110
Physiocrats 57
plague 37, 39
plantation system 55, 178
Polanyi, Karl 169
political economy classical 5, 56–60, 64; criticisms of 60
Pollock, Sheldon 26
postcolonial theory 7, 9, 49, 87–8, 102, 106–9, 114, 121, 124, 146–7, 155, 158, 161–2; misconceptions about 1–2, 20
Prashad, Vijay 148
Prussia 91

Quesnay, François 57

racism 118–20
Ramsaran, Bheri 166–7
Ranapiri, Tamati 169–74, 179
Rancière, Jacques 124
Rawls, John 23
al-Rāzī 40
Rediker, Marcus 95
Renaissance, the 39–40, 98
Renda, Mary 95
'resource portfolios' 33–6
retributive justice 117–18
Ricardo, David 59–60
Roll, Eric 57
Roman Empire 24
Rose-Ackerman, Susan 71–2
Rousseau, Jean-Jacques 108
Roy, Arundhati 9, 124, 136, 141; see also *The God of Small Things*

Sahlins, Marshal 170–4, 177
Said, Edward 72–3
Sartre, Jean-Paul 120
Schiller, Friedrich 72
scientific revolution 37, 39–40
Scottish Enlightenment 58
Second World War 7, 92–4
security studies 7, 87–90; constructivist 93; definition of 90
Sevele, Feleti Vakauta 179
Seven Years War 94
The Shadow Lines 125–32, 136, 141
slavery and the slave trade 5, 11, 49–65, 78, 177–8; abolition of 53, 63, 112, 166–7; absence from study of political economy 56–9, 64; criticisms of 58; in the history of finance capital 59–63
'small wars' 7, 95

Smith, Adam 57–60
social anthropology 168–71, 174
social contract theory 25
South Africa 20
sovereignty 4, 28, 33–4, 41, 44–6, 75, 149, 155–62
Spencer, Herbert 73
spiritual revolution 172–4
Spivak, Gayatri 107, 124
'state of nature' 43–5, 145
Steuart, James 58
strategic studies 89
structural linguistics 171
subaltern histories 147–50

Thornton, Arland 71
time, different conceptions of 5, 60–1, 65
Todorov, Tsevan 75–6, 79
Toussaint Louverture 95
Trouillot, Michel-Rolph 144, 147

United Nations (UN) 25, 155–6, 161, 167; Charter 156, 161
universal values 106, 119

Vattel, Emerich de 45
Venetian trade 35
Venn, Couze 155

Vietnam War 95–7
Vitoria, Francisco di 42–3

Walt, Stephen 88, 90
Waltz, Kenneth 16
war on terror 96, 162
war studies 6–7, 91–2, 96, 103; absence of 88–9, 93–4; 'full spectrum' 94
warfare 36–7, 43, 87–8; definition of 90; as a social phenomenon 92–4; *see also* 'small wars'; world wars
Watson, Adam 16–18, 21, 23
Weber, Max 91, 98
Westmoreland, William 6, 70, 78–80
Westphalia, settlement of (1648) 3, 17, 19, 32–3
William of Rubrick 37
Williams, Eric 52–4, 58
women's rights 20
Wood, Ellen Meiksins 50–1
World Bank 71
world wars 94
Wright, Richard 144

Zong case 61–3

Taylor & Francis

eBooks
FOR LIBRARIES

ORDER YOUR FREE 30 DAY INSTITUTIONAL TRIAL TODAY!

Over 22,000 eBook titles in the Humanities, Social Sciences, STM and Law from some of the world's leading imprints.

Choose from a range of subject packages or create your own!

Benefits for you
- Free MARC records
- COUNTER-compliant usage statistics
- Flexible purchase and pricing options

Benefits for your user
- Off-site, anytime access via Athens or referring URL
- Print or copy pages or chapters
- Full content search
- Bookmark, highlight and annotate text
- Access to thousands of pages of quality research at the click of a button

For more information, pricing enquiries or to order a free trial, contact your local online sales team.

UK and Rest of World: **online.sales@tandf.co.uk**
US, Canada and Latin America:
e-reference@taylorandfrancis.com

www.ebooksubscriptions.com

ALPSP Award for BEST eBOOK PUBLISHER 2009 Finalist

Taylor & Francis eBooks
Taylor & Francis Group

A flexible and dynamic resource for teaching, learning and research.